The Eighth Flag

The Caribbean from 1493-1750 and the mystery of
St. Croix's pirate legacy

Stanford Joines

The Eighth Flag

www.stanfordjoines.org

Latest update March 2021, with new information about 'Buddhoe' from George Tyson, William Cissel, and Deirdre Calley

stanfordjoines@hotmail.com

Cover art by Niarus Walker, niarus_art@yahoo.com

TABLE OF CONTENTS

III. PIRATES

IV. EPILOGUE

V. SOURCES AND MORE

©By Stanford Joines, June 2018

Preface

An island is more than a dot of rock and sand in the middle of the sea. In these pages, you will get to experience the Virgin Islands in times past by meeting some of the people who made it their home.

The Eighth Flag was written on the island of St. Croix. I have held century's old documents in my hands from the British National Archives at Kew, the Archives Nationales in Paris, and the Archives Nationales d'outre-mer in Aix en Provence. In Holland, I had the honor of meeting with Dutch historian Ronald Prud'homme van Reine, and have been in communication with Frits de Ruyter de Wild. While I was able to find and purchase rare, relevant books online, I have also used a lot of archived material available on the internet; websites are included in the bibliography.

I acknowledge that there are many more sources out there; please feel welcome to visit my website (eighthflag.com) or Facebook page (*THE EIGHTH FLAG*), cast off from the dock of spin, and begin a conversation. Historians like to feel they have written the last word, but inevitably something comes to light two weeks later that turns their narrative upside down!

THE EIGHTH FLAG stands on the foundation built by historian and scholar Dr. Arnold Highfield and the careful translations of Dr. Aimery Caron. For more in-depth information, see their work that is cited in the text and in the Bibliography.

He is no longer here;

the wreckage of his storm-tossed boat strews the beach.

Standing on the shattered deck, I feel neither reverence nor fear.

Yet I recognize myself in this wreck,

the thirst for adventure beyond known shores, and

fear while spiralling out of control...

I seek my next adventure

unable to take a warning from his last.

He who would warn me

who was me

is in the past. -SJ

Pirates: Those who take without permission from others what they neither earned nor produced.

Cannibals. Conquistadors. Buccaneers. Pirates.

Visions of cartoon characters dancing around a cauldron with an explorer tied inside. Balboa gazing on the Pacific Ocean. De Leon and the fountain of youth. Pizarro conquering the Incas. Henry Morgan, in red, drinking spiced rum. Smoke curling around Blackbeard as his cutlass slashes through the air. ... all children's tales that mean nothing. Today, we do not know who any of these people were, how they came to do what they did, or why they did it. The struggle for power, freedom, and wealth that shaped the Caribbean for two and a half centuries has, since John Barrie created Peter Pan, been relegated to the same literary section as Barney the Dinosaur; yet, underneath the soil of the modern world, the roots are still there. I started pulling them up on St. Croix, and the roots led to more. Islands connected, nations connected, and legends came to life.

This history of the Caribbean centers on a little island that was an epicenter of piracy for two and a half centuries, the last island to be subdued by colonial "law and order". Officially, St. Croix has flown seven flags. Before the American flag and the Dannebrog, the Spanish came for gold, the Dutch to trade, the English to raid, and the Knights of St. John to be in charge. The French built a colony only to watch it die of fever. From 1493 to 1750, Pirates, Conquistadors, Freebooters, Filibustiers, Corsairs, Buccaneers-- whatever you call them--ruled the Caribbean and made St. Croix their home, stealing at sea whether they had 'permission' to do so or not, and paying no attention to whichever European flag flew over the island. It is time to recognize the eighth flag of Saint Croix. It was black. This is the untold story of St. Croix and a Caribbean long forgotten. Come. Sail with me.

I: CANNIBALS AND CONQUISTADORS

Setting the Stage

The Caribbean of the sixteenth and seventeenth centuries can be compared to the old American West. The excitement of exploring a new world was part of both histories, also the lack of police. But instead of brown scrubland with feral cows, the Caribbean was a deep blue road on which untold riches traveled, creating temptation such as the world has never seen before or since. And instead of a Wild West that lived for a few decades, Pirates sailed the Caribbean for centuries.

Piracy defined the Caribbean's evolution, with Kalinago and Europeans raiding in a vacuum with no law and order. Gold fired imaginations and tempted men to venture onto dangerous seas. Sailors faced hurricanes, drowning, sharks, and fears of the Kraken. Instead of horses, they sailed frail wooden ships at the mercy of storms, uncharted reefs, worms, and rot. There were fierce Carib Indians with poisoned arrows, the twelve-foot-long cannons of Imperial Spanish warships, and to be a captain meant leading men who might at any time slit your throat to take your place.

To understand this Golden Age of Piracy, we must first go back and look at the very different worlds that collided in 1492. On the west side of the ocean, Kalinago pirates sought to enslave the peaceful "Taino". On the eastern side of the great sea, there had been no peace for a long time. Survival in Hispania meant war for over a thousand years.

Hispania

Soldiers of the Roman Empire defeated Carthaginian troops left behind by Hannibal (Numidian cavalry and Greek infantry) in the Second Punic War. After Scipio, Pompey, and then Julius Caesar subdued the Carthaginians and Iberians, Rome ruled the Peninsula for 600 years.

A Germanic tribe, the Visigoths were driven from their homeland by invaders from the east and granted sanctuary by the Roman Empire. Visigoths trained and fought as Roman soldiers in exchange for the promise of a new homeland that did not materialize. Frustrated and unpaid, Alaric and his Visigoths sacked Rome in 410 CE.

To get them out of their city, the Roman Senate gave the Visigoths land in Gaul and the Iberian Peninsula (Hispania) on which other tribes already lived. Defeated by the Gauls, Visigoths were more successful in Iberia and managed to rule the peninsula for three centuries despite constant rebellions from Carthaginian (Catalan), Iberian, and Roman factions.

When Rome fell, Europe plunged into darkness and tribal warfare, and the next great empire rose to take its place. In 711, Tariq ibn Ziyad led an army from Africa that included Berbers, Arabs, Nigerians, Malians (Mandinka), Numidians, and Mauritanians across the Strait of "Gibraltar" (The Rock of Tariq). Many of the warriors were Mamluks –slave soldiers; Tariq himself had been one of them, granted freedom after proving himself on many battlefields. Heavy cavalry mounted on superior Arabian stallions overran the Visigoth army under King Roderic at the Battle of Guadalete, and Hispania became part of

11

the **Umayyad Caliphate** ruled by Al Walid I from Damascus, Syria.

The Umayyad Caliphate stretched from what is now Spain to India. Referred to by Europeans as the Moorish Empire, in 711, it was the most powerful military power on earth. United by the Muslim religion, the Caliphate built a culture with universities, advanced architecture, art, and mathematics that kept the flame of learning alive. Education was mandatory for boys of free Muslim families until the age of 14. Schools called Madrasas were built alongside each Mosque, with courses including geometry, astronomy, literature, and music. Just for comparison, laws for compulsory education would not come to the United States until the 1920s, over a thousand years later.

Imagine a Muslim Europe ruled by Arabs and Africans.

It almost happened.

The Umayyad army invaded France under Abd-al-Rahmân in 722 and plundered France at will for ten years. The Moors had become overconfident by the time Charles Martel forged an alliance of Frankish (Germanic) tribes and appeared before them on October 10, 732. Abd-al- Rahmân did not bother to gain intelligence on this new barbarian force and completely underestimated them. Even so, the Moorish army was only narrowly defeated at the Battle of Tours when Charles' infantry, formed into phalanxes and drawn up behind trees on a steep hill, destroyed the previously unstoppable Umayyad heavy cavalry.

Shortly after the defeat at Tours, the Umayyad Caliphate fell into ruin and split into petty emirates, with the Emirate of Cordoba ruling the Iberian Peninsula. The culture of Moorish

Iberia was tolerant of other religions; Christians and Jews were allowed to own businesses and hold civil service positions, though registered as second-class citizens. Many Iberians, however, could never accept rule by invaders, and "Christian" Iberians fought for freedom for 780 years.

A drought spread throughout northern Africa. With the collapse of agriculture, the Moorish Caliphates declined in power, schools closed, and the wheel of fortune turned again. Martel unified the Franks -basically all of Europe except for England- and created the foundation for his grandson Charlemagne's empire, the first nation-state in Europe since the fall of Rome.

Over four centuries later, Portuguese knights freed their country in 1249, but slavers from Moorish Africa continuously raided the Portuguese coast and took thousands of captives (King, p 54, Fage, pp 393-404). In response, King John and his son Henry built ships, trained soldiers, and attacked the slave ports on the west coast of Africa to rescue their people and prevent more raids. They had with them a modern invention that revolutionized sailing offshore: the compass. With their new ships, Portuguese explorers kept going south, exploring the coast. In a classic turnaround, they captured Africans from the slave ports they raided and sold them into slavery in Portugal. Initially, the raids were for rescue and revenge, but the Portuguese made a lot of money doing this. They soon found it easier to purchase Africans from other Africans, setting a pattern that would continue for centuries and involve millions.

In 1453, Constantinople fell. The ancient road to China, the Silk Road, long defended by the Byzantine Empire in the west and the Ming Dynasty from the east and a significant source of profit for Western merchants, was closed. When Manuel became King of Portugal, he sent sailors ever farther south until, in 1487, Captain Bartolomeu Dias made it around what is today called the Cape of Good Hope and into the Indian Ocean. Spices, silks, porcelain, and the markets of the east lay at Portugal's fingertips.

The Emirate of Cordoba lost territory to several small Christian kingdoms, and, in 1469, the marriage of Ferdinand and Isabella created the united nation of Spain. The Emirate crumbled, and on January 2, 1492, Granada, the last Moorish fortress on the Iberian Peninsula, surrendered.

Jealous of the Portuguese trade with the east but respectful of the exclusive patent for the route around Africa granted by the Pope, Ferdinand and Isabella listened to an Italian trader with revolutionary ideas.

Christopher Columbus and his brother Bartholomew, a mapmaker, knew that the world was round and worked out what they thought was the distance from Spain to China. They based their calculations on the idea that land Vikings had once settled west of Greenland (Newfoundland) was northern China, and so concluded that an expedition sailing west at a lower latitude would reach the spice islands of Indonesia.

To see their dream become a reality, the brothers sought royal sponsorship. Bartholomew went to England but failed to convince Henry VII to back the plan. In France, Charles VIII listened but also declined to be involved in the project. Christopher was able to convince King Ferdinand and Queen Isabela of Spain that it was worth a try, and after the fall of Granada, such a trip was financially possible. Queen Isabela gave Columbus a special directive: "Find new lands, meet new people, and bring them to Christ."

Columbus first encountered the Bahama Islands, which he thought were part of the East Indies, and then a big island he called 'Hispaniola', where he met 'Indians' who called themselves *Lucayo*, of whom he had this to say:

> *"They . . . are all... gentle, timid, naked, and defenseless... unprovided with any sort of iron, they are destitute of arms, which are entirely unknown to them, and for which they are not adapted; not on account of any bodily deformity, for they are well made, but because they are timid and full of terror. . .. But when they see that they are safe, and all fear is banished, they are very guileless and honest, and very liberal of all they have. No one refuses the asker anything that he possesses; on the contrary, they themselves invite us to ask for it. They manifest the greatest affection towards all of us, exchanging valuable things for trifles, content with the very least thing or nothing at all.".* . . (Chanca).

Columbus' letter to Ferdinand and Isabella was ecstatic. He saw that the Indians wore gold jewelry and leaped to the conclusion that there were large deposits of gold in the islands (de Cuneo, "How We Explored the Cibao"; also, Columbus' letter). Lucaya told Columbus of many islands to the south, and he determined on his next voyage to cross the ocean at a lower latitude and explore them.

Columbus took a few Lucayo back to Spain with him, six of whom survived the journey (Columbus' letter). Queen Isabella had them schooled in Spanish and the gospels. Five of those returned on Columbus' second voyage to act as interpreters (M. Paiwonsky, p. 28).

Sailors are brave:

Do you know what it is to sail? To leave everything behind and head for freedom? The heave of the deck, the first spray on your face? Exhilaration! (Then maybe nausea...)

Columbus had some Channel Islanders in his crew. Channel Islanders and Portuguese fishermen had summer cabins in Nova Scotia a long time before Columbus was born. They sailed across the Atlantic every spring in open boats. Leaving the women and small boys at the cabins, the men and older boys would fish the Grand Banks until they filled their boats. The fish were cleaned, dried, and salted before sailing back across the ocean. The fishermen stopped to sell fish and trade for vegetables along the coasts of England and France, returning home to the Channel Islands in time for winter. Crossing the North Atlantic in an open boat with your family twice a year is my definition of brave.

There is evidence that earlier sailors made the trip across the Atlantic, but they were shoved along in front of hurricanes or nor'easters, so that doesn't count. Columbus came on purpose and put all he owned on the line. His crew included criminals, and many of his men didn't understand each other when they spoke. Columbus sailed his little fleet into the middle of nowhere, with no charts (don't tell me a scribble with brown blobs on both sides is a chart), hoping he could find something before he ran out of food and his crew threw him overboard. He came within a day or two of taking a swim.

Do you know what it is to sail? Knowing that once you're out of sight of land, no one will ever know what happened to you if you don't come back? A half-inch of wood or plastic between you hungry fish, with a terrible feeling in your belly that you aren't in control? Some years back, while sailing off of St. Lucia, I was caught in a violent thunderstorm. There was a big, dark schooner paralleling my course about two miles away. After a furious set of lightning strikes, I looked over between bursts of rain to where she had been and saw nothing. Becalmed after the squall, I radioed a small freighter near where she had gone down, which altered course to look for swimmers.

Ciboney

The Garden of Eden

In 1493, the island of Ciboney, or Cibugueria (St. Croix, today) had 32 villages and at least one ball court at Salt River Bay (M. Paiwonsky). According to Bartolome de Cuneo, a young priest who sailed with Columbus, the people were of a tribe that called themselves *Cibao* and were of the same culture as the gentle Lucayo they had met in the Greater Antilles farther north (de Cuneo letter home, "How we subdued the Cibao"). He referred to the island as 'Ciboney.' Michelle de Cuneo, who commanded Columbus' soldiers on the 1493 visit, called the tribe 'Cibu,' and put a Spanish spin on the name of the island, referring to it as 'Cibugueria.'

Europeans later identified five tribes of peaceful 'Indians' living on islands in the Caribbean as belonging to the 'Arawak' culture (A European term), though the Cibao, by then extinct, would have made six.

The Cibao enjoyed centuries of peace until the first wave of 'pirates' arrived. In what was to be the First Battle of Salt River Bay, canoes filled with Kalinago Indians (Arawaks called them "Caribs") scouted a way through the reef and paddled in, capturing the Cibao village and afterward two more..

DNA shows that Caribs and Arawak were from the same Guyanese Amerindian stock, though 500-year-old diaries of the first Europeans on the scene say that Caribs were shorter, more industrious, and cannibalistic. The warlike Kalinaga sailed up the island chain from Guyana and attacked Ciboney, taking over three villages on the island that they called "Ay-Ay".

Ay~Ay

Who were the Kalinago (Caribs)? In three pre-Columbian villages on St. Croix, there are Taino pottery shards and, in one case, a Taino ball court, with Carib detritus on top of them. There are few instances of Arawak warlike aggression, but the Kalinago were warriors. They staged raids on Arawak villages and later on European settlements for two and a half centuries after Columbus arrived. They were excellent sailors and navigators and ferocious in battle.

Columbus and the first European explorers greatly admired Kalinago construction techniques, given their level of technology and the materials available. While Arawak houses blew away in a hurricane, Carib homes were round, the walls packed with hard, dried clay, and more likely to survive a storm. They were also impressed by their methods of cultivation, including terraced fields and irrigation systems using wells (Chanca).

Spanish reports say that Caribs on Ay-Ay had come to an arrangement with the Cibao; at some point, the Cibao had fought back. The Caribs had been allowed to keep the three villages they had captured up to that time but, if they tried for any more, it would be war, and they were outnumbered. Caribs used St. Croix as a base to raid Puerto Rican Taino but left the Cibao on Ay-Ay alone.

Early European visitors wrote that Caribs used Arawak women and girls as slaves for life. Letters also said that Caribs castrated Arawak boys, "cutting the genitals off at the belly", though they would not eat them until grown (Chanca, personal letter to a friend; Steward, p. 25; keep reading). These accounts are by Europeans, some of whom were trying to justify slavery, land grabs, and genocide. There are no letters from Caribs to counter.

Spanish Conquistadores stole from and enslaved indigenous peoples; calling them cannibals made it politically acceptable. In 1503, Queen Isabela made a law that protected Caribbean indigenous people, allowing only "cannibals" to be enslaved. There are hundreds of letters from Spanish soldiers claiming that all of the "Indians" they sold were cannibals, but we can safely assume that was not true, since lying was profitable, and unquestioned.

There are, however, other accounts that cannot be so easily dismissed. The priests quoted below traveled to the Americas as idealistic young men who were predisposed to believe that the accusations of the Conquistadors were lies. These and many other young priests had nothing to gain by calling Caribs cannibals and started out trying to protect them from being so stigmatized. In Europe, well-born priests from political families had ambitions in the church hierarchy, but the young men quoted below had no such opportunities. Their letters were written to family members back in Spain, not to church superiors, and only came to light centuries later.

In 1581 Father Pedro de Aguado traveled to Venezuela to save the souls of Carib Indian tribes. Before the trip, he lambasted Spanish colonial officials for accusing Caribs of cannibalism for their own ends. Letters to his family *after* his missionary journey tell of Caribs eating human flesh (de Aguado, v. 1 Ch. 62, p. 458). The letters did not come to light until years after he was dead.

Jesuit Priest Pierre Pelleprat says he watched Caribs cut off hands and feet from slain enemies and cure them by roasting them slowly over a fire until they became jerky, but didn't see them eat them, only use them as trophies of war which they kept. He wrote letters to protect Caribs from persecution, saying that there was no cannibalism. These letters are still in the museum in Madrid. Some months later, Pelleprat was indeed offered a hand and a foot to share a meal. Horrified and disillusioned, he changed his tune (Pelleprat, p. 71). Those letters, written to his family and donated over a century later, are *also* in Madrid's museum.

Edward Bancroft traveled to report on the Berbice slave rebellion of 1763. Accepted as a friend by Caribs, he wrote that cannibalism was a myth invented by the Spanish colonial agenda. These early letters are available in archives. Later letters say something different. He had to change his tune after seeing the cooked flesh of escaped African slaves eaten in a Carib village. He wrote that Caribs had learned that eating white men brought reprisals, but eating escaped slaves did not (Bancroft, pp. 259-60, 336).

Capuchin missionaries reported cannibalism as a sign of victory in war, but not normal fare. Missionary Lopez Borre-Guerro reported the same. He later quoted Caribs as saying that castrated captive boys gained a layer of fat as they grew that added flavoring to the meat (Carrocera, pp. 84, 103, 186, 199, 200). There are many more letters from young priests who were horrified to discover that Caribs *did* practice cannibalism from time to time, but their messages would be redundant. Start with the bibliography at the end of this book and keep going, if you are curious.

Europeans, practiced in the art of war for a long time, feared and respected Caribs as warriors. That says a lot. After two hundred and fifty years of seagoing guerilla warfare, Britain and France agreed to respect Dominica and St. Lucia as Carib islands in exchange for a cessation of Carib hostilities as part of the 1648 Treaty of Aix-la-Chapelle. That means that Carib ambassadors traveled to Europe and treated with European statesmen as equals. Caribs were treated as a sovereign nation. In 1683, however, Louis XIV sprung a surprise attack to seize the islands, and Britain responded jealously. Britain ended up in control of St. Lucia, and France took over Dominica. Britain forcibly removed Caribs to the island of Roatan off the coast of Honduras, where their descendants live today. France allowed Caribs a reservation that still exists, with 3700 acres and a population of approximately 2700 Caribs on Dominica. This violation of a legal treaty seems terrible, but

European nations treated each other the same way; for instance, Poland was invaded and divided on several different occasions.

A glitch in the cannibal theory is that we don't have any of the bones with 'knife and chewing' marks mentioned by Conquistadors. But would unburied bones have survived in beach environments, with beach erosion, waves, and sun? After some years, saltwater environments erode bone. Even the marrow disintegrates so that there is no way to carbon date them.

Were the Caribs cannibals? Did Pelleprat sell out?

You are the jury.

If there had been no accusations of cannibalism, would history have been any different? Of course not. With its greed, violence, and superior weapons, the European culture would have found another excuse or not bothered with one at all.

Arawak DNA also exists today throughout the Caribbean, integrated into Puerto Rico, Hispaniola, Cuba, and many other locations. They survived quietly, with incredible patience and resilience, much as the black race in the Americas survived centuries of captivity and oppression.

"Caribs, Arawaks to Sign Historic Peace Pact in Dominica"

From *Sunday Mirror,* Georgetown, Guyana, November 17, 1996

Guyana's indigenous people are waiting with much interest to learn more about a historic peace treaty to be signed next month in Dominica between two of the original warring tribes who inhabited the Caribbean prior to colonization.

The event will have a Guyanese angle, which will see the indigenous people from the islands paddling their way to Guyana as was the case with their forefathers many years ago.

According to regional reports, Barbados-born Damon Corrie, a fourth-generation descendant of the last Arawak ruler in Guyana, Amorotahe Haubarira, will sign on behalf of his tribe, while Hilary Frederick, Chief of the Dominica Caribs, will represent the Carib nation.

A statement by Corrie said the ceremony will officially end hostilities between the two tribal nations.   Following the December ceremony, the treaty document will be carried by Corrie and the Carib crew of the historic "Gli-Gli" expedition by canoe to Guyana, where other leaders of both tribes will be invited to ratify the peace treaty.

The "Gli-Gli" expedition project is named after a small aggressive hawk, revered by ancient Carib warriors as a symbol of bravery.

Corrie said the aim of the canoe journey "is to create a valuable document of this ancient technology as well as a symbolic and practical journey re-uniting the islands' ancestral Caribs with their ancestral and tribal homeland."

The journey will take members down the island chain through the Orinoco Delta and into the Barima River of Guyana, then through the river systems of Northwest Guyana to the Pomeroon River."
(http://www.landofsixpeoples.com/gypeace1.htm)

Returning to our narrative, it is 1493. Caribs and Conquistadors meet for the first time on St. Croix. Caribs take one look at Europeans and do not hesitate. Arrows fly. People die. History is made. Sail on…

[2] Modern Caribs traditional sailing canoe *Gli Gli* off of Dominica.

Santa Cruz
The "Warrior Princess" and the Battle of Salt River

To get Ferdinand and Isabella to finance a second, much larger expedition to the Indies, Columbus exaggerated the riches of the islands he had discovered (Columbus' letter). Based on these claims, Ferdinand and Isabella used wealth piratically seized from Jewish citizens through the "Alhambra Decree of 1492", which expelled all Jews from Spain and took their assets (those who stayed could keep their assets if they converted to Catholicism, according to the *Jewish Virtual Library*). They borrowed more money from the House of Fugger in Augsburg, Germany, and sent Columbus back to the Indies with a fleet of 17 ships. [A]

The fleet made landfall between Marigalante, named after Columbus' flagship, and Dominica, so-called because they arrived on a Sunday.

After seeing the Lesser Antilles, Columbus wanted to work his way back to the men he had left behind at La Navidad. In answer to his inquiries, Carib Indians on Dominica gave directions to an island they called "Ay-Ay", where they said other Carib Indians could direct them on to Hispaniola. Following the directions to Ay-Ay, the fleet first followed the island chain north, naming all the islands on their way up until taking a left at an island Columbus called "St. Martin". From there, they sailed west for 90 miles, heaving to off of Ay-Ay in the night (no sailor without charts would ever go into a strange harbor in the dark!) (Chanca, p. 29; de Cuneo, p. 37).

On the morning of November 14, 1493, at "the hour of eating," they sailed along the north coast of "Ay-Ay." Columbus renamed the island "Santa Cruz," and the fleet put into what is now called Salt River Bay, where they saw beautiful green hills rolling down to sapphire water, flocks of pink flamingos wading in the mangroves, and a village surrounded by extensive cultivation. A launch with 30 men rowed to shore, where they 'rescued' Taino captives from the Carib village on the west side of the bay; the Carib elders guarding them ran off into the bush. The warriors (men and women) who knew how to navigate the islands were off raiding Puerto Rico (Chanca and de Cuneo).

Thus, the launch was on the beach on the west side, just inside the spit, when the first canoe of Carib warriors returned from Puerto Rico. In it were four men (two of them recently castrated Taino slaves), two women, and a boy. On entering the bay, the Indians saw the fleet of 17 ships inside the bay. Stunned, they sat in place for a half-hour staring (Imagine walking into your backyard and seeing a UFO). While thus paralyzed, the launch came up behind them. Too late, the Caribs tried to flee.

When they realized that the launch must intercept them, the five Caribs attacked, sending a cloud of poisoned arrows through the sailors' wooden shields and into two men, one of whom would die. Columbus had only wanted to ask for directions; this probably wasn't what he envisioned happening. The launch rammed the canoe before more sailors could be injured, overturning it.

"One of the women was like a warrior princess. She was firing arrows the fastest and deadliest of all. If the launch had not rammed the canoe, many more of us would have been killed. Even in the water while trying to swim to shore she continued firing until we caught up to her and took her captive... One of the Indians had been speared in his stomach, and we thought him killed. Soon we realized he was still alive and was trying to swim toward shore while holding his intestines, which had

spilled out. We quickly caught up with him. He reached for the side of the boat, and we cut his head off."

-*Michelle de Cuneo.*

The Second Battle of Salt River Bay was over; there were new pirates in town. ☠

[3]Spanish caravel

Sometimes in November, the rains clear all dust out of the air and allow for seeing great distances. Tops of hills across the sea to the north were visible on this day, and knowing that he was still south of the latitude he needed for Hispaniola, Columbus ordered the fleet to sail. They had only been at Santa Cruz for seven eventful hours. The "less ferocious" of the Carib women was given to de Cuneo, who found her attractive but a fierce fighter; he whipped her until she agreed to do his bidding. After exploring the other Virgin Islands for several days, the fleet sailed west along the south coast of an island Columbus named San Juan (we know it as Puerto Rico; the names of the island and the main port are swapped, today). While sailing three miles from land, Indian captives allowed on deck for

27

fresh air leaped overboard and swam ashore (Chanca and de Cuneo letters).

Sailors use common sense.

Sailing at night under the stars is magical, but when the stars start to go out, either you're going to get wet and cold soon, or there is land ahead. Another thing about sailing at night is that you cannot see rocks that are below the surface. There's no guarantee you will be able to see what's under the surface in the daylight either, but before the invention of GPS and lit harbor buoys, few sailors tried to sail into a strange harbor at night. By heaving to off Ay-Ay until dawn, Columbus put the sails to work against each other so that his ships parked offshore, practicing common sense seamanship.

Storms, collisions, and equipment failure can all be dangerous at sea, but sailors can use common sense to save themselves from preventable disasters. Columbus failed to use common sense seamanship at least once. The story goes that he took his crew ashore for a Christmas party, leaving the *Santa Maria* on a single anchor with a cabin boy on watch. The ship drug her anchor and was lost on a reef.

Conquistadors
Spreading God's love, through slavery

On Columbus' first voyage, the *Santa Maria* drug her anchor and was wrecked on a reef while the crew was ashore celebrating Christmas. Unable to fit everyone on the little *Nina* to sail back to Spain (the *Pinta* having already mutinied and returned home), Columbus' men built a small fort which they christened "La Navidad" out of the wreckage of the *Santa Maria* (in other words, there isn't any 'wreck' to find, today).

After leaving the Virgin Islands on his second voyage, Columbus sailed past Puerto Rico to Hispaniola, dropping anchor at La Navidad on November 28, 1493. He almost made it in time. The bodies of all 38 of his men were lying on the ground without eyes (de Cuneo). Lucaya had killed them, only some fifteen days before he returned. Whatever the men had done to elicit such a response remains a mystery but must have been horrible. Jails provided Columbus with much of his first crew, but he did not remember that. Columbus wrote that pulling eyes out was particularly barbaric, not realizing that almost certainly birds, crabs, or ants had eaten them. Whatever his feelings for native peoples up to that point, he never treated any "Indians" like people, again (Chanca); but honestly, he may never have treated them like people, anyway.

Ferdinand and Isabella had invested heavily in Columbus' second voyage, based on his promise of gold. If he returned home empty handed, all he had accomplished would have been for nothing. In desperation--and for revenge--he sold his soul. Columbus captured

500 Lucayo Indians to sell as slaves; if he tried to bring them to Christ at all, they must not have understood Spanish. The die was cast. Slavery would shape the Caribbean for the next three and a half centuries.

Two hundred Taino bodies went overboard during the passage; only 300 made it alive (de Cuneo). Seasickness isn't fatal, but Columbus' men carried diseases for which the Indians had no resistance. This was to be the story of European interaction with Indiginous people in America for centuries to come.

Proceeds from selling the Indians paid the crown and provided money for a third voyage. This time, Columbus, armed with the letter below, forced Indians on Hispaniola and Cuba into slavery to work what he hoped were gold mines. A hand was cut off for the first attempt at escape (de las Casas, source 8).

King Ferdinand's letter to the Taino-Arawak Indians (1495):

"In the name of King Ferdinand and Juana, his daughter, Queen of Castile and Leon, etc., conquerors of barbarian nations, we notify you as best we can that... the late Pope gave these islands and mainland of the ocean and the contents hereof to the above-mentioned King and Queen, as is certified in writing, and you may see the documents if you should so desire...

Therefore, we request that you understand this text, deliberate on its contents within a reasonable time, and recognize the Church and its highest priest, the Pope, as rulers of the universe, and in their name the King and Queen of Spain as rulers of this land...

...Should you fail to comply, or delay maliciously in so doing, we assure you that with the help of God we shall use force against you, declaring war upon you from all sides and with all possible means, and we shall bind you to the yoke of the Church and of Their Highnesses; we shall enslave your persons, wives and sons, sell you or dispose of you as the King sees fit; we shall seize your possessions and harm you as much

as we can as disobedient and resisting vassals. And we declare you guilty of resulting deaths and injuries, exempting Their Highnesses of such guilt as well as ourselves and the gentlemen who accompany us (Ferdinand, King)." D

Isabella was still Queen, but Ferdinand left her out of the letter, and she probably never saw it. Bartolome de las Casas, the first Catholic priest in America, a young man whose soldier father had sailed on the second voyage with Columbus, described the murder which followed:

"As for the newly born, they died early because their mothers, overworked and starving, had no milk to nurse them. And for this reason, while I was in Cuba, 7,000 children died in three months. Some mothers even drowned their babies from sheer desperation... In this way, husbands died in the mines, wives died at work, and children died from lack of milk... My eyes have seen these acts so foreign to human nature, and now I tremble as I write... ".

"Since the Admiral [Columbus] perceived that daily the people of the land were taking up arms, ridiculous weapons in reality [wooden spears and bows] ... he hurried to proceed to the country and disperse and subdue, by force of arms, the people of the entire island... For this he chose 2000 foot soldiers and 20 cavalry, with many crossbows and small cannon, lances, and swords, and a still more terrible weapon against the Indians, in addition to the horses: this was 20 hunting dogs, who were turned loose and immediately tore the Indians apart (de las Casas letter)."

As a young man, Columbus owned a copy of the Bible and wrote extensive notes in the margins. How do boys of promise turn into monsters who commit atrocities?

Spanish ships put into Santa Cruz regularly from 1494, using it as the forward base to organize expeditions that colonized what are now Panama, Honduras, Venezuela, and Columbia. According to Floyd, the following put into Santa Cruz between 1493 and 1509:

Antonio Torres with three ships in June 1494

Antonio Torres with four ships in October 1494

Juan de Aquato with three caravels in 1495

Peralonca Nino with three caravels in 1496

No ships in 1497

Pedro Hernandez Coronel with three caravels in 1498

Alonso Sanchez de Carajal with three caravels also in 1498

Ovando with thirty-five vessels in 1502

Columbus with four vessels in June 1502

From 1502 to 1508 there were forty vessels

From 1506 to 1509 there were a hundred and nineteen vessels (M Paiwonsky, p. 134; 39).

In 1508, Columbus appointed Ponce de Leon, a young soldier who had shown ruthless ability during the subjugation of Hispaniola, to be Governor of the Virgin Islands and Puerto Rico. In America, Columbus lost his faith, but de Leon found his, instead. After participating as an officer in atrocities on Hispaniola, de Leon had a spiritual epiphany on his return to Spain. King Ferdinand offered de Leon soldiers for conquest, which de Leon politely refused. Instead, he brought only 50 men—priests and agricultural experts--with him from Spain. De Leon and the chief of the Cibao brokered an arrangement which the Caribs accepted, and de Leon made the Indians of Santa Cruz trading partners. De Leon built churches, and many Indians were baptised (M. Paiwonsky, p. 134).

St. Croix and Puerto Rico were a model example of Europeans and Indians living peacefully together, and Columbus did not interfere with the relationship. He realized there was no gold or silver in the Virgin Islands and decided that having a peaceful place to organize expeditions was desirable. Unfortunately, King Ferdinand, fearing that Columbus had been given too much control, ruined the friendly relations by encouraging men loyal only to him to immigrate to Puerto Rico, with promises of free land and Indian slaves for all. These new immigrants did not answer to de Leon. In Puerto Rico, they took Indian land and made Indians slaves, and Indian reprisals became common.

According to Juan de Santa Cruz:
> "There is a pretty island of Sancta Cruz that the Indians call Ay-Ay but also Cibugueria. It was discovered by the armada of the second voyage of Don Cristoval Colon. It used to be very populated as there were twenty or more Indian pueblos; the greater part of the inhabitants voluntarily became Christians and for a time were our friends for whom they willingly worked. This lasted until Joan de Nievesa, when going to the continent, forced many of the inhabitants to go with him." (M. Paiwonsky, p. 130).

In 1508, Ferdinand signed a contract with Diego de Nicusa and Alonso de Ojeda to settle the Gulf of Urabá on the mainland (Now in Columbia, near the border with Panama). The expedition sailed in 1509 from Spain and arrived in Santa Cruz to resupply just in time for de Leon's term as Governor to expire. Onboard for the voyage was a young battle-hardened soldier, Francisco Pizarro. The new Governor of the Virgin Islands and Puerto Rico, Juan Cerón, helped Nicusa and Pizarro capture 120 Indians of Santa Cruz for use as slaves.

The expedition also acquired a thirty-three-year-old stowaway named Vasco Núñez de Balboa. Balboa had mailed himself in a barrel to Santa Cruz to escape debts in Hispaniola to join a new expedition (Lidz, p. 33). Balboa's barrel was loaded onto a ship, and Balboa revealed himself shortly after the expedition sailed for Urabá.

Immediately after Nicusa, Pizarro, and Balboa sailed for Urabá, seven Caribs from Santa Cruz who were trading in Puerto Rico were killed by Spanish soldiers.

Caribs were felt betrayed, and lashed out. The base in Santa Cruz became unsafe for anyone Spanish, and Caparra was under constant attack. Ferdinand reinstated de Leon as Governor in 1510, but the damage had already been done, and de Leon's vision destroyed forever. De Leon wrote Ferdinand that in reprisal, Caribs in Santa Cruz killed and ate the Cibao chief--and his family--who had befriended and brokered the deal with de Leon (Newton, p. 267-81). Revolted, King Ferdinand issued a Declaration of War against the Caribs of Santa Cruz on June 3, 1511, concluding that, "Before all things, it is necessary to destroy the Caribs of Sancta Cruz." Before an expedition could be organized, Caribs from St. Croix raided Puerto Rico in July of 1513 and burned the town of Caparra to the ground. Ferdinand's fleet arrived in Santa Cruz in 1515, and soldiers made no distinction between Cibao or Carib. Defeated Caribs scattered to other islands from whence they continued to fight, occasionally returning to Santa Cruz over the next 25 years only briefly, to stage raids on Puerto Rico. Whether Cibao were murdered or taken into slavery, Ponce de Leon wrote that Santa Cruz was completely depopulated when he visited in 1515 (Sauer, p. 192). Did he say that to keep survivors safe? Or was it really the end of Indigenous people on Santa Cruz?

Surely Spanish troops could not have caught them all? Swamps and the rough terrain of the west provide hiding places. Wouldn't it have been simple for the soldiers to kill a few and call it mission accomplished?

In Dominica, accounts of Indians raiding livestock and tools, of Indian laborers, and of trading with Indian villages appear in Governor's dispatches every month, century after century. I could have missed something, but to this day, no indigenous people are ever referred to on St. Croix again, not in Spanish, Dutch, English, French, or Danish colonial records. Spain had used the island for years and mapped it well. With orders of extermination and no conscience, my best guess is that Spanish soldiers poisoned the wells, which in the dry season were necessary for survival. It would be a century and a half before other European colonists used the same wells, and by then, nature had long since cleansed them. French colonists built their windmill pump towers directly on top of Indigenous wells, and you can still draw water from some of them today.

Is there any evidence of this murder? Bodies would have remained unburied. Could traces of poison can be detected in bones? Over time in a salt air environment, chemicals and DNA disappear, so that only the minerals and calcium remain --even if you can find bones scattered five centuries ago

Ferdinand and his successors sent conquistadors to take what they neither earned nor produced. That made them pirates. Allow me to introduce you.

Conquistadors of Santa Cruz

Christopher Columbus
The world has never been the same.

Today, children build stands by the road and sell lemonade. Young Christopher Columbus built one in front of his father's store in Genoa and sold cheese squares. Christopher was a very serious boy and read incessantly, but his father sent him off to sea at only ten years old. At eighteen, he fought with the navy of the Republic of Genoa against the Kingdom of Naples. A year later, he was an apprentice agent for the powerful Centurione family, who assigned him to their base in Lisbon. Agents sailed with each ship to conduct business, and Columbus sailed many thousands of miles, from African Guinea to England, Ireland, and probably Iceland. He was very familiar with latitude and longitude and knew full well that the world was round, as any sailor did. Christopher did very well for the company and himself. He boosted his career when he married the daughter of a Portuguese noble and produced an heir. Being part of a noble family gave him entrance to royal courts in Portugal and Spain (Much of the information in this thumbnail sketch comes from the biography of Columbus written by his son, Fernando.)

Able to speak Italian, Latin, Portuguese, and Spanish, Columbus acquired an incredible library for a sailor of his time, reading Ptolemy, Marco Polo, and many books of geography and history.

He wrote notes all over the margins of his valuable books, showing that he not only read them but thought deeply about what they said. He studied the Bible extensively and scribbled all over it as well -- odd considering the cruelties he later oversaw in the Americas.

Trade with China, India, and the Spice Islands had been going on for at least as far back as the time of Alexander the Great. The remains of ladies buried in Chinese silk dating to Roman times have been found in England. For a thousand years, the Mongol Emperor guarded the eastern part of the route and the Byzantine Empire the west. With the fall of the Byzantine Empire in 1453, half of the road was unpoliced and trade ground to a halt. Fellow Italian Toscanelli suggested that it should be possible to sail west to the Spice Islands. Columbus' brother was a mapmaker, and the two sat down to estimate how far it would take to sail from Europe west to the East Indies. No one had ever done it, but they were sure that land Vikings had found was northern Asia, and it would be possible to sail farther south and find the Spice Islands. But there was no way to know how far it was. If it were farther than food and water lasted, anyone who made the trip would die. There was also great risk because, if a storm sprang up, there would be no safe harbor nearby.

King John of Portugal was happy with the brand-new trade route around Africa; Bartolomeu Dias had rounded the Cape of Good Hope and found the way east into the Indian Ocean. The Pope granted the Portuguese a patent for that route that no other nations were allowed to use. Columbus went to Ferdinand and Isabella in Spain. They were busy with the Reconquista until 1492 when Granada fell, but with the long war over and jealous of Portugal's new trade route, they listened.

Columbus offered to risk his life for what he believed in, but he wanted promises in return, in case it worked. In April 1492, King Ferdinand and Queen Isabella promised Columbus that if he succeeded, he would be made 'Admiral of the Ocean Sea' and appointed Viceroy and Governor of all the new lands he could claim for Spain. He had the right to nominate three persons, from whom the sovereigns would choose one, for any administrative position in lands he discovered. He would be entitled to 10 percent of all the revenues from the discovered new lands in perpetuity. He also had the option of buying one-eighth interest in any commercial venture.

The ninety men who sailed with Columbus were worried. What if Columbus was wrong? They knew that, even if he was right, Columbus did not know how far it was to the East Indies. They mutinied, and Columbus made a deal. They would sail no further than half of their supplies would last. If they had not found the Indies by then, they would return to Spain. Columbus agreed.

But Columbus lied. They had surpassed their supplies by a couple of days already when the crew realized it. With seven and a half weeks of supplies, they were past their eighth week. Columbus begged for one more day, promising a coin for whoever saw land first, and when dawn broke on the sixty-first day, land was sighted.

It is hard to imagine their relief. Apprehension evaporated instantly, replaced with excitement that none of the sailors would ever forget.

Though he did not know it at the time, Columbus had stumbled into two new continents. Believing Columbus had sailed to the spice islands, Ferdinand wasted no time. He sent fleets with settlers and soldiers as fast as possible to set up colonies. By the time everyone realized Columbus had found a new world, it didn't matter; the new world represented infinite possibilities. Ferdinand reneged on his agreement with Columbus, creating a struggle that would continue in the courts between Columbus's heirs and the crown of Spain for three hundred years, until 1790.

Columbus made four voyages, exploring most of the Caribbean islands and the Caribbean coasts of South and Central America. On his return to Santa Cruz, Columbus spent some time ashore. Columbus served as the first Governor of Hispaniola, but colonists were very angry with his exaggerations of wealth that had lured them into leaving their homes in Spain. Accusations of cruelty led to his recall to Spain in chains.

There is paperwork to show that Columbus made money by taking Indians to Europe and selling them as slaves on his second voyage. However, many accusations of torture were made by men who were jealous of him, such as Bobadilla, the man who did the most to discredit him and then benefited from it by being named his successor. Columbus was a sailor and explorer who spent little time ashore, and others committed many of the atrocities attributed to him. Regardless, the letters of young Father Bartolome de las Casas give testimony to murder. Columbus as Governor-General was in command as soon as he stepped ashore, so the buck has to stop with him. De las Casas' father was a longtime friend of Columbus who had sailed on the second voyage, and Columbus probably considered Bartolome as a Godson. When Bartolome sailed to the new world with Columbus, he thought of Columbus as a hero. He did not expect to witness the genocide – from inadvertent disease, but also intentional murder-- that he did.

Known as "The Great Navigator," Columbus made significant contributions to seafaring. He is the first to have discovered that the variation between magnetic north and the North Star was changing (the magnetic rock floating in the earth's molten core near the north pole is slowly falling south).

Columbus established the Great Circle Route Portuguese sailors had predicted. Taking advantage of trade winds that blow from the east in the tropics and from the west in northern latitudes, sailing ships did not have to travel against the wind but could sail before it on both outbound and inbound voyages. Ships used the circle route for centuries until the age of steam. Columbus fine-tuned calculations for latitude. He devised the calculations for longitude still used today, though the world lacked a proper timepiece and had to wait three centuries for one to be invented so that anyone could use them.

Sail with Columbus:

> *"For nine days I was as one lost, without hope of life. Eyes never beheld the sea so angry, so high, so covered with foam. The wind not only prevented our progress, but offered no opportunity to run behind any headland for shelter; hence we were forced to keep out in this bloody ocean, seething like a pot on a hot fire. Never did the sky look more terrible; for one whole day and night it blazed like a furnace, and the lightning broke with such violence that each time I wondered if it had carried off my spars and sails; the flashes came with such fury and frightfulness that we all thought that the ship would be blasted. All this time the water never ceased to fall from the sky; I do not say it rained, for it was like another deluge. The men were so worn out that they longed for death to end their dreadful suffering." -Christopher Columbus (Morrison, p. 617).*

Chronic intestinal infection from eating rotten shipboard food during the second voyage sapped his energy and gradually wore him down. Christopher Columbus ended his days with study and prayer in a monastery until the infection killed him at the age of 58.

The Medieval world was not our own. The world Columbus was born into was only beginning to find its way morally. The Catholic church owned slaves; slavery had been practiced throughout the world since the dawn of human history, in every race, on every continent, and had been common in Spain for its entire existence, including the 780 years it was ruled by Africa. The Papal State collected taxes, had an army, and fought wars. His Catholic church was torturing fellow humans for not subscribing its particular doctrine, and as far as he knew, his church was the supreme moral authority. But none of this justifies the mass murder reported by de las Casus. Though warlords had hijacked the Church, Columbus had read Jesus' message of peace and love.

Sailing into the unknown was frightening and dangerous. The little boy with the cheese stand grew up to do both great and terrible things, but regardless of the state of his soul, he changed the world forever. He also unleashed the dogs of war.

Don Juan Ponce de Leon
Looking for Eternal Life, He Found Death

Born into a poor though noble family sometime around 1460, de Leon served as a page in Aragon's royal court, as a squire to don Pedro Nunez de Guzman, and fought in the last battles to drive the Moors out of Spain. He asked to go on Columbus' second voyage in 1493 as one of the 1200 volunteers. De Leon was present at the Second Battle of Salt River Bay.

After finding the remains of the men left behind at La Navidad, de Leon participated in capturing hundreds of Taino slaves to sell in Spain. He returned to America as a Captain serving under Nicolas de Ovando, governor of Hispaniola, who ordered De Leon to put down an Indian uprising. De Leon did so with ruthless efficiency, pleasing Ovando so well that he was appointed Deputy Governor of Hispaniola. Columbus named him Governor of Puerto Rico and the Virgin Islands in 1508.

On his return to Spain, De Leon had a religious experience and found Jesus. Appointed Governor of the Virgin Islands and Puerto Rico, King Ferdinand offered him as many soldiers as he would like to conquer Puerto Rico, but he refused. De Leon took only 50 men, mostly farmers and missionaries. Instead of conquering them, he made trading partners and Christians of the Indians he dealt with (de las Casus letters). He spent considerable time in Santa Cruz establishing a relationship with the Indians, making it the forward base from which to settle Puerto Rico. King Ferdinand replaced him after only a year with Juan Cerón, who ruined de Leon's plan for colonizing Santa Cruz and Puerto Rico, but de Leon served as Governor for five more staggered one-year terms, finishing his last in 1519.

After realizing a brief utopia of sorts under his leadership, it must have hurt him to see that he had just set the Indians up for extermination. Regardless, he continued to function in his duties as a Spanish officer until, in 1519, de Leon turned his attention to some "Islands reported to the north," which turned out to be part of a continent.

De Leon fitted out an expedition that was the first to explore what he called "Pascua Florida," as he landed on Easter, 1521. Legend has it that he was trying to locate the legendary 'Fountain of Youth', but instead he was found, by an Indian arrow, and died a few weeks after returning to Puerto Rico.

Vasco Núñez de Balboa
Mailed himself and his dog in a barrel to St. Croix

The territories of Costa Rica, Nicaragua, and Panama were formed in 1502 as part of the Governate of Veragua by Christopher Columbus. He intended it to be his private estate, but the king had other ideas. Each of the three parts received a governor appointed by the king, and Veragua had a governor who was over them. Into this new Governate of Veragua sailed Vasco Nunez de Balboa.

Balboa was born in Jerez de los Caballeros, Spain, in 1475. His parents were nobles; during his adolescence, he served as a Page and then as a Squire to don Pedro de Portocarrero, Lord of Moguer. He first sailed to the Caribbean in 1500 as part of an expedition looking for treasure along the coast of the "Spanish Main" from Panama to Venezuela. Afterward, the reality of supporting himself in a strange new world set in. Balboa bought some land on credit in Hispaniola and set himself up as a pig farmer. He must not have been a very good one, as he went bankrupt. For debt, Spain sent even nobles and honored veterans to prison.

In 1509, needing to escape his creditors, Balboa hid as a stowaway inside a barrel together with his dog *Leoncico* and mailed himself to St. Croix, a major staging area for Spanish expeditions to America (Lidz, p. 33).

The ship Balboa hid on was loaded with food grown in Hispaniola. Upon reaching Santa Cruz, it was made part of an expedition headed by the new Governor of Veragua, Diego de

Nicusa (Veragua stretched from Panama north into Guatemala). Also with the fleet was the Governor of New Andalusia (Colombia), Alonso de Ojeda. Balboa and his dog emerged from their barrel shortly after the expedition left Santa Cruz.

Captain Fernández de Enciso threatened to leave him on the first uninhabited island they encountered, but the crew pled for Balboa's life, and Enciso decided that Balboa's knowledge of the coast of Panama might be useful. The Captain's brother, Martin Enciso, agreed. Governor Ojeda had hired Martin to be mayor of San Sebastian de Urabá.

Nicusa's ships split off to Veragua, and Ojeda's part of the fleet sailed for San Sebastian de Urabá. On arrival, they discovered the settlement destroyed by local Indians and the Spanish survivors under constant attack. Ojeda took a poisoned arrow in his leg and left for Hispaniola to recover. He asked the men to stick it out for 50 days, which they did, under the command of Francisco Pizarro, after which the unrelenting ferocity and courage of the Indians proved that San Sebastian was not tenable. Everyone was receptive to Balboa's suggestion that they move to a safer location.

Landing in Panama, the group was again attacked by Indians, but victorious this time, they founded Santa Maria la Antigua del Darien, and voted Balboa to be their leader.

Ojeda recovered and found them, but Balboa announced that Ojeda could not transfer his authority from San Sebastian to Darien as, in his opinion, Darien was in Veragua (de Nicusa's Governate), not New Andalusia. The colonists also voted to install Balboa over Martin Enciso.

A few months later, De Nicuesa arrived to take his place as Governor, and the settlers, hating him, forced him onto an 'unseaworthy ship'; he sailed away and was never heard from again. Balboa was then elected Governor of Veragua by the colonists. His first act was to arrest Martin Enciso and send him back to Spain for trying to usurp the authority of the elected Governor of Veragua.

Balboa also sent a good deal of golden trinkets he had stolen from Indians to the King to grease the rails of justice (de Gomara, pdf).

Balboa defeated some Indian tribes and made friends with the rest. Temporarily secure in his position, Balboa proved that he wasn't one of the great liberals of his time. Peter Martyr d'Anghiera wrote that Balboa fed 40 noble--but homosexual--Spaniards to the dogs for food; Indians had learned of the presence of people with this inclination and demanded their deaths. King Ferdinand's brother, one of the homosexuals in the group, was spared, of course (d'Anghiera, <u>De Orbe Novo</u>, v. 1 Ch. 1).

The pacified Indian tribes of Darien slyly used Balboa to hurt their rivals; they sent him to the Pacific side of the Isthmus with tales of Indians eating off of plates of gold. Balboa did not find any such dishes, though he did collect some trinkets and obligingly defeated all of the Indian tribes he encountered. He also discovered what he named the Great South Sea (Magellan renamed it the Pacific Ocean). This increased the size of his Governate of Veragua, just in time for a new governor to arrive. Martin Enciso had managed to convince the King that he should be named Governor of Veragua in place of Balboa.

Pedrarias Davila, notorious for his cruelty, was named by Martin Enciso to be Mayor of Panama, and as soon as he got off the ship, he arrested Balboa. Before he could lock Balboa up, a new message came from the King. Ferdinand ordered Enciso to New Andalusia. The King named Davila to be Governor of Veragua, and Balboa to be the Mayor of Panama serving under Davila, but with Davila to consult Balboa on all things.

With Davila's permission, Balboa had ships built and explored some of Panama's Pacific coast. While Balboa was away, Enciso returned with soldiers under Francisco Pizarro. Davila, Enciso, and

Pizarro accused Balboa of creating a new territory for himself on the shores of the South Sea.

Upon his return, Pizarro's soldiers seized Balboa. Tired of dealing with the troublesome stow-away, Pizarro immediately led Balboa and his four closest friends to the block and had their heads cut off (Lidz, 34-5).

Francisco Pizarro

Friendship meets gold. And murder.

Francisco Pizarro was the illegitimate son of an infantry colonel and a cousin of Hernan Cortes. He was a veteran soldier some 35 years of age when he sailed with Ojeda and the stowaway, Balboa, to Urabáin 1509. He commanded the troops Ojeda left behind in the doomed colony. He fought under Balboa in Panama and accompanied him on the expedition that 'discovered' the 'South Sea.' When Davila arrived from Spain, Pizarro instantly changed his loyalty. Davila had Pizzaro arrest Balboa and bring him back to Santa Maria for execution.

Tales of Cortes' success in Mexico stirred Pizarro's ambition. This Jealousy and rumors of great wealth in Peru led Pizarro to make three expeditions down into that area. In the first two, he was defeated by strong bands of Indians. Before he could try a third, a new governor, de los Rios, ordered him not to try again.

Rios suspected that Pizarro wanted to conquer the Incas, make Peru a new territory, and declare himself its Governor, cutting Rios out of his share of the Inca treasure (exactly what Pizarro had accused Balboa of). Pizarro sailed to Spain and received a commission to do exactly that from King Charles I, who sent Pizarro back with soldiers and the title of governor of all lands he conquered. Pizarro was allowed to bring his best friends along, including longtime comrade Diego Almagro, his executive officer.

Pizarro took 168 soldiers into the middle of enemy territory filled with 80,000 soldiers and attacked. The Incan Emperor Atahualpa was overconfident. Fresh from ruthlessly crushing a rebellion, he brought only 8,000 lightly armed soldiers with him to the small clearing Pizarro suggested. Further motivating the Conquistadors, Atahualpa's soldiers wore headdresses of gold.

Atahualpa arrived carried in a litter made of silver, covered with colorful parrot feathers. Pizarro had his friar approach and offer Atahualpa a Bible, saying as he did so that Atahualpa was now required to become Christian and swear allegiance to the Pope or suffer the consequences. Atahualpa did not know what the book was and didn't care. He was the King of Kings. He tossed it on the ground.

As per Inca traditions, Atahualpa offered Pizarro a golden ceremonial chalice of chicha (corn beer). Told by his spy that he was supposed to pour it out as an offering, Pizarro did. The spy was wrong; this was a precious gift to be consumed by an honored guest.

Furious but patient, another was brought forth. Again, Pizarro poured it out onto the ground. Outraged at the disrespect, Atahualpa ordered his men to attack.

The Inca died quickly. The defeated rarely appreciate technology until it is too late; unspeakable courage was still an essential ingredient, but technology was also in place. Feathered cloaks were no match for armor nor stone for steel. Pizarro took Atahualpa prisoner, and the Incan empire laid down its arms. Spain had just acquired the wealthiest sources of precious metals and the best source of emeralds in the world.

Offered freedom if he paid a ransom, Atahualpa filled a room with gold for Pizarro, and Pizarro accepted it. Pizarro took over the Incan capital of Cuzco, garrisoned the silver mines, and built the city of Lima to be the Spanish provincial capital. He also took Atahualpa's sister and his 10-year-old wife as his mistresses, fathering children with both.

Pizarro planned on taking Atahualpa to Spain, but to his dismay, Almagro executed Atahualpa while Pizarro was off foraging. Pizarro was furious, afraid that the act would spark a rebellion. Furious,

Pizarro led his soldiers to arrest Almagro, and Almagro and his soldiers met them in battle. Pizarro won and had Almagro beheaded.

Almagro's son assassinated Pizarro on June 26, 1541. Pizarro's Spanish wife bore him one child, a son who died with no children, but the ten-year-old widow of Atahualpa was fertile. Pizarro's DNA survives only in mestizos (Prescott, v. 2, p. 288).

Spain set up colonial administrations and trade routes, sent thousands of colonists, and began siphoning off the riches of the new world, quickly becoming *the* superpower of the sixteenth century. The rest of Europe schemed and attacked.

4

Treasure Galleons in Santa Cruz

Fifty years after Columbus' first voyage, the world was changed forever. Huge cargoes of American gold and silver were shipped to Spain twice a year. Additionally, Spain explored the Pacific and established trade routes with China and the Philippines. Some silver went west from Peru on the "Manilla Galleon", returning with silks, porcelain, jewels, and spices. "Corsairs," especially French ones, were so busy in the Caribbean that in 1542 King Charles V of Spain gave a royal decree that ships traveling to the West Indies must attach themselves to one of two convoys, sailing twice per year. Each was required to have at least ten armed vessels of 100 tons and one purpose-built warship. Two convoys left Seville together in March, and the next two in September, sailing down the coast of Africa for mutual defense against Moorish pirates and splitting up at the Canary Islands. Coming into the Caribbean, they carried cloth, farming implements, furniture, grain, brandy, mining tools, etc. for the colonists.

The "New Spain" fleet entered the Caribbean north of Guadalupe, then sailed to reach the south coast of Santa Cruz, which they used as a landmark. In the 16th century, islands the fleet passed upon entering the Caribbean were populated by Caribs, and any men sent ashore for provisions were in danger. It was safer to carry on one more day to Santa Cruz for fresh water and food. From 1515 to the 1630's Santa Cruz was unpopulated, but to this day there is a spring at Caledonia gut that empties in the western anchorage for most of the year. Sandy Point was, and still is, a parking lot for sea turtles several months of the year, though their numbers are far less today. Often described as tasting like a cross between filet mignon and fresh tuna, turtles of Santa Cruz provided a food staple for Puerto Rico and would have been a welcome addition to the food supplies aboard ship as well as a source of profit when the fleet reached San Juan. Because different species nest at different times of the year, you'll still see turtle tracks @ 20' apart along the entire stretch of Sandy Point several months of the year. From Santa Cruz, the fleet continued to Puerto Rico, Hispaniola, and west to Veracruz, Mexico (La America Espanola).

At Acapulco on the Pacific, silver and mercury arrived from the mines of Peru and joined with silks, porcelain, and spices the Manila Galleon brought from the east. Mule trains carried it all across from the Pacific to Veracruz on the Gulf of Mexico. Cocoa from "New Andalusia", Mexican gold, and logwood completed the cargo bound for Spain.

The "South Seas" fleet entered the Caribbean south of Dominica and headed for South America, putting in at Cartagena, Nombre de Dios, and Panama loading gold, silver, emeralds, cocoa, and hardwoods before sailing to Havana. From Havana, the two convoys joined once more to sail for Spain (La America Espanola).

With incredible wealth sailing into the Spanish treasury twice a year, England and France were not able to keep up with the arms race and did not have enough naval strength to take Spain on. The Netherlands, also known as the Seven Provinces or Holland, was in a struggle for independence from Spain and had to find a way to finance its revolution.

With cousins on the thrones of the Holy Roman Empire and Spain, the Habsburg family surrounded France. Across the Channel, England was vulnerable to invasion, unable to finance a navy capable of defeating Spain's. To increase their ability to fund a national defense and undermine the Spanish military budget, both nations allowed private enterprise to close the gap. Entrepreneurs sailed at their own expense to attack Spain's trade, and their home nations denied official responsibility.

National treasuries did not get a 'cut' from plunder in peacetime, but during times of war, these "Buccaneers" were given letters of marque as "Privateers". When sailing as Privateers, they owed a cut to the royal treasury, but received the protection of the royal navy, and were not hung if captured by the enemy. Thus, Buccaneers could be called upon to fight for their country in times of war —and still keep most of the loot. "Cry Havoc, and unleash the Dogs of War!" Buccaneers sailed and caught the scent.

Part II: BUCCANEERS

Spain was a brand-new country in 1492, with no money. They plunged immediately into competition with Portugal to get to India, to the markets of gold, spices, and silks that had made the long, dangerous Silk Road profitable. Christopher Columbus' explorations followed by those of the Conquistadors resulted in huge wealth pouring into Spain, enabling Spain to conquer Portugal in 1580 and rule the whole peninsula. Within a quarter of a century, this new nation became a major power; within a half-century, Spain was the superpower of the western world. Wealth was coming from the mines of South America, however, not from trade or farming, and Spain had no resources for settling the minor islands of the Lesser Antilles. English, French, and Dutch ships swarmed across the ocean; all three raced to weaken Spain, steal her plunder, and to claim Caribbean islands as their own. From the time the first Buccaneers appeared around 1528 until about 1715, they were a major force, if not the major force, in the Caribbean.

Every ship at sea was a potential enemy, so all ships were armed. Merchant vessels could not afford large crew and needed hull space for cargo rather than cannons. Most were rarely a match for a ship of force, but ***Armed Merchant Vessels,*** especially Dutch traders, not only expected to be attacked but to take prizes, and so were often formidable foes, sacrificing some valuable cargo space for a few more cannons. They often carried **Letters of Marque** from their governments authorizing them to take enemy prizes during their trading voyages.

Only Spanish ships were allowed to visit Spanish territory, and Spanish colonists only received goods from home twice a year, which was not enough to meet their needs. Merchant ships in the Treasure Fleet were taxed 20 percent of their *gross* to cover the cost of providing escort warships and to finance the royal treasury. These taxes made merchandise too expensive for their Spanish colonists. The result was that English, French, and Dutch smugglers were greeted warmly by many communities in Spanish America.

Armed merchantmen made such good profits that English governors wrote with frustration about not being able to keep warships on their station; even navy captains were packing their frigates with merchandise and selling it to desperate Spanish settlers in Cuba, Hispaniola, and Puerto Rico, as well as South and Central America. This practice was commonplace from the sixteenth century even up to 1718, when Woodes Rogers was sent with a flotilla of frigates to take Nassau from the pirates. Rogers took Nassau, but the town was immediately threatened both by pirate Charles Lane and a large Spanish invasion fleet. Rogers begged for his frigates to stay and help defend the colony, but they immediately sailed off to trade in Cuba. Fortunately for Rogers, Lane was soon deposed by his crew, and the Spanish force diverted to another fight.

Privateers were privately owned vessels that operated under a letter of marque from their government during times of war, but these vessels were purpose-built pocket warships that were not concerned with cargo space but instead with speed, agility, and punch. They flew the flag of their country. Their government took a percentage, investors took their piece, the captain got a big cut, and the crew got a little. If they took no prizes, no one got anything for their trouble.

Buccaneers (*Filibustiers*) operated *outside* of the law. They were patriotic and did not capture ships of their own nation, but did not have *permission* to take any prizes at all. They operated in peace as well as war, and profits went only to the captain and crew (except in the case of Drake and Hawkins, who gave the Queen a nice cut, calling into question whether they were buccaneers or her partners.). Though Buccaneers sometimes fought in battles on the side of their nation, sovereigns could conveniently claim that they had no control over them. In times of war, Governments issued Letters of Marque, officially making them Privateers, which, if captured, meant they would not hang as pirates.

The Buccaneers were English, Dutch, or French. Whether they worked together, as they often did, or fought each other, they always attacked the Spanish. Some of the most successful Buccaneers wound up as Admirals.

Pirates (*Corsairs*) operated against ships of any nation at any time, for their profit only. Typically, their only loyalty was to each other. A death warrant was on their heads; they were at war against the world.

Buccaneers of England, Holland, and France

English buccaneers started as merchants trading illegally with Spanish colonies.

On November 25, 1542, the Spanish Emperor Charles V abolished the enslavement of Indians in his "Leyes Nuevas." Spanish colonists were rabid for slave labor for their plantations. Captain John Hawkins put a trading expedition together, collected merchandise —mostly African captives-- and sailed into Vera Cruz (then "San Juan de Ulua"). A commercial license was extended to him on May 21, 1565, by Sir Rodrigo Caso, city mayor. The license was signed by Hernando Castilla and Miguel de Castellanos, treasurers; Lazaro de Vallejo Alderete, quartermaster; Baltasar de Castellanos and Domingo Felix, aldermen; and approved by Alonzo Hernandez, the Borburata governor. Hawkins and his investors made a lot of money (de Cordova, p. 515).

On Hawkins' next expedition in 1568 his young cousin, Francis Drake, commanded one of the smaller vessels. The new Spanish Viceroy in Vera Cruz, Martín Enríquez de Almanza, pretended to enter into negotiations to purchase their goods. Other English buccaneers had just attacked the convoy of Captain Don Francisco Luján while on the way to Vera Cruz; Lujan's fleet came limping into Vera Cruz while Hawkins' fleet was provisioning. In reprisal, Almanza ordered Lujan's escort warships to spring a surprise attack. Hawkins and 10 of his crew fought their way to join Drake's ship and escape, but the rest of the ships and sailors were left behind. Enraged at the treachery, more English 'buccaneers' swarmed to the Caribbean, considering anything Spanish to be fair game (de Cordova, p. 515). Corsairs were not successful against the combined strength of the convoys; Buccaneers instead raided Spanish warehouses before the convoys could arrive to take it on board.

The Seventeen Provinces of the Netherlands

were ruled by Charles V, who was also Emperor of Spain, Central Europe (Germany, Hungary, Austria, etc.), and parts of Italy. Charles tolerated Protestants, and the Dutch Reformed Church had become popular. When he abdicated in 1566, he left Spain and the Netherlands to his son, Philip II, who was of a different sentiment. Phillip immediately ordered an Inquisition. Protestants, and those accused of being Protestants, thousands of them, were tortured and murdered without a trial. He appointed a "Council of Troubles" in the Netherlands to encourage people to denounce their neighbors. The Duke of Alba and Philip's illegitimate sister, Margaret, ran the Council. Margaret referred to the Dutch as "those beggars." A noble, William of Orange, led a land rebellion, and Dutch sailors calling themselves the "Beggars of the Sea" armed their ships and set out to attack Spanish shipping. Privately owned vessels and those of the world's first corporations (The Dutch East India Company and The Dutch West India Company) were typically heavily armed merchant vessels, making good profits from smuggling to Spanish colonies and from capturing Spanish ships. The Caribbean became their favorite haunt, sailing out of Tortola, then St. Thomas and St. Croix. Dutch Buccaneers were fighting for their country's independence, so they did not consider themselves rogues. With some exceptions like murderous van Hoorne, they were religious men who commonly held church services at sea.

From 1566, Spain and the Netherlands were at war for 80 years out of the next 125. Spanish colonies and shipping were preyed upon by some of the most notorious Dutch buccaneers of all time, including Captains Joost van Dyk, Piet Heyn, Nikolaas van Hoorn, Roc Brasiliano, Laurens de Graaf, Michiel Andrieszoon, Michiel

Andriez, Yankey Williams, David Marteen, Bernard Speirdyke, Moses Cohen Henriques, and Michiel Andriaanzoon du Ruyter.

French Buccaneers (Filibustiers) in the Caribbean began as poor fishermen from Britany and Normandy, fleeing constant wars, religious persecution, and taxes. They made a living by fishing the waters of the Caribbean and Gulf Stream. They grew vegetables and smoked the meat of deer and boars they had brought over when they sailed across the Atlantic; the animals were allowed to fend for themselves in the bush until needed. The meat was cut into strips and smoked on the "boucan" (English: grill); thus, the settlers were "buccaneers." They sold the meat and vegetables to passing ships. The Spanish king considered all of the Caribbean his own, as mandated by the Pope himself, and was not amused (Pope Alexander VI, Inter Catera). He periodically sent fleets to wipe them out, but wherever this occurred, Buccaneers grew in numbers and activity. In 1629, while the men and boys of Tortuga were fishing offshore, Don Fadrique de Toledo arrived and landed soldiers who massacred everyone they found. He repeated this murder on the islands of St. Christopher (St. Kitts) and Nevis. Upon their return, the fishermen found the corpses of their children and wives rotting in the sun. Naturally, they turned to revenge. This Spanish attempt to wipe out French 'heretic' fishermen who had settled on 'Spanish' islands galvanized a grassroots vendetta and gave birth to the 'Buccaneers' (Esquemelin, A. O., Buccaneers of America, Ch. 1). Vengeful fishermen lying in the Gulf Stream at night seized Spanish ships. Romantic young noblemen using nom de guerres joined opportunistic sailors heading to the Caribbean. Captains Daniel Montbars ("The Exterminator"), Francois Bernier, Jean-David Nau ("L'Ollonais"), Alexander Bras de Fer, Jacques Gendre, "Le Blonde", Bernard Desjean, Jan Baert, Charles Martel, Michel de Grammont, Le Sieur Boissiramé, Honon de Galiffet, Pierre Grogniet, Philippe

Samson, Corneille, Jacques Daniels, and many others sailed for revenge... and gold.

Spain stumbled under the onslaught, and England, France, and the Dutch became stronger. They dared to seize islands as their own, not as illegal outposts for pirates, but as colonies. Officially treating them as trespassers, Spain, for the most part, bowed to reality, with only the occasional murderous response. Not individually strong enough to safeguard their colonies against Spanish aggression, the three European rivals joined in common cause, signing treaties to fight together against Spain and the Caribs no matter what the situation in warring Europe. Thousands of colonists poured into eastern Caribbean islands. As they invaded and took islands they had no 'legal' claim to, they built families, farms, and forts, amid the constant threat of bloody Carib and Spanish reprisals. Buccaneers were their only protection, their only dependable source of supplies, and the main customers for their produce.

Interestingly, the French 'Boucaneer' was used by the English, while the French called the same sailors 'Filibustiers.' In *The Eighth Flag*, to prevent confusion, only the word 'Buccaneer' is used.

Sint Kruis

Decades of war between England and France had
spawned hundreds of privateers and entire communities dependent
on income from privateering for their economy. English privateers
swarmed primarily out of the Channel Islands, and French privateers
mostly from Dunkirk. The lure of preying on the American colonies
of Spain was great, and as they already had the ships, financial
backing, and practice (Bromley, Ch. 10), the next step was to cross
the Atlantic. The Virgin Islands were a convenient staging ground
for raids on Puerto Rico by buccaneers of all nations. They often
worked together, despite relations in Europe, until the last years of
the 17th century. As the Spanish became more aggressive in striking
back, the most popular harbor in the Virgin Islands for buccaneers
was Salt River, Santa Cruz. It was the most defensible harbor for
small groups of ships.

The Virgin Islands were an important buffer to protect against a
Spanish attack on the Lesser Antilles and a convenient base from
which buccaneers could raid Puerto Rico and Santo Domingo.
Ships sweeping downwind from the Virgin Islands could easily
surprise the harbor of San Juan, which was only a night's sail away.
In contrast, raiding Puerto Rico from Jamaica would involve tacking
back and forth for a week. A swift sailing vessel could spot such a
fleet and dart ahead with a warning.

Europe was locked in years of continuous warfare. Navies were
busy protecting their home shores or attacking those of their
opponent. The West Indies was a backwater, with only occasional
visits from powerful warships. Francis Drake and John Hawkins
used Tortola, Saint Thomas, and Santa Cruz to stage raids against
Puerto Rico and Santo Domingo in their day. Dutch West India
Company Admiral Piet Heyns used a base on Tortola established by
Buccaneer Joost van Dyk to stage his attack on the Spanish Treasure

Fleet, but in retaliation for Heyn's destruction of the Silver Fleet, that base was destroyed.

Drake and Hawkins based themselves in the Virgin Islands twice, for a few months at a time, and legends of other 16th century pirates like Jost van Dyke can found in various archives, but Spain allowed no settlements to survive. However, between 1630 and 1650, Spain grew weaker, and military responses became less frequent. Shortly after Spain eliminated the Dutch base on Tortola, the Dutch West India Company built another trading post on St. Thomas (the deJongh and Riis families arrived at this time). On Santa Cruz, this period was more complicated.

Historians say that the Jamestown and Plymouth colonies had difficult beginnings, but they were simple compared to Saint Croix's start-up:

1631: William Hawley brought eighty hopeful **English** settlers from Barbados to farm tobacco on St. Croix. They put into the west end, Sandy Point, where turtles were an easy food source. Fishermen from Puerto Rico were making regular runs to Sandy Point for turtles, so they discovered the English after only four months. **Spanish** soldiers were dispatched from Puerto Rico by Gov. Sotomayor to "eliminate" the invaders (Archives, San Juan, Puerto Rico, Letters of the Governor to the King, 12 February 1632).

1634: French fishermen landed on the west end and built their new homes. Gov. Sotomayor again sent **Spanish** troops quickly, and the village was "eliminated" (from the same archives, letter from April 1634).

1635: English settlers led by a Bucccaneer named Brainsby were sent by Saint Christopher's Governor Thomas Warner to settle Saint

Croix. They arrived at the west end, built a village, planted tobacco, and began logging. New Puerto Rican Governor de la Motta Sariemento sent **Spanish** troops, and their camp was also "eliminated" (from the same archive, letter dated April 1636). The Englishmen escaped into the forest and then returned to St. Christopher. Immediately after, English pirates from Tortuga, tired of paying tribute to Governor, sailed for St. Croix, establishing a base in the harbor of Bassin in 1635.

1636: Dutch: In 1635, Jan Snouck, a sea Captain and trader from Vlissingen, obtained a license from the Zeeland Chamber of the Dutch West Indian Company to plant a colony on the island of Sint Kruis. Snouck enlisted two other merchants, Abraham van Pere, Sr., and Pieter van Rhee. They acquired a vessel and hired Pieter van Corselles to be the Commander. Van Corselles and forty settlers arrived at Basin early in 1636 and found Sint Kruis 'infested with pirates.'

The Dutch ship left immediately and, sailing east, came to Sint Eustatius, where French adventurers under Monsieur de Cahusac had built some structures including a fort during their stay from 1627 to 1629 before abandoning it. The Dutch quickly wrote to the Stadtholder asking for permission to settle Sint Eustatius instead.

(Oude West-Indische Compangnie 22, "Resolutions of the Zeeland Chamber, 27 December, 1635," Algemeen Rigksarchief, Eerste Afdeling,'s-Gravenhage).

(Dr. Arnold Highfield, *Sainte Croix 1650-1695, Antilles Press, Christiansted, VI, 2013, p. 54).*

> In the museum of Oranjestad, on the island of St. Eustatius, framed and hanging on the wall to your left immediately inside, is their "Founder's Letter". This letter first thanks the Stadtholder of the Netherlands for granting permission for the undersigned families to settle on "his" island of Saint Croix. It continues saying that, after a long and arduous passage, the settlers arrived at the settlement of Bassin (now Christiansted Harbor). A group of men went ashore to reconnoiter but immediately hurried back to the ships, having found "the island infested with pyrates." The settlers quickly put back to sea to look for another island upon which to settle. Arriving at the island of St. Eustatius, they found it uninhabited and much more suitable, and asked for his majesty's permission to build there, instead (Museum of St. Eustatius, Oranjestad).

1638: French, English, and **Dutch** settlers cleared land together on the west end of Santa Cruz. They opened trails, built homes, and traded with Carib people in Puerto Rico for two months. A hurricane threw two of their vessels from the west end of Santa Cruz onto the coastal reefs off Coamo, Puerto Rico. Two weakened survivors reached the shore aboard a longboat, and Spanish authorities took them prisoner and interrogated them. A sick Frenchman died within a few days, and they escorted the other prisoner to San Juan, Puerto Rico. "I, Captain-general Iñigo de la Mota Sarmiento (Governor of Puerto Rico) write of these events on 6 April 1639 (Bonet, p. 371)."

1641: British: Charles I granted a patent to the Earl of Carlisle to settle the "Caribby Islands." Sir. William Caverly asked the Earl for permission to colonize "Sancta Cruse" and sailed with his wife, Elisabeth, for St. Christopher, where they convinced Brainsby to try again. Another party was assembled, sailed for St. Croix, and settled this time in Salt River Bay. Brainsby leveled parts of the hill on the west side of the bay and mounted a few cannons.

1642: The Dutch colony of "Sint Kruis": Sint Eustatius was small, dry, and had no good dirt. It also had no harbor safe from storms and was too far from Spanish Islands of the Greater Antilles for easy trade. Jan Snouck hired Buccaneer Louis Capoen and gathered a new group of settlers. They landed at Salt River, where they met Brainsby and Caverly in battle. Caverly received a mortal wound from a pistol but escaped, and Brainsby and eight other officers were hung. British survivors were given a choice: transportation to St. Christopher's or swear allegiance to the Prince of Orange, Stadtholder of the Netherlands (Caverly's widow, Elizabeth, told of these events when she wrote seeking a pension from King Charles II, CSP 1652, #47).

Until the Danes built fortifications in St. Thomas Harbor, Salt River Bay was the most defensible harbor in the Virgins and provided the safest careenage and hurricane hole. It also offered a unique food source: huge middens left behind by Indigenous people show that the bottom of Salt River Bay was once *covered* with oysters, mussels, and other shellfish. Today the bay is not the same. Centuries of erosion caused by agriculture have filled in around the edges and deposited six feet of silt and sand on the bottom. Mangroves have crept into much of what was, in 1642, a much larger anchorage, and only the middens prove that shellfish once lived in the bay.

Alexander Esquemeling wrote of English, Dutch, and French Buccaneers who sailed from Sint Kruis during the Dutch period. Though he didn't sail from Sint Kruis himself, Esquemeling sailed and fought all over the Spanish Main with many who did so (Exquemelin, A. O.; Credit for the confusion in spelling this name belongs to the author. When he retired from Buccaneering and returned to Europe, Alexander spelled his name Exquemeling on his Dutch and French editions and Esquemeling on his English one. He thought people would buy his book quicker if he spelled his name like he was their countryman. Because the editions have passages that are different, they must be cited separately.).

From the 1640s through the 1670s, Captain Joseph Williamson operated his heavily armed trading vessel as a Buccaneer and a smuggler between all of the Leeward Islands. Quick to buy rounds at the bar, he was everyone's friend, always had desirable merchandise for sale, and was invited to dinner at the Governor's house often (Williamson paid him a percentage). Meticulous in his observations, he was *Sir* Joseph Williamson, a spy, and he reported directly to the Admiralty in London. He wrote that many Dutch, French, and English Buccaneers operated out of St. Croix, mentioning specifically that de Ruyter lived on St. Croix for five years in the 1640s. (CSP v. 31 #98), and it makes sense. Sint Kruis was a colony of the Vlissingen chamber of the Dutch West India Company, and Vlissingen was the hometown of Michiel de Ruyter.

Father de Tertre wrote that Michiel de Ruyter, Jan Lifde, Alexandre Bras-de-Fer, and Daniel Montbars ("The Exterminator") operated out of Salt River at this time (de Tertre, trans. Caron and Highfield; Highfield, Sainte Croix, p. 31).

In addition to hosting Buccaneers, records show that 300 Dutch men at arms—craftsmen, merchants, and farmers--lived around Salt

River, and there were also salt harvesters on the West End. In the interest of having enough guns to oppose the Spanish, the Dutch also allowed One hundred twenty French fishing families to continue living in Bassin. Swearing allegiance to the Prince of Orange, 300 British settlers stayed, and two British logging camps operated at Limetree Bay and on the west end (Highfield, *Sainte Croix*, p. 57).

Journals by Buccaneers Exquemelin, Wafer, Ringrose, and others document a half-century of Buccaneering expeditions in which British, French, and Dutch Buccaneers raided Spanish colonies together. Their friendships lasted a lifetime, even after many of them became admirals of rival navies. Personal letters between Robert Blake and Michel de Ruyter, de Ruyter and Abraham Duquesne, Jean du Casse and John Benbow, etc., survive and show that they often visited each other in peacetime, exchanging gifts.

For five years, Michiel de Ruyter helped keep Sint Kruis safe. His routine was to leave Holland after Christmas, sailing his ship *Salamander* to Morocco, where he sold his cargo and purchased the freedom of Christian slaves with the money. He carried them to the Caribbean, where many of those rescued were happy to settle as colonists. In the Caribbean, he based himself in "Sint Kruis," returning to Holland at the onset of hurricane season each August. When de Ruyter left the Caribbean for Holland in 1646, a desperate group was waiting.

SAINT CROIX, AND THE RETURN OF THE KING

1646, British Exiles: Nine years of bloody civil war in England left one hundred thousand civilians dead and nearly as many soldiers. The war came to an end in July of 1646 at the Battle of Naseby, where Oliver Cromwell and his "New Model Army" won a final, complete victory over the royalist forces of King Charles I.

Charles I was beheaded. His nephew, "Prince Rupert of the Rhine", who had commanded the royal cavalry, secured some of what had been the English Royal Navy and loaded the ships with surviving royalist officers and their families. Rupert ordered General James Ley, the Earl of Marlborough, to sail for Saint Croix.

Saint Croix was considered the last 'good' (for its agricultural potential) island still up for grabs. Proximity to the dangerous Spanish base in Puerto Rico had kept nations from committing the resources necessary to build proper fortifications. The English refugees sailed into Saint Thomas harbor and waited a couple of weeks for Michiel de Ruyter to sail back to Europe at the beginning of August. As soon as he left the area, the first of the English fleet sailed south and anchored off the west end of Saint Croix.

Ley left two hundred soldiers under Colonel Sir Braselet to secure the island while the fleet sailed for the better anchorage of Saint Thomas.

The Dutch cautiously welcomed Rupert's first arrivals. Rupert was a great-grandson of William the Silent, Prince of Orange (the founder of the Dutch nation), and more men-at-arms made the island better able to repel a Spanish invasion. The welcome quickly soured when Sir Braselet named himself the new Governor. An argument broke out, and the Dutch governor killed Braselet. English soldiers then killed the Dutch governor. Each elected a new leader, and the new Dutch leader was lured to a parley where he, too, was killed.

The rest of Rupert's fleet arrived at Saint Croix and landed one thousand more refugees. Outnumbered, the Dutch agreed to leave for St. Eustatius. French citizens of Saint Croix did not feel safe and hired an English ship under Captain Paul to take them to Guadalupe. Paul asked a stiff price: titles to their property on Saint Croix. On arrival, Governor Houle arrested Paul for blackmail and seized his ship and cargo, dividing the proceeds among the displaced. Captain Paul remained in jail on Guadalupe until he went insane, at which time Houle shipped him home to England (Crouse, p. 21-24; CSP v. 31, #98).

What flag flew over Saint Croix at the end of 1646? Rupert flew the Union Jack, but he did not represent the government of Great Britain. St. Croix belonged to pirates who had once been British. The flag was a lie; the proper flag was black.

The Greatest Buccaneer of All Time

Ley gave 23-year-old Buccaneer **Captain Christopher Myngs** (ship *Elisabeth*) charge of constructing defenses for Saint Croix. Myngs soon learned of a rich Dutch convoy from a Buccaneer friend and sailed off for plunder. Myngs promoted a 19-year-old Welsh Midshipman, **Henry Morgan**, to Lieutenant and charged him with organizing the defenses of Saint Croix. In his three years on Saint Croix, Morgan improved the Dutch "Fort Flammand" on the west side of Salt River Bay (the island capital). He also added batteries at the northeastern tip of Bassin Harbor and at the west end where Fort Frederick is today (Calendar of State Papers, v.20, #202). Morgan would go on to become known as the greatest of all the Buccaneers. Disappointed in Myngs, Ley appointed a Major Reynoulds to govern St. Croix (Highfield, *Sainte Croix*, p. 59), and he was replaced when Rupert sent Governor Nicholas Phelps (CSP v. 5, p. 1). Fifty-five tobacco farms were cleared and operating within two years, with villages at Basin, the west end, and Salt River.

Parliament tasked **Robert Blake** with creating a new navy for England, and he did an amazing job. Blake took on dockyard corruption, improved warship design, raised sailors' pay, and quickly trained a cadre of new officers. In short order, Blake built a navy superior to any in the world.

Seventeen officers with Royalist sympathies sailed to Holland and turned their warships over to Charles II's exile government. Charles gave the ships to Rupert, who sent the vessels to his younger brother, Maurice, then operating from the Virgin Islands. Never before or since has there been a pirate fleet with state-of-the-art naval warships and such trained, disciplined sailors.

Maurice split his fleet. He operated from St. Thomas with the larger ships, and smaller ones sailed from Salt River on Saint Croix.

Rupert established two more pirate lairs, one in the Scilly Isles and one on the Channel Island of Jersey. He recruited swarms of small pirate vessels in the Channel Islands, gave them Letters of Marque from a government that did not exist, and sent them into the Bay of Biscay and the North Sea. Rupert's vessels captured hundreds of ships of all nations.

After Admiral Blake captured the bases in Scilly and Jersey, he chased Rupert and his warships around the Atlantic and Mediterranean before being recalled to deal with French and Dutch navies.

Rupert rejoined Maurice. Logbooks show they supported Saint Croix by sending large warships to the west end on a rotating basis, where they filled water casks from the spring at Concordia. Spain had no warships in the Caribbean that could stand up to them. Buccaneer Alexander Esquemeling wrote that at this time, pirates sailing out of Saint Croix and Saint Thomas made the waters

surrounding Puerto Rico the most dangerous in the world. Loot was
sent to Charles II's court in exile to build the 'royal' treasure chest.

1647: In hurricane season, Rupert's fleet sailed south to trouble
Trinidad. Puerto Rican Governor Fernando de la Riva Aguero
seized the opportunity to punish Buccaneers operating out of Tortola
and Saint Croix. He first destroyed the Dutch village on Tortola,
where survivors ran into the bush. Aguero's men then sailed to the
west end of St. Croix. They encountered **Henry Morgan** and
more opposition than they were ready for and were thrown back into
the sea (Archives in San Juan, letter to the King, 1647; Highfield,
Sainte Croix, p. 72).

1649: Holy Roman Emperor Ferdinand restored the von Simmern
family (Rupert's brother, Charles) as Elector of the Palatinate of the
Rhine. Rupert left the fleet with Maurice and returned to Charles,
playing politics and claiming the allowance he was now due.

1650: Meleé! The bloodiest year in the history of the Virgin Islands:

1. August: Spain. Governor Aguilera of Puerto Rico sent a
spy to Santa Cruz. The spy drew a map detailing the fortifications
on Saint Croix and reported that Maurice's fleet of pirates had left
Virgin Islands waters for the hurricane season (see map below).
Morgan was no longer on Saint Croix either, as he had rejoined
Captain Myngs.

Aguilera sent Don Lorenzo Perez de Tavora to Santa Cruz with
1200 soldiers on five ships. Troops disembarked at Cane Bay and
marched four miles east along the old Indian footpath during the
night to surprise the Salt River fort at dawn. In the battle on August
20, 120 English soldiers died, and the rest fled into the mangroves
(Exquemelin, A.O.; Raynal, p. 274). Tavora knew his men could
never get the British out of the swamp, but he also knew that they

would not enjoy being devoured by mosquitoes and midges. Tavora offered exile, and the survivors came out of the swamp. Tavora wrote that all of the Englishmen were transported to St. Cristopher.

2. The Dutch heard that Tavora had returned to Puerto Rico and immediately sent soldiers to Santa Cruz from St. Eustatius, sailing in under the cannons of Fort Flammand. Unfortunately for them, a **Spanish** garrison of 60 men remained in the fort, and they opened fire. Dutch survivors were captured when they swam ashore. (Crouse, pp. 26, 27).

3. French Buccaneers invaded, under the orders of history's great bastards: Sieur Phillippe de Poincy, "Lord Ozymont." De Poincy came up with a battle plan and sent Sr. de Vaugalan with 160 men to take the island from Spain. De Vaugalan first took the battery Morgan had built at Bassin, then marched to the fort at Salt River and took it. He freed the Dutch 'swimmers' and sent them home to Sint Eustatius.

1651: Prince Maurice returned with his pirate fleet to Saint Thomas. While formulating a plan to retake Saint Croix, a hurricane hit the Virgin Islands. Prince Maurice von Simmern perished with all of the larger warships; of his fleet, only five small ships survived. Rupert lost his brother/best friend and was out of the pirate business, but the money he had made was already changing Britain's future.

On Sainte Croix, de Poincy granted estates to the most dangerous men on the planet. In 1655 Spanish soldiers landed again but were quickly driven back into the sea by Pierre LeGrand and his Buccaneers.

Rupert's dream came true in 1660. Money from the sale of Rupert's loot helped finance one of the great comebacks of history: the King's return. In 1660, Charles II landed and was quickly asked by Parliament to rule Great Britain. Rupert was no longer a pirate but a Lord again, and soon, Admiral of the Fleet.

Sainte Christopher
Nursery for Sainte Croix

Two Norman pirates, Pierre Belain and Urbain de Roissey brought their ships into St. Christopher in 1625. They found Caribs co-existing with French tobacco farmers and 400 English colonists led by Thomas Warner. They went home to France with the idea of founding the first official French colony in the Antilles, won royal approval, and returned with 240 colonists. Ironically, of all of the Antillean islands, Warner's colony on St. Christopher was also the first English colony in the Caribbean. Spanish raids, neglect, and drought left the colonists in dire straits, but Dutch traders extended them credit and kept them supplied with essentials. English and French colonists had a written agreement: whatever wars were happening in Europe, they would not fight each other but were bound to fight together against the Spanish.

In 1635 the *Compagnie des Iles d'Amerique* was born, with a royal charter to establish colonies on any islands not yet occupied by a "Christian prince," though at this time only St. Christopher had colonists. The *Compagnie* would run the colonies, and a Governor would be named by the King as his representative, governing and defending them but *not allowed to take part in trade*. In 1638, with some 3000 French men on the island (the English side had grown to 6000),

King Louis XIII named Phillippe de Poincy as Governor. De Poincy was descended from Vikings on his father's side, ennobled since the days of Rollo. His mother was of ancient French noble blood (Dube' pp. 244-6, 270).

Bastard

A naval officer, army general, and commander of the Knights of St. John, the Chevalier Phillippe de Longvilliers de Poincy, Knight Commander of the Order of Oyzemont, had joined the Knights of St. John Hospitallers (Knights of Malta) as a teenager. At 19, he was knighted after leading a successful frontal assault against a Turkish fortress. As a young chevalier of the Knights of St. John, he captained privateer vessels in the Mediterranean Sea against the Turks. De Poincy wasn't ordered to attack defenseless Turkish merchants; he was ordered to seek and destroy Turkish pirates. Recalled home to France, he sailed out of ports in Brittany as a "Dunkirker" to destroy English and Dutch shipping. As he matured, he rose to command the base and be an advisor to Cardinal Richelieu, who served as Foreign Secretary and Chief Minister under Louis XIII (Cultru, Ch. 4).

Louis XIII died in 1638, leaving his four-year-old son on the throne. Not only was France at war with Spain – Spain's army at one time approaching within three miles of Paris-- but some of the nobility tried to stage a coup against the young king (the Fronde War), and a civil war was raging. In the Caribbean, Caribs constantly raided French colonies –now located on Martinique and Guadeloupe as well-- from their bases on St. Lucia and Dominica. Unable to send any regular French troops or ships, the new Chief Minister, Cardinal Mazarin, asked the Knights of St. John Hospitallers (Knights of Malta) to administer French West Indian possessions. De Poincy was named Governor of St. Christopher and Governor-general of His Majesty's American Islands by the Knights of Malta and confirmed by the King's regent, Anne of Austria.

Arriving at the French Antillean capital of Basse Terre, St. Christopher, De Poincy immediately set out to build his fortune. He is famous to students of the buccaneering period because as

77

Governor-general of Tortuga and all of the French West Indies, he tolerated the presence of Buccaneers --for a percentage. Piracy may have paid, but doing business with the pirates paid very well.

De Poincy built up the colony on St. Christopher. He built roads, warehouses, wells, irrigation systems, bridges, chapels, a hospital, port installations, and beautified villages. He also created the necessary bureaucratic organization. To do so, de Poincy reached into his pocket. He went further into debt by buying several hundred hectares of land on Martinique for himself, building two sugar factories with six mills, and purchasing 600 African slaves. This ambitious building program led to conflict with the Caribs. By the end of 1640, de Poincy had driven Caribs off of St. Christopher, Martinique, and Guadalupe. Caribs now held only the islands of Dominica and St. Lucia. European nations made a treaty with each other and with the Caribs. Caribs would have those islands unmolested by Europeans if they promised to stop raiding (this is a provision of the Treaty of Aix la Chapelle).

As Royal Governor, de Poincy was explicitly ordered not to involve himself in trade, but he ignored this and set up a system on St. Christopher whereby merchandise and food sent to the colony was stored in his private warehouse. When scarcity drove prices high, he would then sell what wasn't his in the first place, thereby restoring his investment and profiting at the same time. On hearing of this outrage, the boy King's mother had her son sign a Commission for De Poincy to be replaced as Governor-General of the French West Indies by M. de Patrocles de Thoisy. A Capuchin monk brought the official letter to De Poincy, and posted copies of it around the Capital, Basse Terre, in January of 1644. De Poincy, in true pirate form, refused to honor the Commission. Capuchin monks on St. Christopher went among the colonists decrying the crime; they were all jailed, soon sprung by members of their congregation, and fled to Guadeloupe (Cultru, Ch. 4).

A "Patrocles faction" formed on St. Christopher, and a group of colonists demanded that De Poincy honor the King's commission. These people put everything on the line for their King. They made the wrong choice. Not only was De Poincy capable of defying the King, but their boy King would also betray them, and they would lose everything. Most of the militia remained under De Poincy's control, and they began arresting and torturing men known to belong to "The Patrocles". When "Patrocles" members learned that they were to be arrested, they ran and hid in the bush. Militia Captain Grement put a bounty of 10,000 pounds of tobacco on the heads of two fellow militia captains, de la Fontaine and M. Camot, who accompanied them. A citizen accused of posting the King's flier announcing that de Poincy had been replaced was marched through the streets of Basse-Terre naked except for a shirt, carrying a candle. When he reached the square, he was decapitated (Dubé, p. 267).

A 12-year-old boy, Antoine-Marie, was caught and accused of taking food to his father, who was with "The Patrocles". Lit wicks were placed between his fingers, burning them horribly, yet he would not tell where his father was. The ruined fingers were each cut off. A vice made of a rope and two sticks was twisted on the boy's head. This brave young boy would not betray his father, and while the rope was tightening, father De Tertre says that his skull was heard cracking. Priests were able to take his confession before the boy died eight days later (De Tertre 1978, p. 7).

Grement put a tub of bacon out as a trap for the starving rebels. A youth named Jean Duret was caught trying to make off with it. De Poincy cut off his nose and ears, then tired of playing with him and had his head cut off. Brains scooped out, De Poincy used Jean's head in a game of bowls (DuTertre 1978, p. 8). This was no man to have as your enemy.

Captains de la Fontaine and M. Camot sent their African servants to find food. The servants were caught but would not reveal their masters' whereabouts even while their toes were being cut off. De Poincy threatened to throw all wives and children left behind by the rebels into the sea. Fontaine and Camot, who had been hiding in a large tree, made their way to the coast and put to sea in a small dinghy, with no expectations of survival. They were, however, picked up by a passing ship whose captain happened to be a friend. He carried them to France, where they reported De Poincy's depredations and treason to the Queen (DuTertre, 1667, p. 8).

Du Tertre says that all those merely suspected of sympathizing with "The Patrocles" had their possessions looted, were caned and banished from the island. In desperation, some made rafts and set out for other islands at the mercy of the currents. An Irish friar, Father Trinity, put a dozen innocents on rafts that escaped at night. Most drifted downwind to the different Virgin Islands; he steered to Puerto Rico. All of the people with him were murdered by Spaniards when they made it ashore. On his knees making a last confession, he was recognized as a priest and taken to a Dominican monastery. (DuTertre, pp. 5-6). Crouse says one priest who helped load rafts with children was executed for treason by de Poincy the next day. A slave uprising occurred at the same time; de Poincy did not waste time with trials. Rebels were run down and killed. Those who surrendered were quartered: a horse was tied to each limb, and rumps struck with switches (Dube', p. 267).

De Poincy was too dangerous to cast aside. The French needed someone strong to hold on to their islands. France was still at war. Caribs, Spain, England, and the Dutch posed a constant threat to the safety of the French Antilles, and de Poincy was, after all, noble and a distant cousin. The Minister and Regent decided that only an intelligent and ruthless man such as de Poincy stood a chance of keeping the colonies together for the time being.

In 1647 De Poincy was ordered by Cardinal Mazarin to claim Sainte Croix for France. De Poincy determined to kill two birds with one rock; He rounded up 66 men that he *suspected* might back the Queen and de Thoisy against him and convicted them as criminals on trumped-up charges, creating a group of expendables. One of them, Vincent Veillet, known as "La Haye", had long held the office of Court Clerk on St. Christopher; another was weighing master at Customs; the others were mostly militia officers.

DeTertre says that De Poincy would only let them out of prison if they agreed to exile. He wrote that the exiles were sent to "a spacious plantation developed by the English and upon which had been planted quantities of sweet potato and cassava."

Dr. Aimery Caron, who translated deTertre's journal with Dr. Arnold Highfield, believes that the island referred to was Tortola. But de Poincy had just received an order from the King to settle Sainte Croix, and Sainte Croix at the time was under the control of the British royalist exiles. Because Sainte Croix was occupied by people who had no nation to back them up, it was ripe for the taking. Tortola was, at the time, a Dutch island, and the Dutch had many powerful ships. Regardless, the exiled Frenchmen sailed on 'Jean Pinart's small sloop' to an island 'near to Porto Rico' and were put ashore at a large bay near a fort (I believe this was Salt River). Expecting to find some people near the fort, they found only fresh bodies of English men and women spoiling in the sun; de Tertre says the exiles spent their first nights ashore breathing the stench and devoured by mosquitos. DeTertre says that the Governor of Puerto Rico learned of de Poincy's plan to claim the island for France and sent another raiding party. Spanish soldiers drove the French exiles into the hills but took great losses, including the Governor of Puerto Rico's nephew, and soon returned to Puerto Rico. The crew of Pinart's ship fought alongside the French exiles in this battle, and afterward, fearing that the Spanish would return in larger numbers, I believe Pinart then took the exiles to Tortola. Dutch colonists would have welcomed them as reinforcements, as a Spanish raid was anticipated, and a Spanish raiding party did wipe out the Dutch settlement later in the year. Attempting to escape the wrath of Spain, some of the survivors built a raft and sailed it on a strange adventure to several different islands before being 'rescued' and set ashore in Puerto Rico itself, where they were treated well. Ironically, in Puerto Rico, they were guests, not enemy squatters who posed a threat to Spanish claims. Other exiles went to nearby St. John, where the Veillet, or "Vialet" family would live for the next several centuries, establishing itself as one of the leading families of the Virgin Islands even today.

Sainte Croix

De Poincy questioned French buccaneers. They told him that 60 Spanish soldiers had returned to Sainte Croix. De Poincy sent 160 soldiers with the Buccaneers (Raynal, 160 soldiers, p. 275). Included in the invasion force were a couple of dozen battle-hardened fellow Knights of St. John under M. de Vaugalan and some of the most dangerous French Buccaneers of the age. The fort surrendered. Settlers followed, and de Poincy plunged immediately into building the new colony. Within a year, however, the Governor and 200 of the colonists were dead of malaria, and the Buccaneers were off plundering Spanish colonies. **In 1651, de Poincy was allowed to buy the island of St. Croix from Louis XIV (now 17 years old) as his private estate.**

A fierce fighting force must be in place to hold Sainte Croix for France, but France had neither soldiers nor warships to spare. The first thing de Poincy did was to offer land to French Buccaneer captains and fellow Knights of St. John. He then sent engineers and bondsmen to add to the Dutch village around Salt River Bay and build a private residence. The water pump tower remains from his plantation. De Poincy visited but continued to split most of his time between Martinique, where he had extensive holdings, and St. Kitts. He was already over-extended and, at 66 years old, pretty ancient by 1651 standards (Camus, pp.119-125) (trivia: Napoleon's Empress Josephine was a direct descendant of De Poincy).

Pirates Become Planters

St. Croix would have to be attacked before any Spanish forces could invade the Leeward Islands; the Spanish were not comfortable leaving an enemy in their rear. Spain did not want to let St. Croix go. How did de Poincy expect that his colony could succeed where England's and Holland's had not? Fearing a Spanish invasion at any time, knowing that England and Holland also claimed the island as their own, he took a cue from his family history.

At the beginning of the tenth century, French King Charles "The Fat" could not keep Vikings from raiding the coast of France. Wherever he sent his army, they struck somewhere else, overwhelming local forces. Rollo, the most feared Viking of them all, threatened Paris itself, and Charles devised a unique plan. Charles made Rollo a Duke and gave all of Normandy to him as his fief. In exchange, Rollo sent Charles taxes, contributed soldiers to the army of France, and kept other Vikings out. Rollo's Vikings became plantation owners.

If you were low born in France, you had few chances of social climbing, and most buccaneers started life at the bottom of the ladder. The measure of success for Frenchmen was to become a landowner. The chance to settle down and have a family, to make it into the exalted class of estate owners, must have been appealing. The names of many French Buccaneers appear on the militia rolls of Sainte Croix, and history also records that they sailed for France when their country needed them. Many more names found on the maps and census records may have been Buccaneers but only those whose names also appear in the journals of Buccaneers Ringrose, Wafer, and the Exquemelin are mentioned below. Buccaneers were often away from the island, either as pirates supplementing their income or in wartime while serving as Louis XIV's proxy Caribbean navy, so the number of men at arms on St. Croix went up and down dramatically, depending on whether or not France was at war. These fighting men were not farmers, which helps explain why Sainte Croix was never a very productive agricultural colony.

Census records for Sainte Croix during the French period exist only for the years 1680-96. They show a who's who of notorious French Buccaneers and Knights of St. John. Many of their names also appear on maps drawn in 1660 by Gerard van Keulen and by Lapointe in 1671, and their names appear in letters from Governors to the foreign office in Paris. The title "Sieur" appears in front of the names of Knights of St. John of Jerusalem in the census records, and sometimes famous Buccaneer Captains were Knights of St. John, as well.

An invasion force would have to land soldiers at one of six beaches on St. Croix, beaches located where boats could row in. These beaches were: Cane Bay (**Rivere Salee** Quarter), West End (**Pointe de Sable** quarter); the east side of Sandy Pointe (**Pointe de Sable**). the bay in front of where the Buccaneer Hotel currently sits (**Mestre de Camp**); Salt River Bay (**Rivere Salée**), and a beach at Great Pond Bay (where the Boy Scout camp is now located, then called "**Fond de Monery**").

Buccaneer Captain Michel de Grammont, one of the most famous pirates of all time, served as commander –Major- of St. Croix's six militia companies (Highfield, Sainte Croix, p. 520; Johnson, Notorious; Archives Nationale Outre Mer, C&A-18, folder 70-114) from 1670-1678. His estate was in the **Riviere Salee** Quarter (Lapointe map, DuTertre). He led the group of eleven Buccaneer ships that sailed from St. Croix to join the ill-fated expedition of Jean, Comte d'Estrées (Exquemelin, A. O.).

Owning an estate not only raised Buccaneers to a minor class of nobility, but it also allowed them to 'settle down." Pierre le Grand appears in the census records as the owner of Estate LaGrange in **Pointe de Sable** Quarter. LeGrand was a notorious Buccaneer. In 1634, the Dutch West India Company hired him as military commander for Johannes Walbeck's expedition that captured Curacao from Spain. A few years later, with 28 men in a small boat, LeGrand rowed up to a Spanish treasure galleon that had 250 crew one night, and as his men climbed onto the hull of the ship, LeGrand took a hatchet and knocked a hole in their small boat, sinking it for motivation. They took the ship. On Sainte Croix, census records in the 1680's show that he married, and when his wife died, he was left with four daughters to raise. Though he bought indentures to work the LaGrange estate, most ended up sailing with him as crew. Imagine the excitement at the end of a voyage: "Daddy's home!"

Buccaneer Captain and Knight Sieur La Pointe appears in the same census with an estate in the same quarter, with a wife and three children (van Keulen and Lapointe maps; Archives Nationale Outre Mer, cote: 5DPPC/52).

According to census records and maps of the period, Buccaneer Captain Jacques Daniel raised his children on his estate in the **Pointe du Sable** quarter (Archives Nationale Outre Mer, cote: 5DPPC/52). The royal treasurer of the Sainte Croix colony, Duverger, accused Daniel of selling pirated cargoes in Sainte Croix in times of peace (Highfield, St. Croix, p. 503; Archives Nationales, Section Outre Mer, C8A and B14, p. 580).

Captain Sieur Francois Bernier was given land in the **Pond du Monery** Quarter, located around what is now called Great Pond. There is an entrance on the west side of the reef. (Archives Nationale Outre Mer, cote: 5DPPC/52, Highfield p. 520). Originally from St. Barthelemy, Bernier was a Crusader Knight and former militia Captain and Major on St. Kitts (Crouse).

Captain Charles Martel was given land on Sainte Croix in quarter **Mestre de Camp**. His estate was where Gallows Bay and the Buccaneer Hotel are today. Martel had a wife and two sons, Charles Jr. and Jean Roux Martel (below, "St. Croix's Pirate Shipwreck") listed in the census (Archives Nationale Outre Mer, cote: 5DPPC/52, Lapointe and van Keulen maps). The Martel family appears in Sainte Croix census records until St. Croix's Buccaneers sailed off to fight in the Nine Years War, at which time Charles' wife is listed first with the two boys but the next year alone;

the boys sailed off with their father. Captain Charles Martel, his sons, and the rest of St. Croix's Buccaneers were not home when St. Croix was abandoned in 1695 because they were plundering Spanish colonies. Their names appear in accounts of the raid on Cartagena in 1697 (Exquemelin, A. O.; Highfield, p. 520).

With invasion beaches under the watchful eyes of these dangerous men and their crews, more Buccaneers were given estates located on the line of march between those beaches and where settlements were located. Buccaneer Captains Grogniet, Samson, and Sieur de Beguet (one-time Governor of Sainte Croix, Knight of St. John and Crusader veteran) were given land in the Riviere Salee (Salt River) Quarter (Highfield, Sainte Croix, p. 520; Archives National Outre-Mer, C8A-18, #70-114, also census records, cote: 5DPPC/52 and maps of the period), along with eight other battle-hardened Knights.

In addition to the fort at Salt River, a battery commanded the entrance to Bassin harbor that Lt. Henry Morgan had built in 1646 (the French rebuilt the dirt battery with stone and named it Fort Sainte Jean. Danes later made it higher and renamed it Fort Louise Augusta). Another of Morgan's batteries that covered the western anchorage (where Fort Frederick now stands), plus a new sand fort farther north protected the west end (near present-day "Rainbow Beach"). Another small battery at Pointe Española (Long Point) protected the eastern side of Point du Sable (Sandy Point). Finally, a central bastion for the last stand in case of an invasion by overwhelming force was built at "Ste. Ans" and stocked with provisions. At the ruins of 'Fort Augusta,' the remains of the French fort—small, similar-sized stones meticulously placed—form the bottom layer, with Danish era masonry—rocks of every size and shape jammed together with occasional yellow bricks and coral chunks--make up the top layer. This holds true throughout the island so that it is easy to distinguish between masonry of the different periods. The reason is obvious: many French indentures were trained in masonry (just visit France) and had the possibility of freedom followed by entrepreneurship—they would need a good reputation (the fact that almost none would ever actually become free is immaterial). Enslaved masons of the Danish period had no such hope and thus no reason to give a damn (would you?). Besides, Danish masonry was all smothered in plaster, anyway.

In 1653 Prince Rupert sent his brother Maurice to try and retake Saint Croix. Anchoring in St. Thomas Harbor (Charlotte Amalie), Maurice sent spies to check out French forces on the island and found them too strong. He turned his eyes on the Spanish Treasure Fleet, but a hurricane that struck St. Thomas sunk several ships, including his own (70 guns), and scattered the rest. (Esquemeling, A. O.). Maurice perished in the storm with his ship, and private letters show that Rupert was heartbroken.

Where is the wreckage of what had been the Royal Navy and the bones of Maurice? In a hurricane, most ships slam into the shore. Exactly where depends on the direction of the wind when lines parted or anchor drug. Perhaps the bones of ships and Prince lie under the concrete of Veteran's Drive today.

In 1655 Spanish troops from Puerto Rico invaded the west end of Sainte Croix, but French Buccaneers quickly drove them into the sea.

Labor and Militia

De Poincy needed more militia to defend Sainte Croix, especially when the Buccaneers were away, and the plantations needed laborers, but he dared not arm African captives as militia. Puerto Rico was very close, had too many soldiers to take lightly, and Puerto Rico had invaded St. Croix many times in the recent past. He felt that white bondsmen, who held out the hope of freedom if they behaved themselves, could be safely used for both labor and militia. On Martinique, an island much farther from the threat of a Puerto Rican invasion, there were ten times the number of black people as there were white people. On St. Croix, in times of plenty, there was twice the number of white people to black people. In times of drought, war, or disease, more of the white settlers died of malaria or left to go pirating, and the numbers would be about the same. Thus, in the French period, some of St. Croix was built by captive African labor, but white indentured laborers were mixed equally in the labor pool (Camus, pp. 119-125; Crouse, pp. 25-31).

De Poincy spent a lot of money building infrastructure on St. Croix. His engineers built roads and bridges on the old Taino footpaths, and they built cisterns and wind-powered irrigation systems. Colonists cleared land and established 164 plantations. Eighteen were devoted to growing sugar, 31 to food and cattle, and 115 to tobacco, with the rest producing cotton and indigo (Highfield, Sainte-Croix, pp. 232-233).

Tobacco from Sainte Croix was prized above all other from the Caribbean (Crouse). Wool clothing was what Europeans wore. Cotton did not grow in Europe, nor tobacco. Before those crops came to be cultivated extensively in the southern English colonies of America, cotton had to be imported from Egypt or India, and tobacco from Turkey, which made them very expensive. Wild cotton still grows along the roadsides of St. Croix, and wild tobacco did into the 1970s. Indigo was the dye used to make cotton blue

(blue jeans today are this color), but there is no more indigo growing on St. Croix today.

To regain his investment, De Poincy got greedy. Buccaneers did as they pleased, but the only merchant ship he allowed to trade with St. Croix was his. He charged extremely high shipping charges on any goods coming in and on produce going out. According to Father Du Tertre, he shipped only the lowest grade merchandise at the highest prices.

The colonists were desperate for supplies, but they could not afford them even when the ship made its rare appearances. In addition to having insufficient tools, cloth, and food, they suffered horribly from malaria, so that 400 out of 600 bondsmen and free farmers and four Governors who arrived in Sainte Croix in 1650 died in two years (Crouse, p. 28). To gain access to more funds for development, De Poincy deeded the island to the Knights of St. John in 1653, remaining, however, as the administrator of the French Antilles (Crouse, p. 31). The Knights were men hardened in battle in the Holy Land.

In **1655** Knights set fire to the entire island, hoping to dry up the swamps and eradicate malaria. It did not work. The Knights had no interest in farming anyway, so many left after only one year. A couple of dozen stayed behind as plantation owners, de Poincy wanting to have at least a few Knights to lead and train each militia company alongside the Buccaneers.

As de Poincy sent more bondsmen to Sainte Croix, the possibility of an uprising grew. Most were young, teenaged orphans or juvenile delinquents who had been captured and sold by the government, not of their own free will. African captives knew their lot was slavery for life; they also were a powder keg waiting to go off at any moment. Two hundred white bondsmen and some African captives revolted in 1656, set fire to fields all over the island, took over de Poincy's ship, and sailed it to Brazil; it must have been a very tightly packed ship. It took two months for de Poincy to find out what had happened; this was, after all, the only merchant ship that had the authority to go to Sainte Croix. De Poincy sent militia soldiers to stage a witch hunt with severe punishment for any involved (DuTertre 1978, p. 12).

De Poincy had a plan to pacify the indentures. First, newspapers in France carried de Poincy's advertisements for young women who wished for an adventurous life, offering free passage. Prisons sent more. Packed into ships like cattle, many died on the way across. Those that survived were not an attractive lot. Pox scars, crippled limbs, often emotionally unstable, Du Tertre paints a sad picture of watching them disembark (DuTertre 1978, p.11). Women from the poor classes had nothing to look forward to but a life of servitude. Desperate women had perfectly good teeth pulled to make dentures for the rich (Victor Hugo wrote of this in Les Misérables; George Washington had a set of such dentures). Women and men were all used as slaves, whatever their 'official' classification. Father Raynal says that the white women brought into Sainte Croix were sold to the highest bidders on the auction block as slaves (p. 366-369). Few white bondsmen survived their three or seven-year terms, and when their time was almost up, the owners of their bond could add more years to their time for various 'offenses' or 'expenses' they had incurred (whose food have you been eating for the last seven years?).

To further pacify the captive workers of St. Croix, de Poincy wrote to all of the Catholic orders, and even Protestant churches, begging for priests. There was nothing new in this; tyrants have always tried to hijack Jesus' message of love for their own ends. Carmelites refused to have anything to do with it. Jesuits came, and most died of fever; the Jesuits, gifted land by de Poincy to build a monastery at Estate Cane Garden Bay, lost so many priests to malaria that they sent only enough to staff the one monastery. Jesuits returned to Sainte Croix in numbers only after the Danes had mostly ended the threat of malaria on St. Croix a century later.

Only the Dominican order complied, and some "secular priests" (Protestant).

King Louis gave a salary to Catholic priests, and also provided slaves and indentured servants for their use. With this free labor, they built six churches on the island, each 'cruciform,' or in the shape of a cross. Understaffed, they held masses for white and black parishioners, slave and free, but had no time to proselytize to potential new communicants.

The map of St. Croix below (@1650) shows a "Kerk" in Salt River. Built in 1642 for the Dutch colony of Sint Kruis, this Reformed Church may have been the first permanent house of worship on the island. During the Dutch period, it would have served transient buccaneers like de Ruyter. The British allowed some Dutch to remain in 1646, so it would have still been in use. The Spanish probably destroyed it in 1650. Every Reformed Church has a cemetery, with some elders buried under the floor of the sanctuary itself. Today the land is part of a private residence, with the bones of pious Dutch Buccaneers bulldozed off to the side when the hill was scraped to build the house.

Possibly the first French water pump windmill on St. Croix. Some of the original Lignum Vitae wood placed to support the axle is still inside, and there is water in the well. The first French wells were shaped like cans --with no taper. When the Danes took over St. Croix a century later, de Poincy's Salt River Estate was divided into smaller parcels; this water mill is now in Estate Judith's Fancy.

The French used round "horse mills" to process sugar, but in the Danish period larger, tapered windmills were built to crush the cane.

These are the ruins of de Poincy's house on St. Croix, built in 1650, in what is now Estate Judith's Fancy. Newer wings, made with stone but also Danish yellow bricks imported as ballast in the holds of ships, were added a century later. Some original French walls like these were repaired with pieces of brick during the Danish period.

⁵ Above, a water pump windmill at the head of Salt River Bay, up the creek bed. . The mill was still in use for irrigation into the mid-1900s, and has recently been restored by the National Park Service. The tall chimney in the back is a steam mill built after emancipation, used to crush cane in the late 19ᵗʰ and early 20ᵗʰ centuries.

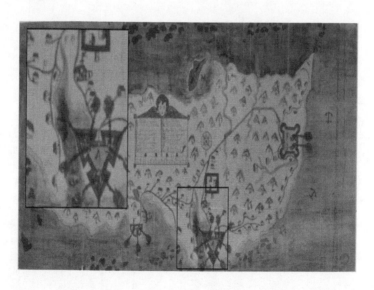

⁶ St. Croix as drawn by a Spanish spy, possibly during the English period, sometime around 1650; there are farms, new fortifications, and a church. The boxed insert shows Salt River Bay and Fort de Sales (Originally the Dutch "Fort Flammand" in 1642, Henry Morgan improved it in 1646. The French named

it *"Fort Salée,"* then renamed it in *1666* in honor of the slain Governor of St. Kitts, Charles de Sales, as *"Fort de Sales." Map courtesy of the Department of Planning and Natural Resources, Department of Archaeology, United States Virgin Islands).*

On this map, North is down. The earthworks of Fort Salé/ Fort de Sales are easily discernable on the Western side of Salt River Bay; the walls are taller than a man still, though overgrown. Somewhere under these ruins probably lie cannons and refuse piles of buckles, bottles, etc. Fortunately, this is on National Park land, and so one day may be excavated.

The map shows roads that comprise part of the still-used road system. On this map is the portion of Centerline Road that leads from Christiansted ("Bassin") to Estate Golden Rock. The Northside Road from Estate Golden Rock to Estate LaReine and on to Frederiksted is on the map also, as is the West End Road out of Frederiksted that follows the shore north and south. The map shows The Northshore Road that goes by Salt River, and on to what is now Davis Bay. The Catholic spy makes a note of the "secular" church (see inset "D"), identified as a Kirk or a Kerk, most probably identifying a Dutch Reformed Church.

The map of St. Croix made by LaPointe and also published by Gerard van Keulen in 1671 shows quite a few more farms.

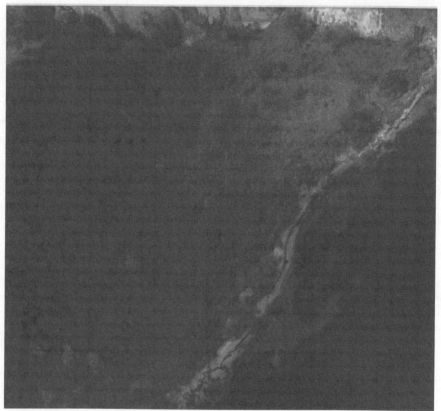

Dutch "Sand forts" began with a six-foot trench, holes for tree trunks spaced inside, the trunks erected, and then loose rock and gravel used to fill the ditch and mound over it. Next dirt was scooped from in front of the walls and piled on top of the rocks. Today you can see the 400-year-old walls of Fort Flammand clearly from space. The ditches filled with stones hold water even in a drought, so that vegetation on top of them is green. The "Star-shaped fort" was not a five-pointed, American star, but more of a flower shape. Foundations of buildings continue south of the fort itself.

Life on St. Croix

A terrible hurricane in 1656 and a new bout of malaria set Sainte Croix back again. St. Croix's Buccaneers had been called to sea for the Anglo-Spanish War in 1654. Between disease and the call of duty, only 50 men capable of bearing arms were on St. Croix when a new Governor arrived from St. Christopher on May 9, 1661.

Francois DuBois was the young Captain of King Louis XIV's personal body guard. But with the Fronde war, Louis did not trust any of his countrymen not to betray him, and so hired a company of Swiss mercenaries for his guard, as well. DeBois quarrelled with the Swiss Captain and, in a duel, killed him. The Swiss Guard threatened to go home if Louis did not take DuBois' head, but Louis was fond of DuBois. Louis exiled DuBois to St. Kitts, sending him with a glowing letter of recommendation to de Poincy, who offered the Governorship of Sainte Croix to him.

After studying the situation, DuBois agreed to take the position only if de Poincy would allow free trade with all ships of nations not at war with France. He also demanded 400 free men for militia who knew how to farm, but could also pick up guns to defend the colony against a Spanish attack. De Poincy agreed and leased DuBois his plantation at Salt River for 30,000 pounds of sugar per year (see above). Officially the governor had to be a Knight of Malta, which DuBois was not, but that was overlooked (DuTertre 1978, pp. 42-43. Upon the death of Francois, his brother Antoine became Governor, and Antoine was a Knight).

DuBois arrived on Saint Croix with 30 men, and five months after that, there were 600 men who could bear arms. Part of that was because a few hundred Buccaneers had just sailed home following the Anglo-Spanish War. Everyone was optimistic, morale was high, and an ambitious building program began. Dubois moved the capital from Salt River to Bassin, where he said the air was better. Salt River became a private yacht club for Crucian Buccaneers.

De Poincy died in **1660**, just after ratifying a treaty with the Dutch, Caribs, and the English to leave Dominica and St. Lucia as reservations for Carib Indians (the Treaty of Aix la Chapelle), which he must have known his King had no intention of honoring. DuBois tried to keep everything as it had been under de Poincy, but Sainte Croix was isolated for a couple of years when the bubonic plague arrived in 1665 (DuTertre 1978, 54).

Each time sailors left for war or malaria struck, there would be a smaller labor pool. White bondsmen were regularly given arbitrary and illegal extensions to their time of servitude, under orders of the Governor. Every Governor of St. Croix during the French period at one time or another did this. In 1665, Buccaneers sailed from St. Croix for the Second Anglo-Dutch War, and Governor DuBois immediately extended all bondsmen's terms of service. Ninety bondsmen ran away to Sandy Point. Father Du Tertre, now on St. Croix, was sent in by Governor Dubois to offer them a full pardon if they surrendered. To his horror, when the starving men emerged, they were imprisoned and beat twice a day for weeks (DuTertre 1978, p.52).

To men of God, faith is everything. To politicians, faith is something to be used to further an agenda. In 1660, Father Jacques DuBois, a Dominican priest, arrived and set up a mission at Fort Salle with a Father LeClerk. They used Sainte Croix as their base for mission trips to other islands. These priests led worship in a Catholic Church, which, according to DuTertre, was built on the side of Fort de Salles. Father DuBois had been especially encouraged by King Louis to preach to Indians on Dominica and St. Lucia. Louis, finally of age and ruling France by himself, planned on violating the international treaty that agreed to leave the two islands to the Carib Indians.

Life on St. Croix for black people was a mixed bag. Sailors were free, as were craftsmen who had arrived as sailors. For people brought in as slaves, though, rules were different. According to DuTertre, an enlightened law early in St. Croix under the Governorship of Francois DuBois set free any female slaves that had been impregnated by a white man and named any offspring of the union as legal heirs. The result was free mulatto families, with some holding deeds to property. Francois' brother Antoine became Governor of Saint Croix upon his death, and repealed that law; the new law said the child of such a union would share the condition of the mother until the age of fifteen for girls, or twenty for boys, at which time they would be free, but did not name them as heirs of their fathers. In 1695 regulations regarding treatment of slaves in all French colonies were codified in the "Code Noir." In it, Article IX declared that if a single free black man had a child with a slave woman, she became free and the child was free (this was to prevent an uprising by black Buccaneers who took slave wives?), but mulatto children would share the condition of their mother for life. Regulations for the code were specific and harsh, with punishments such as cutting off ears for an unsuccessful escape attempt, along with branding (Le Code Noir, Chez Claude Girard, la Grande' Chambre, Paris, 1735).

There were free English laborers on St. Croix from the mid-16th century through the entire French period at Limetree Bay, logging Lignum Vitae. Lignum Vitae is the hardest wood on the planet and is impregnated with natural oil which retards rot and makes it inedible to termites. Prized for centuries to make ships blocks for rigging, it was also used for building well pumps. In the early years of steamships, Lignum Vitae used as bearing material for propeller shafts and was over-harvested to near extinction on St. Croix.

An English diplomat was sent to Sainte Croix to work out an agreement concerning the loggers in Lime Tree Bay in 1661. He brought his wife along for the trip. As an English lady, she was not accustomed to French cuisine, especially not French colonial cuisine. At the formal dinner, several Buccaneer captains were also invited by the Governor. Captain Joseph Williamson ended up sitting beside the English diplomat's wife. She only spoke English; while her husband was speaking French with Governor DuBois, she struck up a conversation with Williamson on her other side. He offered her a dish of cow tongue, which shocked her. "Heavens!" she exclaimed. "Do you know where that *came* from?" "Your pardon, Madame," Williamson replied, passing her another dish, "Might I tempt you with an egg?"

Dutch, French, and English Buccaneers kept the colony alive. After supplies needed for St. Croix were unloaded, plunder was shuttled over to St. Thomas by Danish West India and Guinea Company sloops, and sold. King Louis ordered that St. Croix not trade with St. Thomas under threat of severe penalties, but that was ignored. At times, inventories of goods illegally shipped to St. Thomas were signed off on by the Governor himself, but whenever this came to the King's attention, he did not pursue the matter.

Still served officially only by de Poincy's one sloop, tobacco was rotting in the fields of St. Croix, and colonists were desperate for supplies; as usual, when there was a drought and crops failed, local Buccaneers were away at sea, busy plundering towns on the Spanish Main, and not around to help. On his own initiative, Father DuBois went on a fishing boat to Puerto Rico, where Crucian fishermen introduced him to Puerto Rican fishermen they had met near Vieques (Crab Island).

Father DuBois changed into the boat with the Puerto Rican fishermen, and they took him to meet his fellow Dominican priests at the monastery in San Juan. The Puerto Rican friars arranged for trade between the islands, with the permission of their Governor.

This arrangement lasted only a few months until word got back to Spain. King Philip IV had the Governor recalled and executed (DuTertre 1978, p. 53). Trade with Spain was once again, officially at least, off.

Infrastructure such as roads and bridges had to be built and maintained, facilities and manpower for defense provided, and an administration for government put into place. To cover the costs, King Louis levied expensive import and export duties. Farmers could not pay the taxes and live. Farmers also needed to bring in more food and equipment, and send out more produce, than the occasional French ships could carry. They did what they had to: Dutch traders and local Buccaneers picked up the slack, and by charging too much, Louis caused himself to get little (Raynal, p. 274).

The response was pragmatic. No French naval vessels could be spared. As smuggling was not policeable, the Crown made its money by imposing extremely high land and head taxes, a tactic that would be mirrored by the Danish government a century later for the same reason.

Frenchmen in the Caribbean measured success by how much land they possessed. They were not interested in trade, which they deemed something for lower classes. The Dutch were getting rich off of trade, however, and governments noticed. Holland had created the first joint stock companies ‒corporations—in the world, with the result that they had large amounts of cash for building ships. The DWIC had warehouses at Tobago, St. Eustatius, St. Martin, Guiana, and, until the Spanish destroyed it, Tortola (after which they built a new one on St. Thomas). They were purchasing produce and supplying the entire Caribbean.

England, Spain, and France all had laws saying that only their vessels could trade with their islands. These "Navigation Acts" ensured that colonies assumed some of the costs for maintaining themselves, both by paying duties on what came in and excise taxes on what went out. It also meant price-fixing for shipping costs. The Dutch subverted these laws openly, smuggling as often as possible to the delight of the colonists, and effectively cut de Poincy and the Knights of Malta out of their monopoly. St. Thomas was the "Mart" to which the Dutch carried produce and captured merchandise from Sainte Croix's French Buccaneers. It was also an essential market for merchandise coming into Sainte Croix (Crouse, p. 61; Raynal, p. 447).

In **1665**, Jean-Baptiste Colbert, Finance Minister to King Louis, founded the *Compagnie Francaise des Indes Occidentales* (French West India Company, FWIC). King Louis took responsibility for administering the French colonies in the West Indies away from the Knights of St. John and gave it to the new company. Colbert obtained backers and letters of credit and purchased ships to use in trade. Everyone on St. Croix was optimistic that adequate supplies were going to be coming in at last, and there would be a market for their produce. Those hopes immediately went to hell when in March of 1665 the Second Anglo-Dutch War broke out.

The war between England and France meant that all company resources –food, munitions, and clothing-- were sent to St. Kitts, Montserrat, and Guadalupe, sites of battles between English and French forces. To make Sainte Croix's situation worse, a severe drought hit the West Indies in 1666 that ruined food crops. Months of torrential downpours followed, and four hundred people on Sainte Croix fell ill with fever.

France was in danger of losing her Caribbean colonies, and St. Croix, safely out of the war zone, was not a priority. Crucian Buccaneers sailed for France and were seldom home. While the war lasted, two years of drought killed most food crops on St. Croix. There was no help for the starving island except supplies occasionally brought in by Buccaneers and Dutch traders.

TRADE WARS:
The Second Anglo-Dutch War, 1665-67

The treaty of 1627 between the English and French on St. Kitts originally signed by d'Esnambuc and Thomas Warner called for peace regardless of whether or not their nations were friendly or at war in Europe. Both sides respected this beautiful treaty for many years, but in 1665 it was time to negotiate a renewal. The two Governors on St. Kitts, Charles de Sales and William Watts, signed the agreement. Watts was required, however, to have his superior, Lord Francis Willoughby in Barbados, sign as well. Willoughby lured the French ambassador into long talks that stretched into April of 1666 while preparing an all-out invasion of St. Kitts; messages from the Foreign Secretary informed him that Louis XIV was going to war on the side of the Dutch against the English. England always had the best spies.

Shortly after England attacked Dutch shipping to begin the Second Anglo-Dutch War, Louis signed a declaration of war siding with the Dutch against England, and Willoughby immediately launched his invasion of St. Kitts. The French were surprised, but farmers picked up weapons and fought in several bloody battles. Governor de Sales died in battle, but his battle strategy prevailed. Victors, the bitter French asked all Englishmen to take their families and leave.

Willoughby's career would have been over, had word reached England. Before that could happen, he needed to redeem himself. He commandeered 30 merchantmen, filled them with 600 more soldiers and militia, and sailed for St. Kitts. Willoughby could not keep himself from mischief; on the way from Barbados to St. Kitts, he ordered French flags flown from the mastheads, and the fleet sailed into the roads of Basse-Terre, Guadeloupe. The surprise failed. English ships cannonaded the French ships in the harbor, but the French ships weighed anchor and came out to fight. Winds picked up, turning into a hurricane passing just north of the island. With winds from the northwest, both fleets tried to make for the roadstead of Terre de Haute, the larger of the Isles de Saintes. All but two English ships were driven ashore on the rocks outside of the harbor and destroyed, and Willoughby was crushed to death. Most of the English soldiers survived, however, and they quickly took the island.

Both sides sent for help from nearby islands. Crucian Buccaneers arrived just in time to recapture Terre de Haute, capturing several of English vessels and 200 soldiers.

The French now decided to invade Antigua, and their fleet sailed into St. Johns flying English flags. Surprisingly the ruse worked, and they captured the garrison of the island quickly. The French force was making preparations to invade Montserrat when word came of English naval warships approaching. Dutch ships in the area were hastily recruited to fight with the French, but when the fleets met, the English demolished the French Buccaneers and Dutch armed merchantmen that were not purpose-built warships. English troops speedily retook Antigua and all of St. Kitts, which is where things stood at the end of the Second Anglo-Dutch War (Crouse, 16-42, 43-84). Crucians limped home.

The Third Anglo-Dutch War, 1672-74

Colbert still let only ships licensed by the company trade with French islands and charged high taxes. There were not enough ships, not enough warehouses, and not enough merchandise to supply Sainte Croix, so smuggling was rampant. Frustrated, Colbert obtained letters of marque from Louis for all of the company ships, directing them to take or sink any non-permitted vessel they caught operating near Sainte Croix. This was a great joke. Planters had to show profits to their investors, colonists needed food and a market for their merchandise. FWIC officers took bribes, allowing the smuggling to continue (DuTertre 1978, p. 96, Raynal p.274). Besides that, half of the smugglers were St. Croix plantation owners. Estates were supposed to be paying import and export duties, but instead sold their goods to Dutch smugglers (Raynal, p. 256-8).

Corruption went deep. The new corporate Governor-General of the French West Indies, Jean Charles de Baas Castlemore, published an edict regulating the conduct of "Protestants, Harlots, Jews, Saloonkeepers, and other undesirables" as soon as he arrived in St. Kitts. That was to make Colbert happy back home, but in actuality, he quickly began accepting bribes from buccaneers and Dutch traders. The Dutch Parliament was the largest shareholder in the Dutch West India Company, but many other investors were French, most likely including de Baas. The FWIC formally charged him with allowing trade with the Dutch, which he did not deny, arguing that pity for his people demanded it, but Louis ordered Colbert to let him be (Crouse, p. 96).

The FWIC was going bankrupt. On February 21, 1672, England had just started the Third Anglo-Dutch War when King Louis (the largest shareholder) saw the balance sheet of the French West India Company. The King's shares were now worth more than five million livres *less* (about $50 million in today's currency) than he had invested nine years before (Crouse, p. 103). Louis immediately dissolved the French West India Company. Louis XIV took control as the owner, as well as ruler, of all of the colonies.

Louis blamed the Dutch, as their dominance in trade and refusal to recognize the French Navigation Acts had doomed the FWIC. Louis coveted Dutch bases in Tobago and Curacao. Louis was also uncomfortable having a republic next door (the "Batavian Republic of the Seven United Netherlands," led by a Parliament with an elected executive, Johan de Witt) at a time when monarchs had to keep their people believing in the 'divine right of kings.' Louis joined the English and declared war on the Dutch.

St Croix struggled to survive, still with only 600 men capable of bearing arms on the island in the Fall of 1672, according to an English spy (CSP v. 29, #14). The full census was much larger than that with craftsmen, older people, women, children, and the enslaved population, plus several hundred of Sainte Croix's Buccaneers, who were at sea fighting in the Third Anglo-Dutch War.

The Business of Piracy

With the Third Ango-Dutch War over and Sainte Croix's Buccaneers home, the Chevalier Antoine DuBois, governor of St. Croix, was tried for purchasing stolen and smuggled cargoes to traffic with St. Thomas Governor Jorgen Iverson in 1665. During wartime, St. Croix's Buccaneers were given letters of Marque as 'legal' privateers, so selling their captured cargoes received no attention. In peacetime, however, they and other French Buccaneers continued to sell stolen ships and plunder in St. Croix, and that caused a rift between legalistic officials and those who shared in the profits. It was huge for an English, French, or Dutch colonial Governor to be tried by his Government for using his office to promote business with pirates. Every Governor of Sainte Croix (Sueur's Boissiramee and Begue, Buccaneers themselves, were, of course, complicit) was accused at one time by royal colonial bureaucrats, and especially Governor LaSaulaye, but no charges were ever filed against them. The Domaine Occidental in France wrote back each time anyone complained that they must produce witnesses, but no one would testify (It was not until the evacuation of Sainte Croix in 1696 that witnesses came forward).

The Royal Tax Collector for the Sainte Croix, Monsieur Duverger, wrote down all of the smuggling and pirate activity he saw. He noted pirate cargoes sold, pirate ships sold, Buccaneer cargoes sold, Buccaneer traffic with Saint Thomas, etc., and wrote to the Royal Director of the Domaine Occidental in Paris (this letter is in Aix en Province, in the *Archives Outre Mer*).

Sainte Croix Governor Begue had Duverger's letter brought to him by the post official, read it, and ordered the local militia captain, Major Louis DuBois, to place *Duverger* under arrest. Duverger fled to St. Thomas on one of the vessels he had written about. From St.

Thomas, Duverger was able to send a letter to the Director of Domaine Occidental in France, but the Ministry replied that he must provide collaborating witnesses. Duverger was turned down by every person qualified to give testimony, as they were afraid of reprisal. Begue considered Duverger to be discredited but wanted to keep him close and under control. He also still needed the position of tax collector filled. He talked Duverger into giving up his crusade and returning to work on St. Croix. 'Unnamed' militia officers periodically checked on him and gave threats to keep him 'in line.' De Begue told Duverger that he would have him hung as an embezzler if he talked (Crouse).

The new Danish West India Company in St. Thomas avoided the difficulties endured by St. Croix by persuading the king to proclaim St. Thomas a free port; ships of all nations were welcome as far as they were concerned, with no taxes or duties charged. The governors of St. Thomas also encouraged a lively business with privateers, buccaneers, and pirates. The company bought illegal cargoes cheaply; the governor took a cut and the merchandise sold at below retail to ships from all the islands. Business was booming, but England noticed.

Buccaneers of St. Thomas and St. Croix
Partnership and Mêlée

With the end of the Third Anglo-Dutch War in 1674, English, French, and Dutch privateer captains had the option of seeking commercial cargoes, retiring, or turning pirate. Many of them chose to become pirate, though they continued to style themselves as 'Buccaneers.' This wave of pirates terrorized Spanish villages along the Pacific coast. A small army of 331 English and French Buccaneers sailed from the Virgin Islands with Captains Bartholomew Sharp, Pierre le Picard, and Raveneau de Lussan. Imagine their pluck: to land on the enemy shore of Panama, desert the ships that brought them there, cross unknown jungle terrain and mountains facing hostile Indians and Spanish militia, reach the coast, steal canoes, look for and take ships. Some of the English and French Buccaneers sailed over to prey on Dutch shipping in Indonesia, as well. Several of them wrote journals that are still available in print, such as Bartholomew Sharp, Alexander Esquemelin, Philip Ayers, Basil Ringrose, Raveneau de Lussan, and Lionel Wafer. Esquemelin and Wafer (a ship's surgeon) were naturalists as well as Buccaneers, and documented new flora, fauna, and information about indigenous people (See diaries of Exquemelin, Ringrose, Wafer, Sharp, and Ayers, referenced in the bibliography below; Lussan's memoirs are quoted in Bruney, also cited below).

With no one to police their behavior, few rules, and lots of alcohol, there were many atrocities performed by Buccaneers. There are accounts where murder is so off-hand that it sounds as though they are speaking of what was for dinner. Sainte Croix Captains Gaignet and Le Picard 'adventured' under English Captain Edward Davis. After their apprenticeship they plundered on their own, then rejoined Davis to sack the town of Guayaquil with nearly 500 Buccaneers (Captains Louis and Charles Picard owned estates in Quarter Mestre de Camp on Sainte Croix. Captain Durand Gaignet's estate was in the River Salee Quarter, Sainte Croix). After canoeing up the river to surprise the town, a heated battle ensued which the Buccaneers won. Guayaquil became unsafe, as no one buried any of the dead; there were no officers who could order pirates to do unpleasant tasks. The booty included jewels, merchandise, Church plate in silver, 92,000 pieces of eight, and seven hundred prisoners for ransom, including the Governor.

Buccaneers soon freed two hundred of the prisoners, as enough food could not be found to keep so many hostages. Ransom for the remaining five hundred was agreed upon by both parties at a million pieces of eight. When it did not arrive on time, the Buccaneers made the prisoners throw dice, the heads of the four losers sent to the Spanish officer who had made the excuses for delay. One of the young Buccaneers wrote later boasting of the excellent time they had while waiting for the ransom money, "We had good cheer, well supplied with refreshments from Guayaquil. We had concerts of music; we had the best performers from the city among our prisoners. Some among us engaged in friendships with our women prisoners, who were not hard-hearted." He went on to say that the Buccaneers sexually molested many children of both sexes.

As Spanish forces converged, the Buccaneers accepted 42,000 pieces of eight and made their way back home. Davis and most of the Englishmen sailed west to east around Cape Horn and up to the Caribbean. The rest under Le Picard determined to return overland to the Caribbean. They sailed back to Panama, burned the ships, and began sacking villages and holding people for ransom. At one point, while apprehensive of an impending Spanish attack, fifty prisoners tried to get away. Le Picard's men killed all but four in the melee. Confronted next by a body of Spanish soldiers more than twice their size, the Buccaneers staged a surprise night attack and destroyed it, taking 900 horses. Coming to a river that flowed east they freed the horses, built rafts, and floated towards their goal with bananas and plenty of game available. The force now cannibalized itself; everyone was carrying his own loot. Some French Buccaneers went home to San Domingue; the Picard's and Gaignet returned home to Sainte Croix, but 75 went to Jamaica, where Governor Albemarle took their loot and imprisoned them. When Albemarle died a year later, they were released, but not restored to their plunder or their arms (Bruney, pp. 253-266, quoting from the journal of Buccaneer Raveneau de Lussan, <u>Journal du Voyage au Mer du Sud</u>, pp. 110-117).

In **1682**, Gov. Thomaj Esmitt of St. Thomas seized the British sloop *Gideon* and was reported to be harboring pirates openly in Charlotte Amalie (59: CSP, CEB, (CSP v. 11, p. 4). Pirate George Band was operating out of St. Croix. In 1683, Band captured the British ship *Fox* and gave it to the governor of St. Thomas as a gift. Esmitt sent it to Barbados for supplies, where surprised officials returned to its rightful owners (CSP, CEB, v. LII, #47). Henry Morgan was reported seen in St. Thomas in 1683 by Capt. Joseph Williamson (CSP, CEB, v. LLI, #62).

La Trompeuse

Louis XIV rented many of his smaller warships out to private enterprises (Bromley, Ch. 10). In peacetime, they stayed fit for sea and brought in revenue; when war broke out, they could be recalled to the navy or rented out as privateers. In 1681, Captain Peter Paine took money from investors and leased the 30-gun frigate *La Trompeuse* to cut logwood in Guiana. Paine sailed into Port Royal and Governor Thomas Lynch let him sell the cargo. Paine sub-leased the ship to other loggers, then took off without paying his investors or his lease. The French consul was furious, but it got worse when Pirate Captain Jean Hamlin followed *La Trompeuse* out of port in a small sloop and captured her.

Over the next two years, *La Trompeuse* took many prizes both in the Caribbean and off the coast of Africa. During that time, several frigates from different nations tried to catch *La Trompeuse*. In 1683 the new Governor in St. Thomas was former Governor Thomaj Esmitt's brother, Adolph Esmitt. According to British reports, Adolph was a retired buccaneer himself who financed buccaneer vessels with his own money (CSP v. 11, 1681-85, #1173—Captain Joseph Williamson's letters and others). He was desperate for supplies for his island, intent on increasing his bank account, and happy with the loss of a French naval presence. He broadcast for pirates to trade openly in St. Thomas, and many came to sell their loot. Britain might walk on eggs when it came to France and Sainte Croix, but it was not putting up with this nonsense from a second-rate power like Denmark. On July 31, 1683, Captain Charles Carlisle sailed the 32-gun *HMS Francis* into the Charlotte Amalie and found *La Trompeuse*. When *HMS Francis* entered the harbor, both *La Trompeuse* and Danish Fort Christian (on orders from Governor Esmitt) fired on her. The *Francis* gybed and sailed out, anchoring just outside of the harbor. Esmitt sent a delegation to apologize and invite Carlisle to dinner, which he refused. Instead, that night Carlisle quietly sent in a picked crew in the ships' boats, and they blew up *La Trompeuse* while Hamlyn and his crew were ashore drinking. A big English 'privateer' next to her was sunk in the explosion, as well, but Carlisle's letters express no regret for that. Some of Hamlyn's crew members settled on St. Thomas, but Esmitt gave Hamlyn a small vessel that he filled with plunder he had already off-loaded to a warehouse. This vessel quickly captured a large, heavily armed trading ship, the *African Merchant*, which was owned by her captain, Blankenbiel. Hamlyn gave Blankenbiel the small vessel with its cargo; Blankenbiel wrote later that the exchange was in his favor (Paiwonsky, *La Trompeuse*, p. 68-70). After his cruise, Hamlyn tried to sail into the Pacific, but the Straights of Magellan defeated him, and he returned to St. Thomas, shared his loot, and dined with Esmitt. From there, Hamlyn sailed safely off into history.

Gov. William Stapleton, British Leeward Islands, to Adolph Esmitt, St. Thomas, DWI, August 15, 1683:

> *"I am sorry that your late conduct has convinced me and all the world that the reports of your being a protector of pirates were true. I have affidavits to that effect from some you had on shore, and from the*

pirates themselves… The King of Denmark will not protect you, who are an usurper against my master. If you do not deliver (Hamlyn) or make some atonement for the injuries you have inflicted on the English, I warn you, have a care. I shall come from the Leeward Islands with an armed force, blow you up as quickly as the Trompeuse, and pound any pirate that you may have fitted out." (CSP v. 11, #1189).

On October 28, 1684, a British squadron arrived at St. Thomas, captured the fort, and arrested Governor Adolph Esmitt. (CSP v. 11, p. 1).

A pirate and a madman: Governors of St. Thomas

England soon released Esmitt to Denmark, but Denmark fired him as Governor, appointing Gabriel Milan, a Sephardic Jew from Hamburg whose father-in-law was King Christian's doctor. While Esmitt was being tried for corruption in Copenhagen, his wife Charity, a consummate politician, convinced the DWIGC board of directors that he, and only he, knew the location of a Spanish treasure galleon which had gone down in 1641, the *Nuestra Senora de la Concepcion*. Esmitt was freed and ordered to return to St. Thomas as Governor. Accompanying him on his return was a team of salvage divers. St. Thomians refused to accept Esmitt as Governor again, and Milan had Esmitt and wife thrown into the dungeon of Fort Christian. Directors back home were appraised that England was already busy recovering the wreck of the *Concepcion*, which was nowhere near St. Thomas, as Esmitt had claimed, but off the north coast of Hispaniola.

Milan brought in large amounts of wine along with leaded glass decanters, and following the fad of the day probably even sweetened his wine with lead oxide. It is also possible that the estate he seized as his own had lead pipes, and lead oxide laden paint lined the cisterns of the day. Milan began suffering from cramps and fever, which would not go away—typical of lead poisoning. Already ruthless, and in absolute power over St. Thomas, Milan went mad. He ordered that Adolph Esmitt appear before the court naked. Milan then had an escaped slave *impaled* publicly, which sickened even the plantation owners. Paranoid, he imagined that Captain Meyer, who worked for the Danish West India and Guinea Company, was out to kill him, and ordered the fort to attack the *Fortuna* when she sailed into Charlotte Amalie harbor. Milan sent a leaky old merchant vessel to sea with 40 soldiers and militia with orders to take, loot, and burn all Spanish ships they found, though Denmark was not at war with Spain. This ship found a small Spanish galley off of Puerto Rico and fired a shot for her to surrender. The galley fired one broadside, and Milan's ship fled back to Charlotte Amalie. The captain of the galley sent Milan a letter: "I thought we were meeting Danish friends on the water and was shocked by the attack. Next time, perhaps his majesty can send a better prepared vessel." A quickly dispatched Danish frigate arrived and arrested Milan for treason. He was shipped to Denmark in chains and beheaded (Paiwonsky, _La Trompeuse_, pp193-223).

Shortly afterward, Adolph Esmitt offered his services to the King Karl XI of Sweden to invade and capture St. Thomas for that country, but Karl declined. Unlike Milan, Esmitt then quietly disappeared from history.

In **1688**, the Governor of Sainte Domingue learned that English Buccaneers were selling cargoes from captured French vessels in Charlotte Amalie. He sent a force under Buccaneer (now Major, commanding militia forces in San Domingue) Laurens De Graaf to punish St. Thomas (Burney, p.64). De Graaf's men looted the bank, the fort, and warehouses.

The *Trompeuse* episode and the de Graaf raid ended the brief eight-year period of open pirate trading in St. Thomas definitively. It proved to be a small inconvenience only, with St. Croix just a short sail away.

With St. Croix struggling and unprofitable, Louis ignored it; he was busy fighting the War of the League of Augsburg. Any resources he sent to the Caribbean were for the important colonies of Martinique or Guadeloupe. Also, Louis was making plans to take over St. Lucia and Dominica.

The old smuggling partnership between St. Thomas and St. Croix continued. England did not interfere with English Buccaneers selling directly in St. Thomas, but would not allow French or Dutch Buccaneers to use a harbor so close to the British Virgins. St. Croix was the destination of French and Dutch Buccaneers who sold their cargo to agents of the DWIGC or, for a while, the Brandenburg Company when it, too, operated on St. Thomas (Highfield, p. 503). Small company sloops were used to ferry the merchandise over to St. Thomas. Louis' ministry sent a Royal Tax Collector to gather the usual duties on land, people, exports, and imports. Again, only French ships were allowed to trade with French islands, but they were few and far between, and because of smuggling and the Buccaneers, little revenue came from Sainte Croix on import or export duties. Sainte Croix cost the crown a lot more money than it was returning in taxes. Louis wrote a law that trade between Sainte Croix and Saint Thomas was illegal, promising that anyone involved in that trade would be severely punished, but it was universally ignored (Raynal, 256-8).

Other Buccaneer Activity in the Archives

The *Achives Outre Mer* at Aix en Provence hold letters that mention other Buccaneers and their activities, such as Buccaneer Captain and Knight Sieur Boissiramee, who was appointed Governor of St. Croix after Sieur Antoine DuBois but called away immediately to sea with his ship. His stand-in Governor appealed to the Lt. General of the French West Indies to receive the Governor's salary, since he was doing the job, and won his case (Archives National Outre-Mer, C8A-18, #70-114). Boissiramee was tasked in 1696 to supervise the relocation of French men at arms from Sainte Croix to the new "Sainte Croix" settlement at Cap Francois, San Domingue. He participated with du Casse, de Grammont, and the Buccaneers of Sainte Croix in the sack of Cartagena, was appointed Governor of Marie-Galante, fought in the siege of Guadalupe, and drowned when his ship wrecked off of Cuba (Exquemelin, A.O.; van Keulen map; Archives Nationale Outre Mer, cote: 5DPPC/52).

In gratitude for his leadership in helping Boissiramee organize the removal of citizens of Sainte Croix to Cap Francois in 1696, the King protected Captain Honor Galiffet from a court decision depriving him of his share of the booty after the sack of Cartagena, and named him to succeed Boissiramé as leader of the Sainte Croix settlement at Cap Francois (Crouse). Galiffet's name appears in both census records for Sainte Croix and on period maps (van Keulen and Lapointe maps; Archives Nationale Outre Mer, cote: 5DPPC/52).

Governor Francois DuBois was a soldier, not a Buccaneer, and his brother Antoine (Governor who succeeded Francois) was a veteran Crusader and Knight of St. John of Jerusalem, but Francois' son, Captain DuBois de Montfort, was a Buccaneer, raised on Estate

La Grande Princess on Sainte Croix. De Montfort also raised his family on the estate his father left to him on Sainte Croix. De Montfort regularly sold his captured ships and plunder in Sainte Croix (Archives Nationale Outre-Mer, Gr 498, No. 75, also C&A-9, folders 37-40, 61-63, 73-76, and 156-58; Highfield, Sainte Croix, p. 500). As a young man, de Montfort had been an apprentice under Captain Jacques Gendre of the *Lion d'Or* (more commonly known as 'Captain LeBlonde'). In 1664, when de Montfort was a brand-new young captain, he was attacked by an English privateer under the employ of the Brandenburg Company and wounded in the engagement. Peace was signed immediately after, but LeBlonde paid no attention. The Brandenburg Company had been a partner, with an agent on Sainte Croix, buying pirated cargoes for years, in war and peace; this was a betrayal. LeBlonde sailed up to the Brandenburg Company's dock at Krum Bay in St. Thomas and looted the office and warehouses, leaving employees with no more than the shirts on their backs. To placate politicians, LeBlonde was indicted for piracy on Martinique and sent as a prisoner to France, but his case somehow never came up for trial (Archives Nationale Outre-Mer, C8A 8, folders 216-35, and folder 472).

The End of Sainte Croix

WAR, WAR, WAR! Louis XIV could not stop. In **1688** he invaded the Holy Roman Empire (Germany and Austria) to grab more land, even though his country was virtually bankrupt. The Ottoman Empire was invading from the east again. Louis knew that Emperor Leopold would give that invasion priority, and thus would not have enough troops to guard his border with France. All of Europe was sick of Louis' greed, but no other single army was as strong as that of France, so in this nine-year "War of the League of Augsburg," the Dutch, British, the Holy Roman Empire, and even Catholic Spain united together against him. In the Mediterranean, King Louis sent French Admiral Duquesne in an Italian land-grab, and Dutch Admiral du Ruyter was ordered to join forces with Spanish warships to stop him. In the Caribbean, Louis ordered former Buccaneer -- now-Governor-- Jean du Casse and former Buccaneer –now militia Colonel-- Laurens de Graaf (he was Dutch, but settled with a French wife; the French called him "Baldran de Graff") to invade Jamaica.

Du Casse and de Graaf didn't do anything but burn a bunch of Jamaican farms (including one possibly belonging to a family named "Thatch," according to Baylus Brooks) before returning to Haiti. Elsewhere in the Caribbean, Admiral de Estrees lost a large fleet of the French navy on the reef at Las Aves.

With France's failures, Spain and England saw an opportunity to team up for an invasion of Haiti. Spies notified du Casse of the impending attack. Du Casse wrote the King asking that his old militia command on Sainte Croix be sent to him for reinforcement. Louis XIV ordered that, and more. He ordered that Sainte Croix be abandoned, and all available men-at-arms –members of Sainte Croix's six militia companies with their families and any humans held in bondage to them--be transported to Cap Francois to aid in

defending the more valuable colony. Thanks to the partnership with
St. Thomas, Sainte Croix could be nothing but a liability for the
foreseeable future. Left behind were mulatto children and their non-
French friends. Thus, some of the population of St. Croix stayed
behind; their names are in the telephone directory on St. Croix to
this day (census records from 1680-1696, Archives Nationales Outre
Mer, cote: 5DPPC/52).

Crucians did not make it to San Domingue in time. Buccaneers
of Sainte Croix were busy sacking Spanish colonial towns while
Sainte Croix was abandoned.

De Graaf ended up with only 430 men to defend Cap Francois
(Highfield, <u>St. Croix</u>, pp. 514-20, Crouse p. 213). In February 1695
eighteen hundred English soldiers under General Luke Lillingston
and Commodore Robert Wilmot made an amphibious landing,
while 1,500 Spanish troops invaded from Santo Domingo.
Outnumbered 8 to 1, de Graaf retreated to Port de Paix. While
Lillingston's soldiers busied themselves burning farms, Wilmot led his
sailors in plundering Cap Francois. The English and Spanish
soldiers were jealous of the sailors, and angry, but kept to the plan,
anyway.

Though the English and the Spaniards did not trust each other,
they pulled together again and marched to besiege Port de Paix.
Tipped off that French troops were going to escape at night, they
planned an ambush and butchered the French in the darkness.
While the fighting was moving away from town, Wilmot slipped his
sailors into Port de Paix before sunrise and looted it, once again
beating the soldiers to it. To placate Lillingston, Wilmot let him
have the French male prisoners, probably to sell as 7-year
indentures. Records say the Spanish took all of the women and
children, but don't say what became of them; they most likely were
sold, as well. Afterward, malaria struck the allies, and they fled Haiti
after accomplishing little.

In response to bitter letters from burned out plantation owners, De Graaf was removed from command of the militia by King Louis (Crouse, pp. 178-207, CSP 1696-7, #71). The old Buccaneer finally retired in Petit Goave.

Crucians arrived in San Domingue after the allied invaders had already left. Census records in Cap Francois, San Domingue show that only 71 people from St. Croix settled there, half of them women. Another 25 families were settled in San Domingue estates Leogane, L'Ester, and Petite Riviere, 13 more in La Croix de Bouguets, and one in Port de Paix (Highfield, Sainte Croix, p. 519, from Archives Nationale Outre Mer, Etat Civil, v. 3, pp. 1443-1559.). They were given estates as promised, but those were just burned-out ruins, and there was no food or equipment.

White members of the Salomon family, whose estate on Sainte Croix was just to the north of Ha' Penny Bay, relocated to Leogane, where some of the official records of Sainte Croix ended up (From Leogane, some of the records were relocated to the Archives Outre Mer in Aix en Provence. They are easy to miss, because they are in the boxes of records from Leogane, not Sainte Croix). A descendant, Lysius Salomon, was President of Haiti from 1879 to 1888. A descendant of the mulatto part of the family that stayed behind, Axeline Salomon, also known as "Queen Agnes," helped lead the Fireburn revolt on Saint Croix in 1878. The Girard family descendants still on St. Croix are also descended from the Salomon family.

Some relocated Crucians busied themselves with rebuilding the recently burned-out estates they had been given in San Domingue, but two hundred Crucian Buccaneers set sail immediately under Michel Grammont and Governor du Casse to raid Cartagena. (Highfield, Sainte Croix, p. 520). This would be the last of the Bucccaneers. Tales of torturing hostages for ransom and robbing graves for jewelry disgusted the world, and as part of the treaty ending the war, signatory nations agreed that 'Buccaneers' would no longer be tolerated. Corsairs would be classified as either 'privateer,' with an official letter of Marque for operating in war time only, or 'pirate'--enemy of the world.

The Truth (but no one cared)

Once the colony of Sainte Croix no longer existed, Duverger had the nerve to come forward again. Witnesses, including Dominican friar Eustache Dummy, now stepped forward to substantiate Duverger's claims. On January 20, **1696**, Duverger was interrogated in Martinique. He told of pirate cargos openly purchased in St. Croix by the Brandenburg Company and the DWIGC for transport to St. Thomas. He named pirates, including Captains Corneille, Jacques Daniel, Bernard Desjean (later ennobled by Louis XIV, he led the sack of Cartagena as "The Baron de Pointis"), and Jacques Gendre ("Le Blond"), of the *Lion d'Or* (Highfield, St. Croix, p. 503; Archives Nationales, Section Outre Mer, C8A and B14, p. 580). Captain Jacques Daniel was selling his pirated cargoes to the DWIGC, but he was also the owner of an estate in Point du Sable quarter, Sainte Croix (*Archives Nationale Outre Mer*, cote: 5DPPC/52). The pirate de Montfort was identified as the son of former Governor Francois DuBois and the nephew of former Governor Antoine DuBois.

Duverger named the captured ships that he knew had been auctioned off in St. Croix. He spoke at length about the bribes that Governor de Begue and previous Governor La Saulaye had accepted since at least 1690 when Duverger had arrived and had paperwork to prove his accusations. By the time the truth came out, no one cared. Two hundred of the Buccaneers from Sainte Croix were already sailing their ships to raid Cartagena with de Grammont, du Casse, and de Pointis (Highfield, St. Croix, pp. 514-20), by order of the King. Louis XIV was going to make a lot of money off of the raid.

Honest men could not understand the game of empire their King was playing. Louis encouraged piracy against England, Spain, and the Dutch in times of peace. He needed his Buccaneers to sap the economic strength of France's rivals, without having to accept blame for it. England and the Dutch looked the other way as their Buccaneers did the same thing. The other reason that Louis put up with the Buccaneers is that he needed them to be his proxy naval force in the Caribbean.

Cartagena: The End of the Buccaneers

King Louis ordered du Casse to organize a raid on Cartagena, Columbia, hoping to intercept the treasure fleet --along with everything stored in the warehouses-- before an impending peace treaty could be signed. The order provided no ships and no troops for the expedition. The enterprising du Casse teamed up with a private investor in Paris named Bernard Desjean. Desjean was a veteran Buccaneer, having sailed out of St. Croix and sold his prizes and plunder there (Crouse). As a Privateer, he had been a Dunkirker who served under Captain (later Admiral) Abraham Duquesne. Enobled by the King for his buccaneering exploits, Desjean was now the "Baron De Pointis".

De Pointis managed to raise funds to rent, repair, and man seven ships-of-the-line, three frigates, and nine support vessels that had been laid up in ordinary for lack of an adequate naval budget. On behalf of his investors, de Pointis accepted a commission from King Louis as Commander of the expedition and hired 4000 sailors, soldiers, officers, and marines. The fleet set out for Cap Francois, Haiti, where they met up with du Casse. Du Casse had managed to gather 600 militia (one-third were free black men) and ten frigates coupled with 600 additional Buccaneers and their vessels, counting the Crucian contingent. De Pointis signed an agreement that the Buccaneers would get half of the loot and the fleet sailed, arriving off of Cartagena on April 13, 1697.

The fort guarding the entrance to the bay was massive, with eight-foot-thick walls 35 feet high and 33 cannons, but only 300 soldiers. An English Buccaneer came up with a plan to take the fort, and De Pointis ordered a frontal attack, but the Buccaneers refused to participate; it wasn't the way they operated. French soldiers took the fort without their help, though many died. Two smaller forts commanding the inner harbor were also easily captured, but the formidable batteries of Cartagena itself then opened fire. De Pointis ordered the warships to return fire and ordered field artillery to be taken ashore to batter the defenses. The guns had to be moved from the beach to a hill overlooking the town, and de Pointis ordered the Buccaneers to drag them. The Buccaneers refused. They thought the back-breaking labor unnecessary, suggesting instead that cables be rigged to the hilltop and the cannons winched up. The guns were drug up the hill without Buccaneer assistance, and soon a breach was made in the walls. Though already wounded, De Pointis led his soldiers in yet another frontal assault that got a lot of them killed, but took the city. With nearly one-third of its defenders dead, Cartagena and its remaining 2,800 soldiers surrendered.

De Pointis, mindful of his shareholders, had no intention of honoring his agreement to share the booty with his old buddies the Buccaneers, especially after their refusal to follow his orders. His soldiers looted the city treasury and businesses and levied a hefty tax on citizens before the Buccaneers could get in. The Buccaneers, experienced hands at looting, quickly got among the private residences and began stealing, but this amounted to little compared to what De Pointis had already secured, and this offended de Pointis' sense of honor. De Pointis loaded his plunder onto his rented warships, gave the Buccaneers a pittance, and sailed away. Swindled out of their 'fair share,' the bitter Buccaneers went back in the city and held citizens for ransom. Du Casse was pro-actively discouraging cruelty, but Buccaneers ransacked houses and churches, held children for ransom, and robbed graves. About a million crowns worth of loot was quickly divided (much less than their "fair share" would have been), and the Buccaneers set sail (Crouse, 221-245). When word of the Buccaneers' depredations reached Europe, public sentiment turned against them for good. They were never again to be looked on as adventurous heroes; from then on, they were considered scum.

Thirty English men of war and eight Dutch ones under English Admiral Neville sailed to intercept De Pointis' fleet to try and take the loot for themselves. They found the French fleet but were able to take only a couple of smaller ships before De Pointis slipped away under cover of night. Neville's fleet then found du Casse's Buccaneers. The Buccaneers split up; every ship took a different compass point, returning to Petit Goave by different routes. Neville was only able to capture a couple of small vessels packed with valuable loot.

De Pointis sailed into France with a fortune, more than seven million livres worth. In answer to a petition from du Casse, the King ordered that the Buccaneers be given their fair share. Ironically, bureaucrats stole the money before they could get it. Still at large, Neville next sent his ships under Vice-Admiral Mees to loot Petit Goave. Surprised Buccaneers, including de Graaf and Governor du Casse, were awakened by flames and bolted into the forest (Crouse, pp. 212-245).

Tired of war again and bankrupt, all parties made peace. On September 20, 1697, the Treaty of Ryswick was signed. England and France agreed to go back to the same borders they had before the war.

The Age of the Buccaneers was over. Never again would they be suffered to plunder ships or towns of other nations during times of peace. As part of the Treaty, from this time forward, corsairs would be either privateer, if operating under official Letters of Marque issued by a governor in times of war, or pirate—enemies of all the world. As for the colony of Sainte Croix, it was no more. French maps of the period label the island as "abandonie".

Nature abhors a vacuum. The end of the Buccaneers ushered in a new era: The Golden Age of Piracy.

Pirate University

The War of Spanish Succession, 1701–1714

The Treaty of Ryswick required that property on St. Kitts
be returned to pre-war owners in the same condition it was in before
capture. English settlers had already staked claims on the French
side. Angry with the treaty, they knocked down every French
building and took the lumber. French colonists returning to St. Kitts
found only empty lots where their towns had been and were furious.
Both sides knew that peace would be temporary, and began arming.

The King of Spain, Charles II, had no children and an incurable
illness. He named his nephew, Phillip of Anjou, to succeed him.
Phillip was French, the grandson of Louis XIV. Louis introduced his
grandson at court as "Philip V, the next King of Spain." Other
nations could not allow France and Spain to be united; it would
create a new superpower.

Charles II had another nephew, the younger son of King
Leopold of the Holy Roman Empire. Leopold named his older son
Joseph to succeed him in Vienna and suggested his younger son
Charles for Spain instead of Phillip. Having two brothers rule two
powerful countries was more acceptable than having one man rule
two powerful countries, so King William (England and the
Netherlands) pledged his support to Leopold's plan. When Charles
II died, Europe erupted into war again, with England and the HRE
(Charles to be King of Spain) against Spain and France (Phillip to be
King of Spain). Thus began the "War of Spanish Succession", also
known as "Queen Anne's War" as William died at the beginning and
his daughter took over.

Because England had recently endured a civil war, soldiers loyal
to the Stuarts were in exile in France. The result was an unusual
match-up between enemy generals. The most talented general to

fight in Europe since Julius Caesar led the English and Dutch armies. John Churchill (ancestor of Winston Churchill and Princess Diana), the new Duke of Marlborough, faced off against his nephew James, a very capable Marshall of France. The Caribbean was once again a backwater in the conflict, where empires could spare few resources. Caribbean Governors had to make do with what they could get, using local militia and privateers, as few real naval ships were available.

Most merchant ships hurried to the safety of ports immediately when the war was declared; their seamen were then out of work. Everyone must eat, and it was a simple step to take employment with one of the hundreds of privateer vessels that were soon swarming the waters of the Caribbean for both sides. Wealthy businessmen and colonial governors used their cash and credit to purchase ships and convert them for war.

In Virgin Islands waters, privateers were less likely to encounter enemy warships when going in or out of port. Also, English and Dutch privateers paid no share of the profits to their King when selling their plunder in St. Thomas and French privateers evaded paying their King's share by selling in St. Croix, the "abandoned" island, to DWIGC agents. Observers on St. Croix still reporting to Paris mention especially the successful privateer *Prince Frederick* (Archives Nationale Outre Mer: Petites Antilles Fonds Ministries, cote: C/10D/2, #8, #13).

On land, the first move was made by English Governor Codrington, who in anticipation had already concentrated his militia on St. Kitts. The instant war was declared, his men overwhelmed the French sections. England sent ten small ships of war under Admiral John Benbow to aid Codrington but also to find the Spanish Treasure Fleet. Louis sent du Casse a small fleet of warships to counter Benbow and protect the Treasure Fleet. Benbow and Du Casse found each other, fought to a draw, and returned home. Benbow died a few months later from a wound received in the battle.

The Spanish Treasure Fleet was always an object of interest to Spain's enemies. In 1708 du Casse was in Havana with the New Spain Fleet and his French warships waiting for the South Seas Fleet to join them. On the 15th of May, 1708 an English squadron under Commodore Charles Wager found the South Seas Fleet off Cartagena, Columbia. In the battle that followed, Wagner and his ship attacked the biggest treasure galleon, the San Jose. He should have used more chain shot and aimed less at the hull; the San Jose blew up. Hundreds of bodies flew into the air, and treasure worth more than a billion dollars sunk to the ocean floor while Wagner and his crew watched (Estimates range from 12 to 19 billion dollars in today's American currency). Wagner's fleet destroyed two more ships, the rest made it into Cartagena, and **no more treasure fleets would risk sailing until after the war was over**.

The French were angry that the English had taken St. Kitts, but never again entertained thoughts of settling there. Instead, a French fleet landed enough troops to march up and down the island destroying everything English they could find in an eight-day rampage. In retaliation, an English force invaded Guadalupe. They did want to take the island for England, but could not. The French Governor-General refused to be trapped by the English, choosing instead to keep his command intact but allowing English soldiers and Buccaneers to loot each of the towns before the invaders ran out of supplies and left. George Washington would use the same tactic in the American Revolution.

Louis XIV finally died in 1715 after a reign of 72 years, the longest in European history. Before he passed away, he named his great-grandson Louis (only five years old) to succeed him, instead of Philip. This allowed for peace. Philip would become King of Spain, not Charles as England and the HRE were fighting for. Though related, the King of France would not rule Spain as well, so this was acceptable. In the meantime, Leopold of the Holy Roman Empire had died, and in 1715 so did his older son, Joseph, so that younger son Charles became Holy Roman Emperor. To prevent the creation of a different superpower, one in which Charles would also wear the crown of Spain, the English and the Dutch agreed to back Philip of Anjou as King of Spain, and peace came once again to Europe. Before we leave the age of the Buccaneers, it's time to meet them.

Are you ready to go adventuring? Buckle on your cutlass, take a pill for sea-sickness, and claim a spot for your hammock. One more thing –hide your loot. Always hide your loot.

X. Buccaneers of Saint Croix and the Virgin Islands

Francis Drake

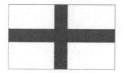

Pirate Admiral

One of the most well-known buccaneers to have walked the beaches of St. Thomas and St. Croix was Francis Drake. Drake was the first of 12 sons born to a Protestant preacher in 1540 in then Catholic England. Father Drake apprenticed his son to the master of a small channel trading ship. When the master died, he left the vessel to 15-year old Francis. After selling it, Francis sailed with his cousin John Hawkins in three expeditions to Mexico, which ended with the incident at Vera Cruz.

From 1528 to 1598, French and English buccaneers, among them Drake and Hawkins (1570-71), were operating out of the Virgin Islands, including the islands of St. Thomas and Santa Cruz (Ogg, p 31).

Drake made one of the most famous voyages of all time a few years later when he captained the *Golden Hind* in the world's second circumnavigation. He captured the 120 ton Manila Galleon (*Nuestra Senora de la Concepcion*, better known to her crew as "Cacafuego"; literally, "fire shitter," or, if you will, "bad fart") and got a nice haul of gold, jewels, and silver. Spain's King Phillip II demanded that he be hung as a pirate when he returned to England. Instead, Queen Elizabeth, happy to have her share of the loot, knighted Drake. Hawkins successfully raided Spanish shipping as well and was also knighted. At this stage of their careers, they became privateers, instead of pirates. Later, both were brought into the English fleet as admirals, helping defeat Spain's great armada of 1588 (Dube'). England loved their pirates. England could deny responsibility for them when it was convenient, and knight them later.

In 1585, Drake sailed to the West Indies, notoriously hanging out in the passage that bears his name through the British Virgins. He left to sail up the coast of Florida, where he attacked Spanish towns. Heading up to Carolina to catch the Westerlies home, he stopped at Roanoke, the first English colony in America, and gave several Colonists' lifts back to England, where they introduced tobacco, corn, and potatoes, all of which rocked the European world.

In his most audacious attack, Drake boldly entered the heavily fortified port of Cadiz, Spain, destroying 30 new ships of war that were assembling to form part of an armada to invade England.

King Henry VIII of England left the Catholic Church in 1534, creating a Protestant (mostly) England. The Pope blessed a Spanish armada on its journey to punish the heretics and bring them back into the fold. One hundred and thirty ships sailing in a large crescent formation, the largest fleet of large ocean-going vessels ever assembled in history up to that time, appeared in the English Channel in July of 1588. Famously, Drake finished his game of bowls after excited messengers ran to tell him of the arrival; he knew that the unwieldy galleons would not be coming very fast. The fleet was to stop in the Spanish Netherlands to pick up an army and invade England. The weather was terrible, but Drake and Howard were brilliant. Drake and Admiral Howard deliberately set eight ships on fire and sent them downwind into the middle of the fleet off of Calais harbor. Some ships caught fire, but the biggest gain was that, though most made it out, they were never again able to organize effectively. The next day the English ships, with their longer-range cannons, proved that the invasion was not going to happen. Unable to turn and sail against the wind for home, the fleet went over the top of Scotland, some over Ireland as well, and many wrecked in terrible storms on the rocky coasts. The blood of many young Spanish men who swam ashore mingled with that of single, Catholic young ladies, resulting in what is known as "Black Irish" and "Black Scots."

In 1595, using the Virgin Islands as a base, Drake and Hawkins unsuccessfully attacked San Juan de Puerto Rico. A Spanish cannonball from El Morro castle passed through Drake's cabin while he was on deck. Some records say that he led a landing party in an assault on La Fortaleza, was wounded in a duel with the Spanish commander, Pedro Suarez Coronel, and retreated to the ships. They returned to the Virgin Islands, attacked Puerto Rico again, and many of the Englishmen came down with dysentery. Drake himself did and the cousins decided to get away from the unhealthy island, sailing over to Panama after receiving information of a treasure fleet in Portobello (de Gomara, Ch. 9). While sailing off of Portobello in January of 1596, Francis Drake died of dysentery caught in Puerto Rico. He was buried in the outer harbor in full armor, lying in a lead-lined coffin. Sir John Hawkins died of malaria shortly after and was buried at sea in the Caribbean, as well. Sir George Clifford sailed to San Juan three years later on his 38-gun *Scourge of Malice* (renamed the *Red Dragon*) and found Puerto Rico unable to defend itself due to that same continuing epidemic of dysentery. San Juan fell on June 30, 1598, but the English left a couple of months later, not wanting to follow Drake to the bottom of the sea.

Pieter Pieterszoon Heyn

Corporate Admiral

Piet Heyn was born to a sea captain from Delf-shaven, a suburb of Rotterdam, in 1577, a citizen of a Spanish province in revolt and a baptized member of the Reformed Church. He went to sea as a boy with his father. Prone to terrible sea sickness when young, he stuck with it all his life. In 1581, William the Silent led the Dutch to a major victory over Philip II's army, leading to the birth of the Republic of the Seven United Provinces. At twenty, a Spanish warship captured Piet and made him serve as a galley slave, chained to his oar for four years until exchanged for Spanish prisoners. Quickly recaptured, he served four more years, until 1607. To have survived eight years chained to an oar as a slave showed impressive resilience. It did not leave him with a good feeling for Spaniards.

From the 13th century, The United Provinces (Holland) had the most towns belonging to the trade guilds that made up the Hanseatic League. Holland was all about trade. The first modern corporations were created in the Provinces as the Dutch East India Company and the Dutch West India Company, starting in 1602. The idea of pooling capital to be able to invest together on a large scale, of fluid but stable leadership and the possibility of liquidation in the event of failure (without personal risk to investors) made Dutch corporations take off in a way that revolutionized the world of business forever. In 1607, Spain signed a truce with the United Provinces (a/k/a "The Netherlands" or "Holland") recognizing their de facto, if not official, independence. Piet Heyn went to work that same year as a mate on a Dutch East India Company ship and quickly made captain.

Sixteen years of adventures at sea and a responsible position in the local government of Rotterdam (due to an advantageous marriage) led to Piet's promotion to vice-admiral for the new Dutch West India Company in 1623. He was sent to raid Portuguese towns and shipping in Brazil, where he bravely led charges against walled cities and met with mixed success; on his second mission, he was far more successful, returning home with over thirty loaded Portuguese merchant ships. Heyn attacked Spanish and Portuguese vessels and towns whether the Dutch were at war with them or not, attacking with dozens of ships, acting on behalf of a company. That made them all Buccaneers. Records show that he was very popular with his crews and captains, that he was appalled by slavery of any sort, and that he treated Africans and Indians with respect (Society of Public Welfare, pp.59-64). Heyn sailed between all of the Dutch trading posts in the Caribbean, and I believe he planned his greatest feat while on Tortola. In 1628, Piet Heyn led a fleet of 80 Dutch ships —all capable of carrying cargo, but also well-armed, with 50 soldiers aboard each ship-- in attacking the New Spain Treasure Fleet. Heyn held the title of "Admiral of the fleet", but not from any navy- from the Dutch West India Company. Heyn's fleet captured or destroyed the entire fleet, the only time in over two centuries that would happen. The long chase ended just outside of Havana when survivors beached themselves to prevent capture. That did not work; Admiral Heyn landed his soldiers, overcame Spanish resistance, and took every ship. Each captain became an overnight hero for the Dutch nation, especially the youngest of all, 21-year-old Michiel de Ruyter. f11, 509,524 (guilders) of loot was taken back to the Provinces and sold. The government's shares alone funded the war effort for eight months. Company investors received a 50% cash dividend at the end of the year (Society of Public Welfare, p. 63).

Heyn was very, very popular in Holland, and school children sing a song praising his adventures even today.

While I believe Heyn launched his attack from Tortolla, there is no proof. My reasoning is in the Spanish response to the raid: immediately after the loss of the fleet, a Spanish force landed on Tortola, where they murdered everyone they could find (DuTertre 1978, pp 8-10).

The Company did not want to pay Heyn the share they had promised; greed kicked in, and they could not part with that much money. Angry, he resigned. He was given command of the Navy of the United Provinces as Lieutenant-Admiral but died within the year in battle against a powerful fleet of Dunkirker privateers, a proxy navy funded by the King of Spain operating out of Dunkirk, France. Guiding his flagship between two enemy ships to fight both sides at once, a musketball penetrated his curiass. Piet Heyn is buried in the Reformed Church that he had been baptized in as an infant, in Delfshaven (Society of Public Welfare, pp.59-64). He is buried *IN* the Kerk. It was not unusual at the time for elders of the church to be buried under the floor of the sanctuary, so that parishioners would always remember that they were standing on the foundation created by their elders. Heyn, however, has a memorial against a wall, a shrine, with a statue of him lying peacefully on top of his coffin.

Today, the very idea of what Piet Heyn did is staggering. A corporate fleet of 80 ships, all commanded by a corporate admiral, with stockholders profiting from the battle! The world has never seen such a thing before or since.

Christopher Myngs

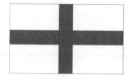

Greed saved his career

Cristopher Myngs began his buccaneering career as a humble cabin boy in the Royal Navy. His intelligence was noticed by his captain, who brought him onto the quarterdeck as a midshipman. He learned fast, passed for Lieutenant at the minimum age, and by age 21 he was captain of the HMS *Elisabeth* serving under James Ley, the 3rd Earl of Marlborough. Ley was dispatched by Prince Rupert to seize and hold the island of St. Croix for England in 1646. Young captain Christopher Myngs was left in charge of preparing defenses for St. Croix when Ley left. While ashore in Salt River, Myngs heard about a Dutch convoy filled with valuable merchandise. Myngs left one of his Lieutenants, 19-year-old Henry Morgan, to build a fort on the west side of Salt River Bay (CSP v. 20, #202). The *Elisabeth* captured the entire Dutch convoy of 12 ships and the two men of war guarding it. Dutch buccaneers cannot have been happy with this, but England cheered Myngs for it.

England exploded into civil war, with Cromwell and parliament against King Charles II. From a humble family, Myngs chose to serve Parliament with Cromwell's General Venable. In 1655, Myngs watched the English troops get thrown back into the sea in Hispaniola but then helped capture Jamaica from Spain.

Instructed to defend Jamaica with no resources, Myngs recruited buccaneers and took the fight to the Spanish, led by his 44-gun frigate, HMS *Marston Moor*. Unable to attack the heavily armed treasure fleet, Myngs attacked towns with warehouses full of treasure before the fleet could arrive to load them, including Tolu, Santa Marta, Cumana, Puerto Cabello, and Coro, where a quarter of a million pounds sterling fell to Myngs' Buccaneers. Eye-witnesses reported that he was unnecessarily cruel and murdered many civilians. Myngs divided the loot with his men but then was arrested for not having anything left on his return to Port Royal with which to pay the King's, or the Governor's, share. The angry Governor had Myngs imprisoned in England. Myngs was waiting trial when Cromwell died, and Charles II regained the crown. Charles freed all of Cromwell's political prisoners, including Myngs.

Myngs was given command of the 34-gun HMS *Centurion* and returned to the Caribbean to gather a French, Dutch, and English fleet of buccaneers that sacked Santiago (Cuba) and Campeche (capturing 150,000 pieces of eight and 15 ships). Records show that several French and Dutch Buccaneers, including Edward Mansvelt, sailed with Myngs in these raids. Once again, witnesses said that he murdered civilians unnecessarily. Colonial Spanish officials called Myngs a mass-murderer and asked Charles II to execute him. Instead, Charles knighted him, and made him a vice-admiral; he had learned to set the royal share aside when sharing the loot.

In June of 1665, Admiral Christopher Myngs once again fought under James Ley, the Earl of Marlborough, part of Prince Rupert's squadron of the white, when the English and Dutch fleets met at the battle of Lowestoft. Marlborough took his 70-gun *Old James* to the rescue of a ship about to be captured and died in the attempt. After the battle, Myngs took over Marlborough's division and was himself killed a year later in the tremendously bloody Four Days Battle of the Second Anglo-Dutch War. De Ruyter sent Vice-Admiral Johan de Liefde's squadron to surround Myng's division. Liefde's ship

Riddershap van Holland locked yardarms with Myng's *Victory*; in the din and smoke, a musket ball tore through Myng's cheek, and another smashed his left shoulder. He died after his ship limped back to London. A musket ball felled Lifde during the last great fleet action of the Third Anglo-Dutch War, The Battle of the Texel. An admiral's uniform marked you as a target, as it would Horatio Nelson at Trafalgar a century and a half later.

Prince Rupert of the Rhine

Jan Hus taught at the University of Prague, where he introduced the reforms of John Wycliff and preached against the sale of indulgencies. That threatened the income of a lot of powerful people, and he was burned at the stake as a heretic in 1415. His followers created the first Reformed congregation in Europe, and it became the largest denomination in Bohemia.

Martin Luther broke away from the Catholic Church a century later, and a century after that, Holy Roman Emperor Ferdinand II was ordered by the Pope to clean up his province of Bohemia and bring it back into the Catholic fold.

On May 23, 1618, three Catholic members of the Council of Bohemia returning from Rome told Reformed members that they were condemned to death by Ferdinand, and all other Reformed congregants were ordered to convert to Catholicism or face the same fate. Reformed Council members responded instantly, by throwing the three out of a third-story window. They survived because of a miracle according to the Pope, but actually because of the coincidental passing of a cart full of cow dung. The Province of Bohemia quickly declared its independence and elected Rupert's father, Frederick, their King. Ferdinand called on his army to put down the revolt, and The Thirty-Years War began.

Prince Rupert von der Pfalz-Simmern was born in August of 1618, during his father's short rein. Bohemia's army was destroyed within months, and Rupert's family escaped to Holland. Rupert's mother was the daughter of King James I of England and Scotland and Queen Anne of Denmark. Rupert's first cousins included future

English Kings James II, Charles II, William I, and George I of England. His father's grandfather was William the Silent, Prince of Orange, Elector of Holland, and leader of the revolt that secured independence from Spain.

In Holland, young Rupert attended the Dutch Reformed Church and was known as "the Devil," for his terrible behavior. Aggressive and super intelligent, Rupert first fought as a soldier in the last Reformed Bohemian regiment at the age of 14, in Prince Maurits' Dutch army. A Colonel at age 20, he was taken prisoner during the Battle of Westphalia. Imprisoned in Vienna, he had an affair with the daughter of his jailer and made friends with Leopold, young brother of King Ferdinand, who gave him a white poodle Rupert called 'Boy' that accompanied him in battle many years. King Ferdinand offered him a cavalry command in the army of the Holy Roman Empire if he would give up his Reformed faith, but Rupert refused. Ferdinand offered him the command anyway, but Rupert still refused. Ferdinand then released Rupert on the promise that he never fight against his army again.

Rupert was twenty-two-years-old when he crossed the English Channel to take command of his uncle's cavalry in the English Civil War. 'Boy' fought with him in every battle, running alongside Rupert's horse, until he died in the Battle of Marston Moor. Rupert then got a pet monkey that rode his horse with him into battle. A lot of people thought that Rupert was into witchcraft, and the animals his familiars.

Rupert fought well and won many battles, but the royalist cause was lost on the battlefield of Naseby in July of 1646, and once again, Rupert was a man without a country. King Charles I was captured and later executed. Gathering a small fleet, Rupert sent one thousand refugees with General Ley, third Earl of Marlborough, to establish an exile base on Saint Croix.

In August of 1646, the fleet anchored in St. Thomas harbor. As soon as Michiel de Ruyter sailed north for hurricane season, Ley sailed to Saint Croix and put the refugees ashore with two hundred troops to build a pirate lair. Twenty-three year-old Captain Christopher Myngs of the ship *Elizabeth* was left to prepare defenses for the island, but Myngs quickly sailed off after a rich Dutch convoy leaving the task to nineteen-year-old Lieutenant Henry Morgan, who built one battery on the northeastern point of Bassin Harbor, and another where Fort Frederick now stands on the west end of the island. Exiled English pirates sailed from Saint Croix in swarms, leading Buccaneer Alexander Esquemeling to say that at this time, the waters surrounding Puerto Rico were the most dangerous in the world.

King Louis XIV of France appointed Rupert a Field Marshal, and he fought to the end of the Thirty-Years War. In 1648, royalists in England revolted, and seventeen warships sailed to Holland to return Charles II to England. The revolt was put down by Parliament before a surprised Charles could go aboard, so he gave Rupert the vessels and a free hand to do as he pleased. Rupert was now in command of the most powerful fleet of pirate ships ever to sail the Atlantic or Caribbean Seas. No mere ragtag bunch of renegades, Rupert had seventeen naval vessels, crewed by professional officers and sailors.

Rupert established two more pirate lairs in the Scilly islands and on the Channel Island of Jersey. Sailing from his three pirate lairs, his ships captured hundreds of prizes of every nation, including England, France, Holland, Sweden, Denmark, and Spain.

England made General Robert Blake an Admiral, had him reorganize the navy, and sent him after Rupert. Rupert's pirate bases took a massive amount of loot, but Blake attacked and put an end to the Scilly Islands base and the one on Jersey. Blake cornered Rupert's fleet in Portugal. Escaping in bad weather, Rupert sailed for the Mediterranean, where he narrowly escaped Blake again.

In 1650 Rupert sailed for Saint Croix after learning that Puerto Rico had surprised and captured his base. Rupert's brother, Maurice, arrived first and anchored in St. Thomas harbor while he sent spies to reconnoiter. At this time, a hurricane hit the Virgin Islands. Most of Rupert's ships were lost, including the powerful *Defiance* with his brother on board.

With only five ships remaining and having sent most of his loot away to cousin Charles II, Rupert returned to Europe. Rupert's older brother, Charles, had converted to Catholicism and been restored as Elector of Bohemia by Emperor Ferdinand. As a family member, an allowance was due to Rupert, and he went to get that set up. In the few months Rupert was in Bohemia, he took up art, and created some of the world's greatest mezzo-tints. At the same time, Rupert wrote romantic letters to the pretty young woman serving Charles' wife as a lady-in-waiting. Charles' wife, Louise, found the letters and thought were for her. She let Rupert know she was interested. Charles discovered the letters, and he became angry on two accounts. At first, Charles thought Rupert was after his wife. Rupert assuaged his fears, explaining that his interest lay with the young lady in waiting. That was worse; she was Charles' mistress. In this way, Louise found out about the affair and divorced Charles. The young lady-in-waiting became pregnant—with which brother's baby no one knew---and it was time for Rupert to leave.

Oliver Cromwell, the hope of English democracy, sent Parliament home and set himself up as a dictator. In 1658 Cromwell died, and Cromwell's son ruled only a few months before he was deposed. The experiment in republicanism having failed, Charles II was invited to return to England as King. Rupert was no longer a renegade but instead a member of the House of Lords, and a Duke. Rupert accepted a commission as a Rear Admiral in the British navy that had been chasing him only a few months before. He fought as a squadron commander in the second Anglo-Dutch War at the Battle of Lowestoft, again in the Four Days Battle, and in the St. James' Day Battle.

Rupert invented a superior cannon, the *Rupertino*--which saw limited use due to its expense--and was made Admiral of the Fleet in time to join with the French and lose the Battles of the Schooneveld and Texel to Dutch Admiral de Ruyter. Rupert finished his naval career as the equivalent of "First Sea Lord," chief administrator of the Navy.

In retirement, Rupert became an entrepreneur, ramping up the slave trade by helping create the Royal Africa Company, and he chartered the Hudson Bay Company in Canada, serving as Canada's first English Governor and having a territory named for him.

Returning to England, Rupert became a prolific and respected inventor. He set up a laboratory in Windsor Castle and helped found the Royal Society. He took two mistresses at this time, fathering an illegitimate child by each. Rupert's son, Captain Dudley Bard 'Rupert', died at nineteen years old in the siege of Buda. Rupert's daughter married into the Howe family, and Rupert was the grandfather of some noted eighteenth century soldiers with that name. As an older man, Rupert hooked up with an actress but had no children with her. He was one of the few Admirals of the seventeenth century to die of old age.

Henry Morgan

Fight hard, and party 'til you die

Historians do not know when Morgan was born, but most certainly have it wrong. His birthday is often put as "somewhere around 1635," but must have been sooner, because in 1646 he was a 19-year old junior officer on board the buccaneer vessel *Elisabeth*, assigned by his captain Christopher Myngs to begin construction of defenses on Saint Croix including improvement of Fort Flammand (Calendar of State Papers, Colonial Series, America and the West Indies, v.20, entry #202).

The island of Jamaica was taken from the Spanish in 1655, after which 5,000 English settlers were scared to death that Spanish troops would be sent from Havana to exterminate them. England did not have the time to worry about Jamaica. Embroiled in the civil war, it took Parliament and Cromwell nine years to beat the Royalists, and the country was bankrupt. Governor Sir Thomas Modyford could only hope to defend the island with a naval force of buccaneers, which included Myngs and Morgan. It didn't hurt that he took a cut of the loot they brought home to the island.

Alexander O. Exquemelin was born in France near the border with Holland. He served as a surgeon with Henry Morgan and wrote of their adventures upon returning to Europe. He is the most important source for our information about the depredations of the Buccaneers. He published in Holland as

Alexander Esquemelin, in France as Alexander Exquemelin, and in England as John Esquemeling. Each edition has slightly different adventures and some different pirates, so each has been cited separately.

After helping construct Fort Charles to protect Port Royal, young Henry Morgan received a Letter of Marque and took the fight to the Spanish. According to Alexander Exquemelin, who sailed with him on most of his expeditions (English, French, and Dutch buccaneers raided together in the early years when it was everyone against the Spanish on the west side of the ocean), Morgan was murderously ruthless and cunning, an amazing leader of very difficult men. He led buccaneers in sacking Puerto Principe, Porto Bello, Maracaibo, and Panama.

On April 23, 1680, in one of the bravest (or dumbest) attacks ever, Morgan took 68 men in five canoes and attacked three Spanish men of war. Cartagena Bay, though large, pinches off at the entrance, and large castles guarded each side. To enter uninvited was to be destroyed. Leaving his ships anchored in a bay fronting the Caribbean Sea, Morgan hand picked his best 68 men and had them strip naked, put their hair into ponytails and rub them with charcoal, and shave their beards. They took three Indian canoes and paddled into the bay as 'Indians.' Pulling into mangroves near the fort at the town, they scaled the walls and subdued the guards in the middle of the night, then locked the sleeping soldiers inside their barracks. Morgan's men then thoroughly sacked Cartagena, and Morgan sent a note demanding a large ransom for the city's leading citizens. The Governor responded quickly. He sent three frigates to take Morgan out. Facing the large men of war and ten times the number of men, Morgan could have paddled ashore and run into the bush, but that was not his style. Instead, three canoes with zero cannons and 68 naked men attacked three large men of war with 97 cannons and over 700 men. Rowing as fast as they could for the nearest frigate, Spanish cannons could not aim fast enough to keep up with the little canoes, or depressed enough when they got close. The other frigates could not fire for fear of hitting their fellow Spaniards. Morgan's carpenter was armed with a rawhide maul and some wooden wedges. He drove one between the rudder and the transom of the first ship so that it could only sail in circles. The Buccaneers were expert shots, even from the tossing canoes. They targeted the helmsman and anyone they could find on deck, and when survivors ran below to escape the fusillade, pirates quickly scrambled aboard and locked the companionway doors, imprisoning the Spanish sailors and soldiers below and taking over the ship. Leaving only a few to guard the prisoners, Morgan and his men jumped back into their canoes and rowed for a second. These men did not run below but instead crouched behind the bulwarks, and when Morgan and his men boarded, sixty men took on over two hundred. In furious hand-to-hand fighting, the pirates were victorious, and the third ship ran for her life (Esquemelin, A. O.).

I do not want to think about the reception given the third Captain when he returned to face the Governor.

Only Henry Morgan could have talked his men to marching against huge odds through swamps filled with mosquitos, snipers, and malaria, all the time convincing them they would get fabulously rich. His exploits included using only canoes with a handful of men to capture Spanish warships in broad daylight, and his men sacked cities defended by impregnable walls with ten times the number of soldiers. The primary source of these adventures is Buccaneers of America, Exquemelin's book (1). Keep in mind that while it is the most important primary source for Morgan's campaigns, Morgan was enraged at his murderous portrayal, and won a lawsuit against Exquemelin for libel. Morgan was not square with his crew after Panama but kept far too much loot for himself and the English Buccaneers. Exquemelin never forgave him, and thus the bad press.

Regardless, if Morgan committed even a small number of the murders that Exquemelin accused him of, he was one bloodthirsty pirate. Be that as it may, Morgan made Modyford and himself quite rich, was knighted, appointed Lt. Governor of Jamaica, and died of alcoholism (cirrhosis of the liver) in 1688. Despite Exquemelin, Morgan was held in extremely high esteem by sailors. Jamaican Governor Albemarl ordered a formal state funeral, and had Morgan put into a barrel of rum to preserve his body until friends could arrive. Albemarl also declared a period of amnesty so that notorious pirates of every nation could attend. Appropriately, the entire city cemetery, including Morgan's grave, sank beneath the sea during the earthquake of 1692.

Bartholomew Sharp

"...you can never predict when they're going to do something incredibly stupid."

Born around 1650 in London, Bartholomew Sharp wrote that he first sailed as a pirate in 1666. He landed in St. Thomas, Virgin Islands, during the Second Anglo-Dutch war serving as mate on a privateer. William Dampier says that Captain Sharp took part in the 1779 raid on Porto Bello. By the Third Anglo-Dutch War and in the Franco-Dutch War he was raiding Dutch shipping in the Leeward Islands from St. Thomas. After the Franco-Dutch War in 1678, Sharp collected 331 Buccaneers for a daring plan. Several of the Buccaneers who had served together under Henry Morgan -- Ringrose, Wafer, Ayers, Dampier, and Sharp himself-- participated, and are famous today for their journals (see bibliography below). The journals of Sharp and his men constitute the most chronicled of all Buccaneer adventures.

Sharp and his men landed on the Caribbean coast of Panama and marched overland in 1679, while England and Spain were at peace; they gambled on being able to capture Spanish ships in the Bay of Panama on the west coast. Landing in mud, sleeping on dirt while being devoured by mosquitoes and midges, and seizing very little loot, Sharp and his men made a considerable nuisance of themselves on their way across the isthmus by raiding poor villages. On reaching the Pacific Ocean, they stole canoes and paddled out to five deserted ships they found at anchor. They took three of them; for a flagship, they used the *Santisima Trinidad*, renamed *Trinity*. They then set off to the south in a flotilla consisting of the three ships, a couple of small captured sloops, and the canoes. For two years, they pillaged and burned poor villages along the coast. Their diaries showed that though men from both sides died while fighting, they did no murder. Sharp explained in his journal that they were well aware that they were outnumbered at all times, and allowed that in the event the Buccaneers were captured, they wanted some chance of being treated as prisoners of war (though there *was* no war, at the time). Too long without any success, Sharp's crew deposed him, but then reinstated him when he claimed to have information on a treasure galleon sailing from Peru. The information was correct. Sailing in a small square of sea while they waited, it appeared on schedule, and, after a hot battle, Sharp's men captured it, only to find it loaded primarily with 700 large slabs of dull grey metal they assumed to be lead. Keeping only one of the great slabs for use in their bullet molds, they threw 699 overboard.

They stumbled onto another treasure galleon, the *Consolación*. The galleon tried to outrun the pirates and struck a reef off of Santa Clara Island. The crew may have taken some of their treasure off before the pirates could arrive; at any rate, they set fire to the *Consolación* . She burned, and then slid underwater to the foot of the reef. Spanish Legend has it that Sharp's men went ashore to steal whatever the crew had removed, could find nothing, and murdered the 350-man crew out of spite. Neither Sharp's, Ayer's, Wafer's, Dampier's, nor Ringrose's diaries say this. It would be out of character --they had not caused deliberate bloodshed up to this point-- but be that as it may, Santa Clara Island is known to this day as Isla de Muerto (Dead Man's Island). Sharp's men let an enormous treasure slip through their hands: 146,000 pesos of silver, with additional stacks of gold and silver ingots, went to the bottom of the sea.

Homesick and broke, the pirates made plans to return home. Spanish villagers bragged that the King of Spain had sent many troops to block their return across the Isthmus to the Gulf side. In response, two of the vessels sailed east to the Spice Islands, and Sharp and his men sailed the *Trinity* from west to east through the Straights of Magellan, the first documented tale of sailors doing so, which for ships of that age was very dangerous. After months of horrible storms and near starvation, with most of them naked as their clothes had rotted off of their backs, they returned to the Caribbean and put into Barbados, where they were not welcome. Spain had reported their piracy to England, and the King had commanded that, upon their return, they be hung. They were also turned away by the Governor of Antigua but finally landed on Nevis, where the Governor allowed them to stay long enough to provision. Taking their rusty firearms ashore to the local gunsmith to have them cleaned, he asked them why they were making bullets out of silver.

... Silver. ...S i l v e r. **...*SILVER*!** The 699 huge slabs they had thrown overboard were worth £150,000 at the time, which would be equal to tens of *millions* of British pounds today.

Though they knew a death warrant was on their heads, Sharp and his crew had the gall to sail for England and turn themselves in. Having the nautical charts of the West coast of South and Central America captured from the galleon, Sharp was confident that the windfall would cause them to be welcomed, instead of hung. On reaching England, Sharp and crew were jailed, but lack of evidence --no Spanish witnesses came forward in England-- led to the crew's being set free after a couple of years. Sharp was set free sooner, having presented the Spanish nautical charts of the Pacific coast of South and Central America, compiled by Spanish mariners over centuries, to the Admiralty, the equivalent today of capturing the plans for the latest stealth bomber and taking them to a rival country. King Charles II rewarded him with a commission as Captain in the Royal Navy and command of the sloop *Bonetta*, fitted out to search for the wreck of the Spanish treasure ship *Concepcion*. Sharp declined the appointment and returned to the West Indies.

On January 29, 1684, Sharp was given a commission by the Governor of Nevis to "take and apprehend savage Indians and pirates" (CSP V. 53, #18). A few months later, Sharp took his ships around Cape Horn and up the Western Coast of South America. Captain Swan on the 16-gun *Cygnet* had onboard Basil Ringrose, one of Esquemelin's old comrades who kept exact journals we have to this day. Ostensibly a business voyage, Spanish colonists would not trade with them. The 'businessmen' quickly turned pirate, holding villages for ransom, but were unlucky at that, as well. Ringrose and many of the pirates died while raiding the village of Sentispac, Mexico, on February 19, 1686. Returning to Nevis, Sharp was tried for piracy for taking an English ship, the *Josiah*, and for his raids on Spanish towns in the Yucatan peninsula. A witness for the prosecution accused Sharp of being "A pirate, an absconding debtor, a cattle thief, a traitor who sold his services to the French, and guilty of contempt of court for cleaning his pipe with his subpoena." A verdict of "ignoramus" (Latin, literally "there is nothing there to see", i.e., there was no evidence) was returned. Sharp was set free, and in 1688 the Duke Albemarle reported Sharp to be the "Commander" of the sleepy, barren sand island of Anguilla. After a few months, he was bored with Anguilla. Sharp and most of the white crew members elected to accept the hospitality of the Governor of St. Thomas. Sharp's black crew members, free men doubtful of their treatment at the hands of the Danes, and the rest of his white crew opted to remain on Anguilla. Their island-built sloops continued fishing and smuggling between islands for centuries.

After the second world war, Britain could not afford to keep non-profitable colonies. Anguilla was paired with St. Kitts and Nevis as a new republic. Anguilla was horrified; they were convinced that St. Kitts would take advantage of their less populated island and keep all of the taxes for themselves. Anguillan fishermen invaded St. Kitts on June 10, 1967, briefly taking over Government House, refusing rule from St. Kitts and demanding to stay part of the British Empire.

Britain declined to accept the island back. The international community considered Anguilla to be part of the 3-island nation, but Anguilla sent neither taxes nor representatives to St. Kitts and did not allow any Kittitians on their island. The Premier in St. Kitts wrote the British Foreign Office that mafia drug lords had taken over Anguilla, begging Britain's help to force Anguilla back into union with St. Kitts. On March 19, 1969, in a comedy of errors, British paratroopers stormed Anguilla. They met only a leader brandishing a Bible and a few sleepy fishermen. The world laughed at Britain. Anguilla's wish was granted, and they were allowed back into the British Empire.

Sharp retired to St. Thomas, quicky spending whatever money he had managed to steal over his career, and was soon imprisoned by Danish authorities for debt. The prison on St. Thomas was his residence at the time Admiral Benbow visited in 1699 looking for Captain Kidd. Sharp died in jail in 1702 and is buried somewhere on St. Thomas.

(Information for this sketch comes from: Ringrose, A Buccaneer's Atlas, pp 30-33; Bucaniers of America v. 2 pp 271-72; Dampier, pp 12-36; and Pringle, from his chapter entitled "Bartholomew Sharp").

Michiel Adriaanszoon de Ruyter

Buccaneer, Admiral, Hero

Born March 24, 1607, Michiel (Adriaan's son) de Ruyter (the rider) was the son of a former sailor and soldier who earned his living by delivering beer barrels to pubs. Rumors suggest that Adriaan's father was a Scottish soldier who fought for Dutch independence as a mercenary. Michiel's mother was also the daughter of a soldier. A lot of pubs lined the waterfront, so he had plenty of opportunities to watch ships sailing in and out of his hometown of Vlissingen, inspiring the young boy with the wonders of the world. Growing up in the Reformed Church, it is possible that at Synod gatherings, he met and played with another Reformed Church youth from a parish only a few miles away in Dieppe: Abraham Duquesne, whose distinguished naval career would closely parallel Michiel's own. Throughout Michiel de Ruyter's career at sea, he read the Bible to his crew every Sunday (Grinnell-Milne, p. 78).

According to biographer Grinnel-Milne, Michiel was a lazy, inattentive schoolboy, dreaming of going to sea, quick to play tricks on everyone, and quick to fight other boys. Milne says,

>*"At ten years of age, while workmen are repairing the principal steeple of the Reformed Church in Flushing, Michiel climbs the scaffolding and then mounts the ladder to the cross on the dizzy pinnacle above. Honest burgers of the good town see a little figure there, calling out boyish impertinences, who waves his cap without the slightest indication of fear. Tired of his fun, he prepares to descend. The*

upturned faces of the crowd afford no encouragement, for it can be seen that the workmen have removed the ladder, and the boy must slide down the steeple as best he can. With his nail-shod boot he kicks away a slate, and his foot finds purchase on the wooden bar that is under it. His other foot is lowered, and again a slate crashes into the street, while he finds footing on the thin supports beneath, and so as slate after slate falls, Michiel slowly moves down the steeple, reaches the scaffolding, and now the street, where his father takes possession of him. This courage and cool-headed, unerring thinking in the presence of great danger announced who he was to the world." (G-M, pp. 4-5)

His father got him a berth as a cabin boy on a friend's ship as a bosun's mate's boy when he turned eleven. On board, his best friend would be a small African boy employed in rope-making, named on the ship "John Company," who would sail with Michiel for forty years.

At 15 years old, already a bosun on a man of war, his name appears on a muster roll for a company of Dutch musketeers fighting an invading Spanish army, as the crew of the ship was employed ashore as artillerymen. Buying a horse, Michiel also distinguished himself as a cavalryman. Back afloat, he boarded a Spanish vessel, was wounded in the head with a pike, and taken prisoner. He and two companions escaped and made their way through Spain, France, and Belgium to return home. The journey took a year. Michiel learned French and made friends as he worked his way through the length of France.

At 16, the Dutch House of Lampsin hired Michiel and sent him to Ireland. He initially worked as a clerk and an agent for the warehouse, learning to speak Gaelic fluently. At this time African ships were making raids on the coasts of Europe, especially Ireland and southwest England. Between one and a half million and three million Europeans were captured and shipped to African slave markets to be sold (John Smith, later Captain John Smith of Jamestown fame, was one. John was taken with his father and uncle when he was 15 years old and sold as a sex slave to an African woman. He escaped at 17 and got on a ship. His uncle and father died chained to oars of Moorish galleys). After a raid on the Irish coast by African slavers, Michiel requested that the company give him a ship to trade with the Moors so that he could rescue his friends (G-M, p. 15).

The company gave him command of the armed merchantman *Den Graewen Heynst*. His ship successfully fought off five Algerian privateers at once to enter the harbor of Salee. The inhabitants greeted him as a hero, celebrating his seamanship and bravery, and Michiel became friendly with the local ruler. The Moors respected him so much that on one occasion, when his ship was lost on a reef, inhabitants of a nearby town helped him recover his entire cargo (G-M, p. 23). Driving a hard bargain for the cloth he brought to trade, Michiel used the profits to buy as many Christian captives from the slave market as he could. Michiel would spend much of the money he made over his lifetime buying captured Christians – Dutch, French, English, Irish, Germans, even Hungarian-- from African slave markets and transporting them to safety; estimates range from 2500 to 3000.

Milne recounts that returning from Salee, French pirate La Land captured de Ruyter's ship. La Land asked him if he was thirsty. De Ruyter recognized this as a trick question, as the pirates all leaned forward to hear his answer. Michiel replied, in excellent French, that he was. "Would you prefer wine or water?" the pirate captain asked. Michiel replied, "If I am a prisoner, give me water, but if I am free, give me wine." That was the correct answer, and Michiel and his ship were allowed to go free. Over twenty years later, while escorting a Dutch convoy, de Ruyter took on a small fleet of Algerian and French pirate ships. Capturing the first, De Ruyter came face to face with its captain- La Land. He treated La Land well but had to turn him over to the authorities to be hung. La Land's ship turned out to be leased to him by the King of France, and Louis had to be compensated for it from de Ruyter's prize money!

Another incident involved a better armed 'Dunkirker privateer' chasing de Ruyter. Part of de Ruyter's cargo was butter. He had the crew smear some of it all over the deck. One account says that chickens just slaughtered for dinner were instead hoisted into the rigging. He sent his crew down below and ordered absolute silence. When the pirates boarded, none could keep their feet. Imagining witchcraft at work, they scrambled back to their ship.

Though at 21 the youngest captain in the fleet, de Ruyter was no wet-behind-the-ears captain when he sailed on the right wing of the Dutch fleet under Piet Heyn to take the Spanish Treasure Fleet. Every one of Heyn's captains became a national hero; de Ruyter had already been a hero at 15, but this exponentially boosted his reputation. (De Ruyter was not the only 21-year-old who commanded a warship in history: for instance, Christopher Myngs was Captain of the *Elisabeth* at 21 years old, and Horatio Nelson commanded the tender *Little Lucy* at 18, the brig-of-war *Badger* at 19, and as a 21-year-old Post-Captain commanded the frigate *Hichinbrook*. De Ruyter himself had already commanded *Den Graewen Heynst*, and his son Engle would be a Captain at 19, as well.).

A map drawn at the time showing the position of Heyn's ships when they captured the Spanish Treasure Fleet identifies captains of vessels. This map is on display at the Rijksmuseum in Amsterdam, and a copy is on display at Piet Heyn's tomb at the Oude Kerk (old church) in Delft. De Ruyter is identified as captain of the vessel on the outside edge of the Dutch right flank.

De Ruyter married in 1633, but his wife died in childbirth, leaving him with an infant daughter. Michiel wanted to be near to his little girl, so he took a job as navigator on a whaling ship, which only worked the northeastern Atlantic.

Jealous of wealth pouring into Holland from trade, England and France looked the other way as their buccaneers raided the Dutch coast. Worse, Spain armed 100 French privateers to operate out of Dunkirk (then part of Flanders, known as the Spanish Netherlands), with a license to attack all Dutch commerce. For three years, de Ruyter captained *de Vlissinge*, a private armed vessel charged with destroying them. He sailed against such legendary "Dunkirker" captains as Bernard Desjean (later an admiral of France, the 'Baron de Pointis') and Abraham Duquesne (later the 'Marquis' Duquesne, Admiral of France and de Ruyter's personal friend). De Ruyter impressed someone. In 1640 he was made a vice-admiral in the Dutch Navy aboard the 26-gun *Haze*. His squadron helped the Portuguese navy defeat the Spanish in the Battle of St. Vincent. How did de Ruyter make Admiral at 33 years of age? Though young, de Ruyter was a legend. He was one of Piet Heyn's captains. Four hundred years later, Dutch schoolchildren still sing of the taking of the 'Silver Fleet'; you can listen to it on YouTube.

After the war, he bought the armed merchant vessel *Salamander*, resuming his career as a Buccaneer and trading extensively in the West Indies and Morocco.

As a Buccaneer commanding his ship *Salamander* in the Caribbean between 1641 and 1646, De Ruyter improved Dutch maps of the Antilles, and, according to de Ruyter's descendant, Frits de Ruyter de Wilde, was responsible for determining the boundary between the French and Dutch sides of the island of St. Martin. According to British spy Sir. Joseph Williamson, de Ruyter lived on and operated out of Santa Cruz for five years. Given his activity in the Caribbean at the time, it makes sense that he was involved with establishing the colony of Sint Kruis. Other Dutch islands in the Caribbean -Curacao, Sint Maarten, St. Eustatius, Saba- are desert islands with poor, rocky soil. Sint Kris was a jewel, much larger, with rich soil and plentiful rain. Many nations wanted Sint Kruis, and only de Ruyter's reputation kept it safe, even if only for four years.

De Ruyter actually lived on *Salamander*, not on land. Returning home from his stint as an Admiral serving with the Portuguese navy in January of 1641, he began a cycle he repeated for six years. He left home in the first week of January, sailing for Morocco. Selling the cargo of cloth and cheese, the money was used to buy freedom for Christian slaves. He brought those he freed to the Caribbean, and operated out of Sint Kruis from February through August, sailing home to Vlissingen at the onset of hurricane season, and spending September through Christmas with his family. After de Ruyter sailed home in August of 1646, Prince Rupert and the Earl of Marlborough, hanging out in St. Thomas harbor waiting for him to leave, captured Sint Kruis for England. Royalist generals, they had just lost the Battle of Naseby, and no longer had a country. They brought one thousand still-bloodied refugees with them and two hundred soldiers.

From 1646 to 1650, de Ruyter served as Holland's ambassador to the Algerian ports of Salee, and later to Morocco as well. The Caliphate run by the Ottomans out of Constantinople was falling apart. Local Beys turned more and more to piracy, preying on the many Dutch ships trading in the Mediterranean. They paid no attention to any central authority, which is why de Ruyter had to deal with individual cities. De Ruyter became an expert in the complicated politics of the area and bought the freedom of many more Christian captives in the slave markets. Ironically, his diplomacy was mostly undone by fellow countrymen; Dutch merchants who had ships captured by the Algerian pirates turned vigilante and outfitted corsairs of their own. Those ships were ordered to take any Algerian vessel they found and sell their cargo in Spain; Algerian captives were sold into slavery in Spanish markets. The Dutch corsairs paid no attention to differentiating between ships of cities de Ruyter had forged new treaties with, and those he had not.

De Ruyter's second wife died in 1650, leaving him with five children. He was devastated and decided to retire from the sea. He returned home, remarried quickly, and planned on staying home to be a family man.

England blockaded Dutch ports and started the first Anglo-Dutch war. Michiel came out of his very brief 'retirement' to command, and fought so brilliantly at the Battle of Plymouth that Admiral Tromp made him a squadron commander. From 1652 until his death in battle in 1676, De Ruyter was an admiral in the Dutch navy. During the First Anglo-Dutch war, de Ruyter often found himself commanding fleets against English Admiral Robert Blake. The two men, both Reformed Church members, were old friends, and in brief periods of peace they visited and exchanged presents.

As the Spanish threat diminished, countries lured their captains from buccaneering by giving them high ranks in their navies. One of the first to take such a commission was Captain Christopher Myngs. While operating out of St. Croix in 1646, Myngs exploited his friendship with Dutch captains to gain information, which enabled him to capture a 12 ship Dutch convoy. A few years later, he is rumored to have cheated the French and Dutch buccaneers who fought with him out of their fair share of plunder after raiding Campeche. It is safe to say that Dutch sailors had no love for Christopher Myngs. In the Four Days Battle, a squadron of De Ruyter's fleet under Admiral Liefde to surrounded Myngs' flagship, and Myngs was fatally wounded. Thousands of sailors were killed in this bloody battle; Repairing ships cost so much that England could not afford to press the war for months afterward.

Michiel de Ruyter was born into a cruel world where slavery was a fact of life. He could not save everyone; he set about to rescue Christian slaves by using most of his money to buy their freedom, but he could free only a small amount; he certainly could not purchase freedom for all slaves, or stop the trade. For the second part of his career, he was an officer of the Dutch Navy; as such, he followed orders. When the English fleet captured Dutch West African trading ports Gorée and Elmina, de Ruyter was ordered to take a Dutch fleet to recapture them, which he did, in 1665, although in a sign of respect, Gorée actually surrendered before he even arrived. I have been able to find no evidence that De Ruyter had anything to do with the slave trade that operated out of those ports. He neither created it, condoned it, nor participated in it. He followed orders and put his country's flag back on the forts; the trade was going on, regardless of his personal feelings against slavery.

De Ruyter's most famous exploit was the Battle of the Medway in 1667, possibly the craziest, most audacious attack by a fleet in history. The plan was hatched by Johann De Witt and his brother, Admiral Cornelis De Witt, while de Ruyter was ill. English General Holmes had just teamed up with Prince Rupert and his fleet to hurt Dutch trade by attacking and destroying more than 100 merchant ships anchored by a small fishing village. While there were few casualties, rumors of English atrocities against civilians stirred the Dutch population to anger. De Ruyter recovered just in time to lead the adventure. Dutch sailors would have followed no other Admiral in such a risky venture. At the mouth of the river, the scared sailors almost mutinied; only their 'Bestevaer' (grandfather) de Ruyter was able to calm them, comfort them, and give them the confidence to proceed. English ships were towed up the river to their base by launches with oars. Over five days, unable to use sails, the Dutch fleet of unwieldy ships of the line was swept up the river Thames as the tide came in, through the heart of enemy land almost to London itself. The Dutch ships anchored in the river periodically when the tide turned against them until they made it to where the largest part of the English fleet was lying at their moorings. Townspeople and farmers along the river must have been shocked to see the huge

Dutch battleships passing by! Half of England's navy was destroyed. Tides carried the Dutch fleet back out with its prizes, including the English flagship. De Ruyter did as he always did after a battle; he swept his cabin and tended to his chickens (G-M, 27).

The lifeblood of the Dutch nation was trade. De Ruyter would go on to win a dozen battles, protecting Dutch trade for many years to come. He could not, however, protect the Republic, or his friend Johann De Witt. In 1672, England, France, and Sweden launched surprise invasions by land against which the Dutch army was inadequate. The Dutch army fell back in disarray. Many blamed the De Witt brothers. The Hague's civic militia seized the De Witt's, shot them, hung their naked bodies, and cut out and ate their livers. Despite this atrocity, the militia mob acted in an orderly manner according to witnesses, as though planned. William of Orange, the royal heir, widely considered as having instigated the riot, was installed as Stadtholder. De Ruyter must have been appalled, but continued to serve his country under William. As Stadtholder he now served as what we might today call a President, as the States General still controlled the money. He wouldn't be a King until he invaded England and took the crown from his uncle James in the Glorious Revolution of 1688.

With the outbreak of the Second Anglo-Dutch War in 1874, Admirals de Ruyter and Binckes sailed the Dutch fleet to the West Indies. Once in the Caribbean, they split, with Binckes ships going to protect Tobago (Binckes and many of his men -and their families- died in the bloody battles that followed. France took Tobago). De Ruyter sailed to Saint Croix.

"On the 19th of June the fleet was about latitude 34" north. In three divisions, Engel de Ruyter being sent in advance to order provisions, the Dutch sighted Madeira on the 18th, Tenerife on the 24th, and de Ruyter arrived in the harbor of Santa Cruz before his son got there, so that he had to obtain some necessaries." (G-M, p. 206)

From St. Croix de Ruyter raided the English island of Barbados, sinking all of the English vessels in the harbor, but his fleet took a pounding from the masonry fort. De Ruyter needed to find an island to careen ships that had been holed below the waterline, and cut trees to replace masts. De Ruyter brought the Dutch fleet back to St. Croix to refit before attempting to take the island of Martinique from the French. Though a French island, the Governor of Sainte Croix at the time was a 'Moor' and had no problem with it (DuTertre 1978, p. 13) (CSP, V. 17, p. 43-44). De Ruyter had such confidence in his friends on Sainte Croix that he took his Dutch fleet to provision at Sainte Croix, then after Barbados returned to repair and re-provision, at a time when Sainte Croix was a French royal colony and Holland was at war with the French!

It seems most likely that the fleet anchored on the west side. First, ships of the line, even Dutch, would draw too much water for Salt River, and could not point close enough to the wind to round the sand bar and enter. Second, Bassin would have been scary; Round Reef is in the middle of the cut, and even with it marked today, many boats run into it. Today there is a channel dredged to 25 feet, but at the time, it was probably too shallow even for Dutch ships of the line to enter. Lastly, the west coast is where the best trees are, and that is what they were after.

The fleet left St. Croix with fever on board but still had a chance at success. Martinique was caught by surprise when the sun came up on the 19th of July when they saw the Dutch fleet off of Fort Royal. Unfortunately for De Ruyter, the wind died; while his ships lay motionless, the French had plenty of time to prepare their defenses. By the time the wind returned, it was too late. An amphibious landing made by sick marines was defeated with heavy losses, and De Ruyter sailed back home. De Ruyter's son Engel, captain of one of the vessels in the fleet, wrote that the Dutch Admiralty poorly supported the expedition, mentioning that bullets supplied to the troops did not even fit their muskets (G-M, p. 209).

The Dutch Reformed Church had many congregations on the other side of Europe in Hungary. Hungarian ministers went to seminary in the Netherlands. In 1671, most of the Hungarian population belonged to the Reformed Church and was allowed to practice their religion under the Ottoman Empire. Holy Roman Emperor Leopold I invaded and 'freed' Protestant Hungary, with no intention of leaving. New Pope Clement X ordered a purge of Protestants from nations ruled by Catholic monarchs. Leopold had over 300 Hungarian Reformed Church clergy arrested and tried for blasphemy and treason. Forty-one were marched to the sea and sold as galley slaves; 30 survived the long march and chained to oars. It was a famous incident in Europe and especially noted by Reformed Church members like de Ruyter.

Abraham Duquesne was de Ruyter's biggest fan. He studied all of de Ruyter's and tactics and venerated him highly, believing him to be the greatest living admiral. The two captained ships and led fleets against each other for most of their careers. In the English Channel, a young Duquesne captained a 'Dunkirker' privateer as a proxy for France hunting Dutch trading ships, while de Ruyter captained a privateer hunting 'Dunkirkers'. In the Caribbean, both captained privateers against the Spanish. In the Baltic Sea, Admiral Duquesne's French warships led the Swedish fleet against de Ruyter's Dutch and Danish fleet. Duquesne was knighted by the King of Sweden and de Ruyter by King Christian IV of Denmark. During the Second Anglo-Dutch War, Duquesne sailed as a squadron commander under Admiral de Ruyter, when France and Holland briefly combined fleets against the English. At that time, Louis XIV was so impressed with de Ruyter that he honored him with France's highest military award.

In 1676, de Ruyter was sent to command a combined Spanish/Dutch fleet against a French fleet under Duquesne in the Mediterranean. Having spent his whole life with Spain as his enemy, this must have seemed strange indeed. After fighting

Duquesne's fleet to a draw in the Battle of Stromboli, de Ruyter took the fleet into Naples for repairs. While there, he learned that a galley with 26 surviving Hungarian ministers was in the harbor. De Ruyter bought their freedom. There is a large statue of de Ruyter in the town of Debrecen, Hungary, commemorating this event (G-M, p. 230).

De Ruyter ran into Duquesne's fleet again on April 22, 1676, in the Battle of Augusta. Half an hour into the battle, a cannonball struck the instep of de Ruyter's left foot, tearing off most of it, breaking two leg bones, and throwing him seven feet down to a lower deck. Bleeding out and fighting to stay conscious, he continued to direct the fight and subsequent retreat while prostrate on the deck. When Duquesne learned that his friend was injured, he stopped the battle. De Ruyter was taken to a hospital on Sicily, but the wound became infected, and he breathed his last a week later as he quoted the 63rd Psalm, "...I think of you, God, through the watches of the night." Admiral Duquesne helped embalm his body, burying de Ruyter's internal organs and heart on a beach near Syracuse, Sicily. King Louis XIV ordered cannons all along the coast of France to fire in salute as de Ruyter's body sailed by on the way home (G-M, p. 241). De Ruyter's body lies in the Reformed Church (Nieuwe Kerk) in Amsterdam.

Michel de Grammont

Hurricane!

Michel de Grammont was a famous French nobleman turned Buccaneer. He was born in Paris either in 1645 or 1650 but was forced to leave France after he killed his sister's suitor in a duel.

De Grammont began his buccaneering career around 1670 by capturing a Dutch trade convoy that was worth about 400,000 livres ($4 million in current US dollars). On his next cruise, he ran aground on a reef and sunk his ship. De Grammont went to Tortuga and bought another vessel. Sailing out of Tortuga, he made acquaintance with Governor de Poincy; he next appeared on St. Croix, as a plantation owner and member of one of the six militia companies between 1671 and 1678, rising to the rank of Major and commanding the militia (Archives Nationale Outre Mer, cote: 5DPPC152; Highfield, Sainte Croix, p. 520).

At the beginning of the Franco-Dutch War of 1678, Michael de Grammont and ten other French buccaneers who lived on St. Croix sailed to join the Comte de'Estrees for the raid on Dutch Curacao. The combined French fleet wrecked on the Las Aves Reef. Only three Buccaneer ships, including De Grammont's, survived, and he sailed back to St. Christopher for help. Elected commodore of the remaining French Buccaneers, he led six ships with 700 men in the capture of Maracaibo, Gibraltar, Trujillo, and La Guairá. At Cumana, 50 Buccaneers led by Grammont and English buccaneer

Thomas Paine defeated 2,000 Spanish militia and sacked the town (CSP v. 10, 1677-1680 #'s 604, 642, 665, 687-90, 718, and 741). De Grammont was wounded by a sword cut in this battle.

In 1682, de Grammont accepted a privateering commission from the Governor of Petit-Goave. He and Nicolaas van Hoorn teamed up with Laurens de Graaf and Michiel Andrieszoon (not de Ruyter) to sack the Treasure Fleet warehouses at Veracruz. Unable to take the town, they captured hostages and held them for ransom. When the Governor only paid a fraction of what they asked, van Hoorn proceeded to behead the hostages. When de Graaf returned to the camp, he was furious at the murder of innocents, and dueled van Hoorn; van Hoorn died a few days later.

De Grammont and de Graaf sailed their ships to sack towns along the Florida Atlantic coast, and in 1685 returned to the Caribbean to sack Campeche. Again, the Buccaneers could only take hostages from citizens captured outside the walls. The Governor refused to pay it, and de Grammont insisted on executing some of the hostages. De Graaf again refused to allow it; they had a falling out and split up.

Peace with Spain came, and to reign in the Buccaneers, English, Dutch, and French governors were empowered to grant military commissions of advanced rank to the most successful of them (something that did not sit well with more conventional veteran commanders). Tarin de Cussy was appointed Governor of Saint Domingue by Louis XIV. De Graaf, though Dutch-born, accepted a commission as an infantry major from de Cussy, commanding French militia on the north shore of San Domingue. De Graaf fought as a French soldier in several campaigns to get the Spanish out of St. Domingue and helped lead an abortive invasion of Jamaica. De Grammont was appointed Major in command of the Southern coast of Saint Domingue, but could not resist one last cruise on his ship before acceding once again to life ashore (Crouse,

p. 147). De Grammont sailed back up towards St. Augustine in the fall of 1686, into the eye of a hurricane. He was never seen again.

John Benbow

Treasure Island's Inn was named for him

In Robert Louis Stevenson's book, <u>Treasure Island</u>, the Hawkins family Inn is named "The Admiral Benbow." John Benbow was born on the 10th of March, 1653. He rose to become one of England's greatest heroes. Benbow was the son of a tanner. A tanner scraped the flesh off of cow hides, then paid people for their piss (if they had a pot to pee in), cured the hides with the piss, and sold the leather. In a class-conscious country like England, you cannot get much lower than that. Records show that John's father died when he was still very young. Some sources say that his mother died around the same time. The Bristol orphanage was full; the Justice of the Peace found a naval captain who agreed to take John on board as a cabin boy. With all of those disadvantages, John Benbow enjoyed important advantages: he was smart, respectful, brave, and very lucky. After a few years in the forecastle, he was invited to become a midshipman —a young gentleman in training to be an officer-- by his captain, Arthur Herbert. At 25 he was a Master's Mate, which means he was involved with navigation. One more step would make him a Sailing Master, as high one of low birth could normally go. In a series of bloody battles in the Mediterranean, he impressed Arthur Herbert so much that Herbert used his influence to have Benbow commissioned a Lieutenant. He soon proved himself and made Captain. In periods between wars, while on half-pay from the navy, Benbow captained private armed vessels and then bought his own 'frigate,' sailing as a Buccaneer both in the Mediterranean and in the Caribbean between 1680 and 1688. During this time, he became friends with French Buccaneer Jean de Casse. Both would later be given commissions as Admirals in their nations' navies. Benbow was called back into the British Navy in 1688, commissioned a Rear-Admiral by Herbert, now "Lord Torrington," and given command of the Leeward Island Station for the Royal Navy. One of his first tasks was to apprehend Captain William Kidd who was known to be sailing to the Caribbean from the Indian Ocean. Benbow put into St. Thomas but could not find him; he came very close, as Kidd was just a few miles away in St. Croix at the time. The Danish Governor assured Benbow that the only English pirate on St. Thomas at the time was Bartholomew Sharp, who was in prison for debt (Ringrose, Atlas, p 32).

When the War of Spanish Succession broke out, Benbow was ordered to support Governor Codrington in the Leeward Islands and Governor Beeston of Jamaica, but also to take and destroy the Spanish Treasure Fleet. To counter, Louis XIV sent a much more powerful fleet of 32 warships, led by the 98-gun *Marveilleux*. Fortunately for Benbow, death, disease, scarcity of food, and desertion plagued the French, and rather than use the fleet and its 12,000 men to strategic advantage, the fleet had to return home having accomplished nothing, leaving only a remnant under Admiral Jean du Casse to convoy the Spanish Treasure Fleet (CSP 1702, #163).

Informed by spies, Benbow intercepted the Treasure Fleet. Benbow fought his flagship furiously, but except for one other ship that fought hard, and two that fought a little, the rest of his ships held themselves out of the fight. The captains signed a petition later saying that they could not participate in the battle as their ships were in 'poor condition,' but the unspoken feeling was that noble blood would not fight under a cabin boy, the son of a tanner. (Crouse, pp 261-65). After fighting his ship extremely well, taking a bad wound in the leg, and being in a position to almost capture the French flagship, he was forced to let du Casse go. Du Casse wrote Benbow immediately afterward, "I had little hopes, on Monday last, but to have supped in your cabin; but it pleased God to order it otherwise. I am thankful for it. As for those cowardly captains who deserted you, hang them up; for, by God, they deserve it." The cowardly captains were court-martialed in England, and two were shot. Benbow died of his wound a few months later (CSP 1702, #936, #1063; 1703, #123). Britain loves their lords, but could never abide with cowards.

Jean-Baptiste du Casse

Death sailed with him

Born in a small fishing village on the Bay of Biscay, Jean was baptized by his grandfather, a minister in the Reformed Church, in the fall of 1646 (Protestant/Huguenot). As a young man, he signed on as an apprentice on board a French East Indiaman, learned seamanship and navigation, then became a junior officer on a slave-trading vessel. Du Casse managed to save his money, bought a small privateer in Saint Domingue, and had quite a successful career as a Caribbean buccaneer, operating out of St. Croix. Tiring of piracy, he sailed his ship to France and offered half of his loot to Louis XIV, who granted him a commission as a lieutenant in the French Navy.

St. Christopher's (St. Kitts) had been divided peacefully between French and English settlers with a non-aggression pact for over a century, but that could not last forever. In 1689 Captain du Casse and Captain Jean Fantin attacked English settlements on St. Christopher. Not surprisingly, a handful of English sailors serving under Fantin, including William Kidd and Robert Culliford, mutinied and took the ship. Kidd was elected captain and immediately joined her to the English squadron. Ashore, du Casse helped defeat the English forces; English colonists were forced to give up their land and relocate.

After du Casse left, the English squadron returned immediately and retook St. Kitts for themselves. Culliford and most of Kidd's crew, not interested in patriotism, mutinied and put their short-termed captain ashore. Culliford took the ship to the Indian Ocean and began pirating out of Madagascar, where Kidd would meet him again. The grateful English Governor of St. Kitts gave Kidd a captured French sloop, which he sailed to New York.

In 1695, St. Domingue Governor de Cussy was killed fighting a Spanish invasion force, and du Casse was appointed his successor, with orders to get there fast and to repel the next attack. Before he left the leeward islands for his new position, du Casse helped defeat English assaults on Guadalupe and Martinique. He lingered in Martinique to make arrangements for the militia to sail with him to St. Domingue, but before he could, the Governor and many people on Martinique died of a nasty epidemic of malaria. Du Casse fled with his fleet to St. Croix, but instead of leaving fever behind, he transported it to St. Croix, changing its history forever. The epidemic would kill many people on the island, helping convince King Louis to abandon it (Haring, Ch. 12). If not for this, St. Croix may never have been Danish, or American. The same fever went on board when de Ruyter brought his fleet to Sainte Croix for repairs soon after, and may have been responsible for his failure to take Martinique.

Arriving in St. Domingue, du Casse rounded up buccaneers who had accepted French commissions, including Laurens de Graaf and Jean Sieur Bernanos, L'Orange, and Bernard, and invaded Jamaica. Port Royal had just been devastated by an earthquake that plunged half of the city underwater, and he saw an opportunity to loot. He burned 50 plantations, stole all of the sugar, burned fields, and carried away 1500 slaves. A legend says that one of the farms burned belonged to a family named "Thatch." That theory attempts to explain how Edward "Blackbeard" Thatch took to the sea.

The expedition was a failure. Tails between their legs, de Casse, de Graaf, and Bernanos returned to St. Domingue. In a surprising and uneasy partnership, the English navy transported Spanish troops to St. Domingue and landed 600 of their own to attack Cap François. French forces abandoned the town and retreated to Petit Goave. Bernanos died in an attempt to lead 150 women and children to safety. The English used their brief alliance with Spain to cripple French forces in the Caribbean but did not want Spain to have all of Hispaniola. They deserted their new Spanish friends and sailed off with all of the food supplies. Unable to eat, Spanish soldiers had to give up the fight and walk back to their half of the island (Crouse, 271).

In retaliation, King Louis ordered du Casse to raid Cartagena. Lacking resources after the crippling raid on Cap Francois, du Casse wrote his old friend Bernard Desjean, once a Buccaneer operating out of Sainte Croix and now the "Baron de Pointis" –a former "Dunkirker" foe of de Ruyter's and comrade of Duquesne. De Pointis gathered investors, leased ships, hired soldiers, and sailed to the Caribbean to join du Casse, who added what his surviving French militia and the Buccaneers from Petit Goave and Sainte Croix. De Pointis and Du Casse looted goods worth 1.4 million francs, which won them each one-fifth of the loot and du Casse the rank of vice-admiral. It was the last time buccaneers would fight alongside French soldiers, however. De Pointis pulled a surprise exit, taking off with the militia, soldiers, and loot, cheating the Buccaneers out of their fair share. Furious, the buccaneers looted Cartagena again, doing better for themselves the second time around. They resorted to brutality, and du Casse was unable to stop them. Torture and murder of civilians led to a cry of outrage from the world.

The perception of buccaneers forever changed. No longer thought of as adventurous heroes, they were now considered to be scum. They either settled down as citizens or turned pirate (Crouse, pp. 155-291, Du Casse, pp. 159-236.).

Du Casse was a very active man and involved in dozens of actions around the Caribbean during his career. He successfully led the defense of Haiti during the War of Spanish Succession, served as Governor of Saint-Domingue for 12 years, and was made a member of the prestigious "Order of the Golden Fleece" by Spanish King Charles II. The charter of the Order includes a promise by the King of Spain that he will never go to war without consulting the Order first. In nearly 600 years, only 1200 men have been tapped to serve in this order, with 41 serving at the beginning of the 21st century. Du Casse retired a rich man and died in 1715. The Age of the Buccaneers was over. With the War of Spanish Succession as the pivot, it was time for a new age, The Golden Age of Piracy, and St. Croix was to take a lead role once again.

III. Pirates

The Flying Gang

A new generation of privateers was born in Port Royal, Jamaica, during the **War of Spanish Succession, 1702-1712**. Colin Woodard quotes Edward Long, who was in Port Royal at this time, and called it "The receptacle of vagabonds, the sanctuary of bankrupts, a toilet stool for the prisons, as sickly as a hospital, dangerous as the plague, hot as hell, and wicked as the Devil… the dunghill of the universe". Merchant sailors caught in port when the war broke out had difficulty finding berths home, as ships stayed in port to avoid the cloud of privateers which poured out from Havana.

The Governor of Jamaica, Archibald Hamilton, was given no resources with which to defend the island against a Spanish invasion. At the same time, he saw no problem with enriching himself through the war. Killing two birds with one stone, he advertised for

privateers and gave letters of marque to 30 vessels. Benjamin
Hornigold (Edward Thatch served with Hornigold), John Cockram,
Josiah Burgess, Henry Jennings (Charles Lane served with Jennings
on the 4-gun sloop *Diamond*), and many others sailed. Jean Martel
(sloop *Revenge*) captained one of these.

      Interestingly, Martel served as a double agent, convincing the
English that his name was "John Martel" while secretly reporting to
San Domingue. Olivier Levasseur (LaBouse), well-educated and
from a wealthy family, sailed as a privateer for the French against the
English. Many merchant sailors deserted their idle ships for a
chance to eat, and even share in real profits.
On August 28, 1712, a hurricane struck Port Royal, destroying 54
ships. A week later, news came that the war was over. Sailors from
the privateers were on the beach, with few merchant berths
available.

The Golden Age of Piracy and the First Catalyst: The Navigation Act of 1684

There were two catalysts for the Golden Age of Piracy. In 1684, Parliament, at the instigation of the Tory party—many of whom were ship owners--enacted **The Navigation Act**. It said that no ships could trade in anything of value with British colonies in America unless the vessel was *built in England*, and *owned exclusively by persons who lived in England*.

American ships? They could carry rocks, or rot, for all Parliament cared.

But with the 'Glorious Revolution' only a few months later, a Dutchman took the throne. William was backed by the Whig party, and did not worry about the Navigation Act. In quick succession, The War of the Grand Alliance, The Great Northern War, and the War of Spanish Succession kept Britain busy. But in 1714, with the Treaty of Ryswick, peace came, and American merchant ships flooded the seas. Parliament was once again in the hands of the Tory party, and Prime Minister Spencer Compton wrote to James Stanhope to 'Enforce the Law' or be replaced.

But what was James Stanhope to do? Send British warships to capture 'British' merchant ships? Colonial vessels were supposed to be British. It would be sure to start a revolution (it did, eventually). A month after Compton's letter, Spanish pirates operating out of Havana began capturing vessels, taking thirty-eight in two months. Checking the registry of these vessels reveals that these ships were not French, Dutch, and certainly not English. They were all *American*. The captured vessels were sold in Havana with their cargoes. Adult crew did not make it to Havana, but seventy boys 13-18 years of age were thrown into the dungeon of El Morro Castle, directly underneath the office of the Governor of Cuba, Laureano Castellanos. And the British navy did nothing.

Did James Stanhope have Spanish connections? Yes. His father was the British Ambassador to Spain, and James may have attended the University of Salamanca, when a young Isadoro Casada Rosales was also a student. By 1715, Rosales was the 'Marques de Monteleón,' and Ambassador to the Court of St. James in London. Stanhope's father negotiated over Gibraltar with Jacinto de Belver, the 'Marques de Pozobueno,' who knew James Stanhope very well. In 1715, Belver was in London almost as often as he was in Madrid, as he was Spain's top diplomat in northern Europe. And of course, both Rosales and Belver were acquaintences of Laureano Castellanos, the 'Marques de Casa Torres.'

What do we know for sure? American ships were eliminated. Castellanos made money from selling the ships and cargo. And the British navy ignored it. Castellanos wrote that his pirates took American vessels 'because they had Spanish coins on board,' but of course they did--in 1715, Spanish coins were the most common medium of exchange in North America (CSP 1716, #158).

One of the captured ships was from Marblehead, Massachusetts, with an eighteen-year-old first mate named LeCraw, who was the ranking officer of his crew after the Spanish killed the older men. LeCraw's ship was crewed by boys of Marblehead between the ages of thirteen and eighteen. Home after a season on family cod-fishing schooners, fathers stayed home for the winter with wives and smaller children while teenaged boys signed on for a Caribbean cruise. A local merchant bought salt fish from the fleet and corn meal from Salem, then sailed his ship for Port Royal with teens LeCraw, Girdler, Laskey, Pittman, Conway, Ross, Martin, and more. Together, they represented a who's who of Marblehead's sailing families.

LeCraw's ship was carried into Havana and sold with her cargo. The boys were thrown into the dungeon in the Castilla de los Tres Reyes Del Morro, along with some 60 boys from the other ships (adult prisoners had been murdered and thrown into the sea. Adults did not sell well at the slave market). Castellanos allowed LeCraw to write a letter to Governor Archibald Hamilton in Port Royal, offering to let him pick up the children for a ransom if he wished, otherwise they would be sold at the slave market (Calendar of State Papers).

Hamilton forwarded the letter to King George, who was furious. George wrote that 'We must teach this French child on the throne of Spain a lesson.' He ordered Hamilton to send some of his privateers from the previous war to pick up the children and take them to 'fish the wracks' of the Spanish Treasure Fleet 'recently thrown onto the strande of Florida.'

In December, Captain Henry Jennings was commissioned by Governor Hamilton to take two Royal Navy sloops, HMS *Barsheba* (Jennings' flagship, with Vane) and HMS *Eagle* (Captain Benjamin Hornigold, first mate Edward Thatch), pick up the boys held in Havana, and take them to 'fish the wrecks.' Jennings took along eight other small sloops. Jennings was given room for improvisation in what was obviously supposed to be a slap in the face to Spain intended to answer the outrage of the capture of British ships.

The Second Catalyst: Ubilla's Treasure Fleet Sails into Hell

7 San Pelayo, reproduction of the flagship of Don Pedro Menendez de Aviles

On the edge of Hell

Labor Day weekend, 1999. It was my last chance for a vacation before students would return to my classes, and the National Hurricane Center website showed nothing in the Atlantic. A recently graduated crew member, Hunter, wanted to come, his mom said, 'sure.'

Thirty-six hours after dropping my mooring at the St. Croix Yacht Club, the anchor splashed into the sandy bottom of Marigot Harbor, St. Martin. Everything on the radio was in French--which we did not understand--so, for the next two mornings, after breakfast at the Pattisserie, we checked the weather posted on the door of Sunsail Charters--sunny, with a 20% chance of showers--and then headed to Orient Bay.

On the third afternoon, we were on the boat making tuna fish sandwiches when someone yelled, "St. Croix! *St. Croix!*"

The fisherman stood in his boat, looking at our transom. "You from St. Croix?"

"Yes."

What the Hell you doin' 'ere?"

"What?"

"There's a Hurricane comin' tonight. Have you extra anchors, and line?"

"No."

"Then get home, now!"

"But, the weather report at Sunsail?"

He laughed. "That report hasn't changed since they went on vacation two weeks ago."

The swells grew through the evening and we put our lifejackets on. There was electricity in the air, and a brooding power in the ocean. When the first band slammed into us, spray flew from the tops of the waves, wind screamed in the rigging, and *Windflower* broached. The world turned on its side, and the sea poured into the cockpit. Standing on the side of the lazarette, I turned the bow into the wind expecting the sails to shred, but they held, and *Windflower* righted herself.

I tied Hunter by the tiller and myself to a lifeline so I could take the sails down. With the jib thrown down the forward hatch and the main tightly wrapped, Hunter and I shook hands, yelled at each other that it had been a privilege being friends, and I sent him below.

I tied myself in and prepared myself for a long night. The rain was blinding, stinging like bees; I put a snorkel mask on so I could keep my eyes open. Lightning struck the water so close, and so hard, that the boat lurched sideways with each strike.

Soaking wet and freezing through the long, dark, terror-filled night, we sailed on the hull alone, steering angles down the waves, my teeth chattering to apocalyptic tunes in my head. On each crest, I yanked the tiller hard to keep from broaching, praying I would pull at just the right moment, praying that nothing broke. Every minute was an eternity of cold.

A little after midnight the wind suddenly dropped to the low 30's, then only upper 20's between gusts; the storm was sliding north-- we had only skirted it. Waves became less dangerous, less steep. Hunter came up. We were exhausted, but I insisted on putting up a big genoa. Wrapping my legs around the pulpit, every wave put me under water and tore the cloth from my fingers. I finally got it hanked on, poled the sheet out, and, somehow, we raised it. Dacron cracked like gunshots until it drew, whipping sheets tore from our hands, and then we raced through the ten-foot swells, spray flying, carving through the waves.

Approaching St. Croix, darkness was broken only by flashes of lightning and lights ashore that blinked between blasts of rain as we threaded our way between Channel Rock and the southeastern tip of the Buck Island Reef. In the shadow of Buck, we raised a small piece of mainsail and changed to a small jib so that we could reach up around the rock line if we made it into Salt River Bay. I knew the beach light should be at 230 degrees on the compass against the house lights behind it for us to find the small entrance through the reef, but the lights appeared only in glimpses before disappearing again with each new downpour. A thousand feet of water shoaled to fifty in a second, and the already huge waves piled up higher, lifting our stern and shoving us forward as fast as a train.

Rushing toward the yet invisible reef, my heart was in my throat; there was no turning back against the power of those waves. To port, White Horse Reef blasted spray into the sky. Lightning struck continuously, thunder roared like cannons, and rain fell in sheets. I told Hunter that if the boat hit the reef we would swim ashore--wind and seas would push us there, anyway.

> Exhausted, freezing, and scared, the buoy startles me when it looms into view and rushes by, six inches from the side of our boat, and we sail safely into Salt River Bay.

The Spanish Treasure Fleet, which had not sailed during the entire war, was bursting with gold and silver. New Spanish King Phillip V, facing bankruptcy from the cost of the war that gave him his throne, issued a decree: "As much treasure as possible must be brought immediately from the Indies without regard for any costs or dangers involved" (Newton, p. 267-81). Juan Esteban de Ubilla was the admiral tasked with organizing the fleet and getting it to Spain. He wrote the Governor of Cuba, begging him to delay the fleet's departure from Havana. Like any sailor, he was afraid of hurricane season. As a veteran sailor, Ubilla would have also seen the signs of an impending storm. But with the King's orders, the governor could not agree to any delay, so Ubilla sailed to his death with his fleet on July 24th (Newton, pp. 267-273). The second catalyst for the Golden Age of Piracy had arrived, on the reefs of Florida.

Hurricanes are cyclones. In the northern hemisphere, the wind moves in a counter clockwise direction. Some storms arrive after a cloudless day, but the day before most storms the sky is odd. Wind becomes faster the higher you go, so at the lower levels cumulus clouds may exit the storm in one direction, high stratus clouds in another, and cirrus clouds at the top in yet another. When you see that, run.

In a hurricane, you cannot sail into the wind; you can only pick your downwind angle. The hurricane Admiral Ubilla predicted slammed into the fleet, and sometime around 2 a.m. on July 31, 1715, Ubilla's ships began crashing into the coast of Florida near present-day Vero Beach. Some of them were able to steer to the beach of their choice, but others were dashed into the reefs. All but one ship of the fleet of 12 were lost. Admiral Ubilla and many families –twelve hundred men, women, and children-- lost their lives. Admiral Salmón had the survivors piece a sailing launch together from the wreckage and sent it to St. Augustine. Local Indian militia was quickly organized and dispatched with food for the survivors. They were also instructed to guard the wrecks and recover the treasure, estimated to be some 14 million pesos (de Francisci, p. 10).

Jennings was ordered to 'fish the wrecks,' but having the boys dive up a penny at a time was not his style, and, after all, he was supposed to teach Spain a lesson. During the previous war, he had captured French militia uniforms. He put them on the boys and adult sailors and taught them to march, drum, and parade so that they appeared to be regular army soldiers. He next captured a Spanish mail ship and got the exact position of the Spanish salvage camp from her captain, Pedro de la Vega. Jennings then landed and marched to the dune just south of the Spanish camp.

Admiral Salmón had sixty-five regular army soldiers and one hundred and twenty Indians at Palmas del Ayr when, at dawn, Jennings' boys marched to the top of the dune just south of the Spanish camp, formed up, and fired a volley. As confused Spaniards and Indians crawled out of their tents, drums rolled, the colors marched to the fore, and Jennings sent a note under a flag of truce: "We have you outnumbered and surrounded; surrender, or die." Salmón met him halfway up the dune and offered 37,000 pieces of eight if he would go away. Jennings refused, demanding the entire pile of 120,000 gold escudos and silver pieces of eight, and Salmón surrendered. He could not have been pleased when he saw children stumbling about in uniforms too large for them.

Salmón required that Jennings sign a letter saying that, in exchange for the 120,000 coins, Jennings would free his prisoners and molest the camp no further. That was actually an article of surrender, an act of war. To Jennings, it was righteous reprisal for the capture of British ships, and he believed he acted with the authority of his King.

Jennings, his boys, and his men returned to Kingston, probably celebrating the whole way, and the boys prepared to go home. But in the meantime, the water began to boil. In retaliation, Governor Castellanos sent an expedition that captured 24 more English and Dutch vessels logging in Mexico and sent Indians from St. Augustine to wipe out a fledgling British settlement at what is now Jacksonville, Florida.

Treasure hunters flooded to Palmas del Ayr, men like Samuel Bellamy and his friend Paulsgrave Williams, son of the Attorney General of Connecticut. Sam needed to make money so that he could return to Massachusetts and marry his love, and Paulsgrave needed money to prove to his wife that he could support her, so that she would return to him with their two daughters.

Kings wrote to each other. Philip wrote, "Florida belongs to Spain, the treasure belongs to Spain, and the attack on Palmas del Ayr was an Act of War!" George responded, "What about my ships?" At this time, it must have become obvious to George that the King of Spain did not know about the capture of any British ships. It is likely that George now found out that his own Foreign Minister was behind it all, and had two choices: Accept responsibility for ordering the attack on Florida and go to war, which would result in tens of thousands of casualties and bankrupt the British treasury, or deny any knowledge of it, instead sacrificing a few dozen privateers and children.

British Foreign Secretary James Stanhope met with Spanish Minister of State Pozobueno in Paris to come up with a solution to avoid war. If my guess is true, those foxes knew full well what had caused this entire mess, but there is no way they could let anyone know. The deal Stanhope and Pozobueno made was for both nations to recall the governors, and hang all the sailors as pirates. King George signed the order recalling Hamilton and declaring everyone involved with the attack on Florida to be pirates. Philip ordered Castellanos to be recalled as well, and his privateers hanged.

Castellanos' privateers had no intention of surrendering to be hung. They turned to piracy. British sailors did the same. When the ship arrived in Kingston with orders to hang Jennings and his crew, sailors rushed to warn them. Jennings and his crew sailed for Nassau, deserted after the Spanish raid in the previous war.

Captain Benjamin Hornigold acquired three large canoes, each with oars, a single square sail, and the capability of carrying 30 men. He took with him John Cockram, Edward Thatch, and 90 more volunteers, and they too sailed for Nassau. This was an adventurous feat, as it meant rowing and sailing for hundreds of miles in open boats, against the trade winds. On the way, they returned to Palmas, but had to settle for only a small ransom before sailing for Nassau as well (CSP 1716, #158).

Located on New Providence Island in the Bahamas, Nassau had been burned four times during the previous war. It no longer had a government, had no defenses, and was positioned perfectly for pouncing on Spanish ships traveling back to Europe. Thanks to Columbus' 'Great Circle Route,' in 1715 eighty-seven percent of all British maritime traffic passed through the Caribbean. Initially, Jennings and Hornigold refused to take British ships. Jennings wrote to James Stanhope asking him to intercede for them, but instead, Stanhope sent a spy to Nassau to list the names of Jennings' and Hornigold's crew.

Dozens of young men like Sam Bellamy and Paulsgrave Williams sailed for Florida to pick treasure up off the beach. Because the camp had been strengthened, they were driven off by the garrison (CSP 1716, #158), though some were able to dive up a little farther along the beach. But when they sailed into Nassau to buy groceries, the spy added them to the list of pirates who were trying to steal Spanish treasure. When the list was published, and sailors in Nassau realized that they could not go home. Jennings and Hornigold drew up a set of 'Articles,' for what they called the 'Flying Gang,' which everyone signed. The treasure hunters were now brothers, sailing together against the world in order to survive. Under the leadership of captains Jennings and Hornigold, New Providence Island became a virtual 'Pirate Republic' (CSP 1716, #408).

Articles were drawn up by each ship's crew as well, respecting the code to which the Flying Gang adhered: captains got two shares, quartermasters, gunners, carpenters, sailmakers, and bosuns one and a half, and the remaining men one share (Similar articles had been drawn up by buccaneers of the previous generation: see Dampier, Ringrose, Avery, Sharp, etc.). The men voted on everything; the officers were elected and could be voted out at any time, the captain in unquestioned command only when in battle. Disputes had to be settled ashore. Gambling was not allowed on board ship. The quartermaster was in charge of all looted money and merchandise, an esteemed and authoritative position, which also provided a check to the captain's power. Plunder was stored by the quartermaster until being divided in front of all. The Flying Gang created the world's first disability pay --wounded sailors would be paid off according to their injuries. Stealing from the ship or a crew member, or timidity in battle, meant death or marooning. Those fancy captain's cabins on pirate ships in the movies? They did not exist. Most officer cabins were torn out; everyone slept on the gun deck, together. Where a cabin remained, it was free for the use of all. The first to board in battle were accorded first dibs on the weapons and clothing of the passengers and officers of captured ships, as a reward for their courage.

In the beginning, Hornigold and Jennings remained loyal to their countrymen, refusing to take British ships. But British Governors sent warships to destroy them, and they got angry. They also knew something British Foreign Secretary James Stanhope would wish they did not. James Stanhope had an older brother, Charles. Charles, Secretary of the Exchequer, had the idea of a win-win policy that proved instrumental in the future of the British Empire. Britain needed thousands of bureaucrats to function, but few signed on to travel half the world away and die of an unnamed disease. To help recruitment of the best and brightest, the Stanhope brothers were instrumental in the creation of the world's first government retirement plan. Eleven percent would be taken out of every check, and civil servants could retire to a life of ease when they reached a certain age or years of service.

But where to invest the eleven percent? The Stanhope brothers knew just where to put the money.

James Stanhope had another problem. Though Parliament resented competition from American ships, they needed more ships for the growing trade with Asia. But if someone borrowed the money for ship and cargo and sent it out, they might well lose it to reef, rock, hurricane, or piracy, and debtor's prison awaited (What made America great, really? The Jews invented credit, the Dutch created corporations, but America gave us bankruptcy laws).

In 1688 a fellow named Edward Lloyd turned 60 and felt he was too old to work hard anymore, so he looked for an easy retirement gig. He decided to open a coffee house in London. Unfortunately for him, so did 99 other people in the same year, so Ed had to be creative to get people to choose his establishment. He decided to offer free coffee and scones to ships captains--people would come to hear tall tales of the sea (advertisements, *The London Times*). Soon, the kind of tales the captains had to share caught the ear of ship owners. They weren't interested in 'Moby Dick.' What cargo did you take to Bombay? How much did you sell it for? What did you bring back? Did that madras cloth bring more profit, or tea?

The Stanhope brothers began frequenting Edward Lloyd's coffee house and offering to insure ships and cargoes. The Stanhope's put their own money into the pool as well, as did Spencer Compton, Prime Minister of the British Empire, and his majesty, King George.

Thanks to the Great Circle Route pioneered by Columbus, 87% of all British shipping passed through the Caribbean. Jennings and Hornigold realized that if they took enough British ships and valuable cargoes, they would bankrupt the underwriters of Lloyd's of London, and thereby ruin the retirement plan of the British Empire. They would also bankrupt the Stanhope brothers, the Prime Minister, put half of Parliament in debtor's prison, and bankrupt the King himself. King George would have no choice but to offer them a full pardon, and they would all be able to return home.

The Flying Gang—the boys of El Morro, young treasure hunters, and the veteran privateers, together with those who stepped forward to join them, took on one of the greatest empires on earth. And they won. The Skull and Bones triumphed over the Union Jack, and the pardon came. When Jennings saw the first pardon, he sent it back, with comments. George was forced to write a second, in which he stipulated that not only were they pardoned for the crime of piracy, but that they were also protected from civil litigation by anyone who thought they still had a right to ships or cargoes they had taken (See appendix for the actual pardon).

Pirates came in every race and hue. General Peter Heywood, the military commander of the Jamaica station sent to replace Hamilton, had this to say about the pirates between Hispaniola and Puerto Rico: "There is of these pirates of all nations, those to westward are generally Spaniards, and some few French, but most mulattos, Quarteroons, and Negroes." (CSP 1716, #212). To the East, records show that one-third to one-half of the pirates were black (CSP 1717-18). While all of the pirates knew that capture meant doom, Black sailors had a different lot when captured: they were sold instead of hung.

Pirates had no desire to fight. They had no belief in a God of Valhalla, they wanted to live to enjoy the next party. They neither wanted to risk being shot, or, by firing their cannons to sink their prey, losing the loot. And, with only some exceptions, they did not hurt those they captured. Instead, they came up with scams and hype to scare merchant seamen into surrendering quickly. The best source for learning how the pirates acted toward their prisoners can be found in the Calendar of State Papers and by reading court depositions made by prisoners after they reached home. The myths of wanton murder were exaggerated by the pirates themselves to keep people on both sides safe.

On the deck of a prize, pirates could yell to the captain for permission to torture the captives, elaborating bloody stories of what they had supposedly done for the benefit of those listening. Captains would say something like, "I let you torture the last ones, let's roll the dice for the lives of this crew." Inevitably, the roll would favor allowing captives to live, and, after taking what they wanted, pirates would allow the prize to sail on its way. Sometimes the theater was over the top. Blackbeard put fuses in his beard and under his hat to look like the devil himself, but records do not show that he actually killed anyone. Bellamy stripped his men naked, tied their hair into ponytails and rubbed it with charcoal so they were all brunettes. They painted primitive designs on their bodies, and Bellamy would yell that his deal with his crew of canibals was that they could not eat crews that surrendered. Who wants to take a chance on being eaten, when you can just let them take the furniture in the hold and you'll go free? There is no record of Bellamy or Blackbeard killing a single one of their captives, and most merchant ships and crews survived to be captured more than once.

Some records of torture are real. Ned Low, Tom Anstis, Charles Vane, and many other pirates had been abused by their captains when in the merchant service (very common at the time, as captains were all-powerful at sea, and no court would hear complaints from sailors). These pirates held a grudge. They would ask captive crews if their captain was a fair man, or if he was he buggering the cabin boy, stealing wages, or whipping them for no reason. If the answer was the later, Ned and others would torture and murder the captain to send a clear message to captains all over the world to treat their crew fairly or they could be next. Once Ned and others descended into alcoholism, they also sometimes tortured captains if they thought money was hidden on board.

Blackbeard began burning captive ships from New England for revenge after Bellamy's survivors were hung, and he wasn't the only one, but the crew was allowed to sail home with another vessel or left ashore somewhere alive.

The pirates captured bigger ships and spread out from Nassau. Some sailed West African waters, others headed for the Indian Ocean to emulate Captain Avery's success, but many came south to cruise the windward and leeward islands of the Caribbean (Lesser Antilles). They needed a base where they could careen, split their plunder, fence their stolen goods, find recreation, and refit, out of sight of policing vessels. St. Croix was their choice. Neither honest merchant ships nor naval vessels came to St. Croix, and stolen cargoes could be fenced easily to planters in the British Virgins, Puerto Rico, but especially to the Danish West India and Guinea Company, whose agents transported the merchandise to St. Thomas on a fleet of small sloops (Creque, "French St. Croix").

A New Generation

The Devil to Pay, and No Pitch Hot

Buccaneers were involved in the struggle to wrest control of the Caribbean from the Spanish. They were either after revenge for Spanish atrocities, part-time pirates, or "legitimate" privateers working for rival European nations. By 1700, however, the Buccaneers were retired, employed as naval officers, or dead. Spanish power weakened by the last decades of the 17th century, so the years in which Buccaneers of England, France, and the Netherlands worked together against Spain were over.

At this time, half of England's population stood six inches shorter and lived less than half as long as their upper-class countrymen. Half of England's population were living at starvation levels. Farm laborers could not afford to buy the eggs they raised for their masters. Eight thousand people moved from the country to London each year, and that was just about enough to keep up with how many died. Human excrement was dumped from balconies, water sources were contaminated with sewage, and wages for the new arrivals gave them worse living conditions than slaves. One-third of all babies died within the first year of their lives. Orphans swarmed the streets. Fevers, measles, smallpox, rickets, and intestinal worms plagued the people. Wages were minuscule, and debtor's prison awaited any who could not meet their obligations when they fell ill

(Munich Dept. of Economics—citation in bibliography; Ogg, pp. 33-34).

In Devonshire, boys escaped by going to sea. Once at sea, sailors were promised pay after reaching port. Once in port, they learned they would not be paid until after the ship left on its next voyage. Anyone who quit after reaching port lost his wages. When paid, they often just got IOU's which could be traded for coin only at an 'unnamed point in the future.' Sea captains had absolute authority, and without any checks or balances, often turned tyrannical, whipping their men at will and even stealing the wages of their crew. Sailors were, essentially, slaves. To question a Captain was mutiny, and severely punished both at sea and ashore.

On the West Indies Station, British men of war routinely lost between one-quarter and one-third of their crews to malaria every year--it was known in the British navy as the "Station of Death." To keep warships operational, the Admiralty got permission from Parliament to press crew from merchant vessels in the Caribbean as needed. Naval vessels routinely stopped merchant ships in the Caribbean and took whatever sailors they wanted. The Navy paid only half of what the merchant marine did, and discipline was harsh.

Either way, merchant sailors had a miserable existence, and it is no wonder they often volunteered when pirates stopped their ships to plunder (CSP, 1716-1717).

Pirates also recruited indentures being transported to colonial fields against their will. In 1716, at the instigation of Royal Governors and Parliamentarians who owned plantations abroad, the British Colonial Records Office issued carte blanche licenses to transport boys and young men who had been kidnapped from their homes, removing the previous requirement of court documents proving conviction for a crime. Kidnappers received bounties for 'recruiting' laborers for colonial plantations, and public officials were bribed to look the other way. Gangs roamed the English countryside (CSP, 1716, #505).

The Royal Governors were alarmed at the influx of black captives and desperately wanted a poor white population to balance them, cheap labor that could also serve as militia in the event of a slave uprising. Further, in case another nation invaded, they felt that they could arm the white indentures as militia. These indentured servants would be slaves for a defined period of seven years. During those seven years, they were treated worse than black slaves, fed less, and worked harder. They did not represent as much of an investment, and there was no reason to try and keep them alive past the seven-year mark. Do you treat a rental car as well as your own? Have you ever washed, much less changed the oil, in a rental car? Many anguished parents wrote the King to complain about the kidnappings, but the letters were unread. King George I had a problem: he did not speak, or read, English, only his native German. His secretary did not either, speaking and writing only in German and French. The King had no ear for his people (CSP 1716, Colonial Records, Preface, vii and viii, 123, etc.).

Few people ever set out to become pirates. The first 'pirates' of the Golden Age were just treasure hunters. When they found themselves forced into piracy, they captured ships and needed more crew. The pirates had no trouble recruiting kidnapped youths or African captives headed for bondage. Pirate ships and crews proliferated so quickly that for 21 years Royal Governors refused to visit any of their territories that required sea travel on anything smaller than a frigate, for fear of being captured (CSP 1716, multiple letters).

Pirate Paradise

Louis XIV could not get the plantation-owning Buccaneers of Sainte Croix to pay taxes, but the island was a constant drain on the French treasury. Until he could figure out how to make it work, he abandoned it, but warned other nations not to visit, or it would mean war.

The island transitioned smoothly into the Golden Age of Piracy. What made St. Croix perfect for pirates was a peculiar set of circumstances. First, the island had no government, and no police. Second, malaria, the scourge of the Caribbean, was known to infest St. Croix in a big way, and no warships wanted to risk the health of their crews. Third, Salt River provided a careenage to clean ship bottoms and make repairs. Fourth, Salt River Bay was as good a hurricane hole as any in the Caribbean. Lastly, St. Thomas was just a five-hour sail away and provided a ready market for stolen merchandise.

With no Cats Around, the Mice Play:

In 1675, in what would be the only time the French navy would ever try to police St. Croix, a French fleet sailed into Salt River Bay with cannons blazing, sinking a DWIGC ship that had just loaded pirate cargo. In response, Danish Governor Jørgen Iversen Dyppel began allowing pirates his protection in Saint Thomas. Dyppel's successor, Thomaj Esmitt, continued the policy. In answer, a French naval squadron sailed boldly into Charlotte Amalie in 1678 and blew several pirate ships out of the water, even as they lay at anchor under the guns of the fort. The Danish government complained to France, to no avail. Denmark had no naval presence in the Caribbean (CSP, v. 10).

A few months later, neither did France. During the Scanian –or Franco-Dutch-- war, Admiral Michel de Ruyter brilliantly destroyed much of the French navy in the Battles of the Schooneveld. Most of the rest of the French navy sunk in a debacle on Aves Island reef. Louis XIV wanted to take Curacao, as it was strategically placed to control trade with South America. Louis sent ten ships of the line, each one representing one-tenth of the French GNP for an entire year-- plus three frigates and five transports to accomplish this. Instead of allowing his admirals to command the fleet, he felt it necessary to put a noble, the Comte de Estrees, in charge. De Estrees had managed to head up disastrous attempt to take Tobago Island from the Dutch, but was given a second chance and overwhelming superiority that was successful.

William Dampier, a British naval officer, privateer and sometime Buccaneer, learned of this event from some of the survivors. He says that after crossing the Atlantic, the French fleet put into the island of St. Kitts to re-provision, where they joined eleven Buccaneer vessels that had sailed from St. Croix under the famous Michel de Grammont. The combined fleet set sail for Curacao. Three small Dutch privateers sent out by the Governor of Curacao to look out for the rumored French fleet ran into it head on. Turning back towards Curacao, the Dutch ships faked slow speed to allow the lumbering ships of the line to keep up while angling slightly north of the rhomb line to Curacao. De Estrees was paranoid the tiny ships would warn Curacao ruining their element of surprise, and gave chase. De Estrees' Admirals told him it was not necessary to worry about them--against 700 cannons and 4000 soldiers, 20 cannons and 120 soldiers would not win, even if warned. The arrogant and tragically stupid de' Estrees would not listen. When night fell, the Dutch ships kept their stern lanterns lit to make sure the French could follow and led the French fleet onto Aves Island Reef (Dampier, p. 221; Haring; CSP v. 10, 1677-1680 #'s 604, 642, 665, 687-90, 718, and 741.).

Aves island is in the middle of absolutely nowhere, 225 miles west of Dominica and 340 miles north of Venezuela. The Dutch ships darted through or around the reef, but the entire French fleet piled right onto it. Every ship was lost. Only three of the Buccaneer vessels avoided destruction. Leaving the sailors and soldiers who washed ashore, de Grammont took the three remaining buccaneer vessels back to St. Kitts for help.

It would be many years before France could project a naval presence into the Caribbean. British naval vessels continued to patrol the Windward, Leeward, and Northern Virgins, and the French islands that lay in between the British ones were under constant observation, but not St. Croix. There were no police watching St. Croix.

Malaria (ague)

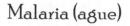

From 1600 to 1820, the British navy lost one-quarter to one-third of their sailors on the West Indian station every year to malaria (sailors called the West Indies "The Station of Death"). In 1695, a particularly bad malaria epidemic wiped out a large portion of the population on St. Croix. Naval vessels stayed away from St. Croix.

Why did malaria kill most everyone but the pirates of St. Croix? Indigenous peoples of Peru made a tincture of cinchona bark that cured fevers, even malaria, and shared this knowledge with Jesuit missionaries who introduced the treatment to Europe around 1640. Surprisingly, no one paid attention. Gentlemen in England did not have to worry about malaria, but the bitter taste of the "Jesuit's Bark" did become popular to flavor cocktails. Privateers of Port Royal grew very fond of adding it to their rum. To this day, cinchona bark is boiled, and the juice is added to soda water to make "tonic" for cocktails with gin. Cinchona bark is one of the spices ("various Venezuelan barks") used in Angostura, and one of the 56 herbs blended into Jägermeister. Today, we know of the juice boiled from cinchona bark as 'quinine,' and every school child knows it is the cure for malaria.

The British navy added rum to sterilize fetid water aboard ship, but the Admiralty was NOT providing herbs to sailors for flavoring.

Be that as it may, pirates were the survivors, the ones who lived while fever killed so many others. "Captain Johnson" (Notorious) says that Blackbeard came to St. Croix to *recover* from fever.

Safe Haven

To catch prey, and to escape from police vessels, the bottoms of pirate ships had to be clean. Hundreds of plant and animal species thrive in tropical waters and cling stubbornly to ship's hulls. Captains could send the crew into the water to scrape the grass around the waterline ("boot strapping"), but to get the torredos, barnacles, and fungus, careening was necessary. Careening meant removing cannons (and everything else) to lighten ship, then hauling her onto a sand bar, leaned her over onto a smaller hull, then scraping and even burning the growth off. This made a pirate vessel extremely vulnerable to police. For the average two-week period of cleaning, Pirates had to find a location off the beaten path of policing vessels, and one that did not put the pirates out of the 'game' for too long. Salt River Bay, St. Croix, with its beautiful hurricane hole and sheltered beaches, off the beaten track but near enough to get back into the game quickly, an island that anyone with any sense was afraid to visit (malaria!), with only one small entrance through the reef and cannons placed strategically to guard it, was ideal for the pirates. The island offered fresh water, game, fish, shellfish, and fresh fruit, including native limes to prevent scurvy. The locals welcomed pirates for their money. Records are sketchy at best; there was no colonial government, no newspaper, and so no records of any sort were kept on the island. What we do have--interviews with pardoned pirates and former 'pressed men', also many letters from Governors of other islands to the Governor of St. Thomas, give ample evidence of a vibrant pirate base on St. Croix (Johnson, Notorious; CSP volumes for years 1699-1733).

HURRICANES AND PIRATES

Today, sailors who live on boats often choose to head south to Trinidad for hurricane season. Why didn't pirates go there?

Trinidad is considered a great place to hide for the season today, but before copper sheathing and modern bottom paint, it was terrible. Torredo worms and barnacles grow in the Gulf of Paria far faster than anywhere else in the Caribbean. Copper sheathing was not made affordable for ships until the nineteenth century. Torredo worms are so bad there that they determined the fate of Trinidad.

Alerted by spies, Spain dispatched two ships of the line to defend Trinidad against a planned English attack in 1796. They did not understand a government where the king did not control the money. The King had to wait six months for a new session of Parliament to fund the expedition, and Parliament only gave him the money for two frigates. But by the time the frigates arrived, the more powerful Spanish battleships had already sunk in the mud of the Gulf of Paria, their bottoms completely eaten away by torredo worms. Trinidad transferred to English control. Trinidad was now the southernmost island of the "arc" patrolled by the British Navy.

Plunder: The Business of Piracy

Most of what pirates captured was cargo such as food, cloth, molasses, human captives or indentures, tools, etc. Cargo had to be turned into cash. In the Age of Buccaneers, the Danish West India and Guinea Company (DWIGC) and the Brandenburg Company in St. Thomas were happy to meet this need.

From 1672, "The Brandenburg Company," a German company operating out of St. Thomas, and the Danish West India and Guinea Company (DWIGC), bought pirate cargoes cheap for resale. King Christian V himself signed the charter for the DWIGC, and was by far the leading shareholder. Stockholders made up a who's who of Danish nobility, many of them royal, and Danish government employees who made more than 300 rigsdalers a year were required to use 10 percent of their salary to purchase DWIGC shares (Dookhan, p. 61). Financial records of the Danish West India and Guinea Company were kept by Jewish accountants referred to as "those Italians," and they doctored the books. There are huge gaps still unexplained in the bookkeeping during this era under columns to record where merchandise originated. Go to Denmark, hold the ancient papers in your hand, and see the blank spaces for yourself. That is highly unusual, because merchandise has to come from *somewhere*, and if any people pride themselves on keeping exact records, it is the Danes! (Rigarkivet)

From the time the Danish West India and Guinea Company seized St. Thomas from the Dutch in 1672 until 1721, dividends were high. King Christian V declared St. Thomas a free port, which meant that all merchandise for sale was *outside the customs territory, with no records kept, and no taxes levied on goods purchased or sold.* St. Thomas became one of the busiest trading ports in the Caribbean. Then as now, directors for corporations must show a profit or be replaced, and shareholders to this day are not always informed about unpleasant ways in which Directors keep the dividends coming.

King Christian was playing the same game all of the other monarchs were playing. As Denmark's head of state, he was complicit in abetting piracy that damaged the economic might of his nation's rivals. But he also *personally* profited from it. He made a profit off of French Buccaneers, he profited from British Buccaneers, and he profited from Dutch Buccaneers.

St. Thomas was the Wal-Mart of the Caribbean. Charlotte Amalie harbor filled with merchant ships of all nations, there to buy merchandise below retail. And, as often as not, it was their own merchandise! Colonial records show that over 100 ships were destroyed in Charlotte Amalie Harbor by one hurricane alone during this period.

For the brief period of 1672-83, Danish Governors invited pirates to sell directly to the DWIGC in St. Thomas, but that ended with the sinking of the *Trompeuse,* so the company went back to dealing with St. Croix. The letter below is typical of dozens still in archives today (CSP 1716-17, CSP 1717-18):

October 7, 1718

"I should have visited the Virgine Islands long since, but have been prevented by frequent reports of the pirates resorting there... I observe about the complaints made to His Majesty about the illegal trade being carried on between HM plantations and this French settlement. ... It is almost impossible to prevent them from carrying on an underhand trade for all the many bays we have about the island.

Governor William Hamilton (Leeward Islands, Nevis) (CSP 1717-18, p. 57, 134)."

With the end of the Age of Buccaneers, the DWIGC smoothly transitioned into the Golden Age of Piracy. Eye-witnesses wrote that known pirates were regularly seen partying in St. Thomas, even though their ships and captains were not there. Numerous complaints from Governor's to corporate directors back home insisted that merchandise meant for their islands was being sold on St. Thomas (CSP 1716-17, CSP 1717-18). Between 1715 and 1726, an estimated 2000 pirates aboard 20 to 25 ships kept a steady stream of merchandise flowing from St. Croix to St. Thomas (Brooks). There is no record of a single Danish ship taken by the Flying Gang in the Leeward Islands other than a small sloop captured by Blackbeard which he took to St. Croix (he didn't know the 'deal'). On arriving in St. Croix and learning the scoop, he immediately let her go (Johnson). In other words, the way to sail safely through the Caribbean was to fly a Danish flag.

With the end of the Age of Piracy, when the DWIGC could no longer purchase pirate cargoes on St. Croix (1750; see Owen Lloyd, below), it was forced to declare bankruptcy (Rigsarkivet). But, as Saint Croix went from being a pirate nest to being just another hell-hole built around slave labor, the DWIGC was re-chartered and re-purposed from selling stolen merchandise to selling stolen *people*. King Frederick V and the DWIGC turned Charlotte Amalie, St. Thomas, into *the* largest slave market *in the world*.

The most famous pirates in history are about to sail into Salt River, Saint Croix. The bars are open; soon Blackbeard, Martel,

Bellamy, La Bouse, and many others will row ashore. Tap into the beer, and bring out the rum. Never forget the rum. ☠

Pirates of ST  : Part 1

Captain Jean Hamlin

He did it right; he retired and disappeared

According to the British <u>Calendar of State Papers</u>, Captain Peter Pain leased the *Trompeuse* from the French Government for trade purposes. The French were uncharacteristically at peace at the time, and the ship was idle. Hamlin captured *La Trompeuse* while operating a small pirate sloop with 120 men crammed into her. (Paine was later imprisoned for not returning the *Trompeuse* at the end of the term of lease).

The *Trompeuse* took 18 English ships off of Jamaica, causing Jamaica's Governor, Thomas Lynch, to send two ships after him. The first missed him; the second, HMS *Guernsey*, found Hamlin off of St. Croix but was outpaced by the freshly careened ship. Lynch recruited retired pirate turned pirate-hunter Captain John Coxon to bring in Hamlin; Coxon was unsuccessful. (Marley, 2010).

Early in 1683, Hamlin began attacking English ships near Hispaniola (letting a French ship go free; he wouldn't capture a French ship), returning to St. Thomas where Danish Governor

Adolph Es mitt helped him sell his plunder (for a cut, of course). Hamlin sailed for Sierra Leone off the African coast in May, capturing seventeen Dutch and English vessels. Some of his crew split off under a Captain Morgan, taking a prize ship with them, and Hamlin returned to St. Thomas. Hamlin had reportedly been very cruel to the crews of captured ships, leading Governor William Stapleton to call him "John Hamlin, the arch-murderer and torturer." (CSP, Volume LI, No. 57).

On July 31, 1683, Captain Charles Carlisle, aboard the 32-gun HMS *Francis,* sailed into the harbor and found French pirate Jean Hamlin on his 30-gun ship *La Trompeuse*. *La Trompeuse* had been in Charlotte Amalie before, and the French crew enjoyed the bars and girls of St. Thomas. *La Trompeuse* had since taken many prizes both in the Caribbean and off the coast of Africa. There had been several frigates from different nations looking for *La Trompeuse* for two years. Hamlin considered himself a Buccaneer, as he did not take French ships. France considered him a pirate; he had, after all, stolen a warship that belonged to the King.

On entering the harbor, both *La Trompeuse* and Danish Fort Christian (on orders from Governor Esmitt) fired on HMS *Francis*. The *Francis* gybed and sailed out, anchoring just outside of the harbor. Apprehensive and regretting his arrogance, Esmitt sent a boat to Captain Carlisle desiring to make amends, inviting Carlisle and his officers to dinner the next evening. Carlisle was having none of that. As soon as most of the pirates were in the bars in town that night, Carlisle and his men rowed two small boats into the harbor, boarded *La Trompeuse*, and set her on fire. She blew up, taking a large English 'privateer' nearby with her (CSP v. 11, 1681-85, # 364-366, 431, and 668). Esmitt helped Hamlin escape. Some of the crew just settled in Charlotte Amalie, where their descendants are today. Boys in "Frenchtown" are still given nicknames at birth as they have been for centuries: "Boogie", "Dog", etc.

Hamlin formed a new crew late in 1684 for his ship *La Nouvelle Trompeuse* (The New Trickster), which had been fitted out in New England. Hamlin left for his old refuge at Île-à-Vache, and next sailed to Brazil. There are few records of his subsequent activities, though some of his men later signed on with privateers Jacob Evertson and Jan Willems. After Willems and Evertson died in early 1688, their remaining crew sailed with pirate Captain Peterson (CSP v. 11, #576-593). According to legend, Hamlin had several sons that grew into the family business, naming their vessels *Trompeuse* in honor of their father. One of these may have been the last pirate ship on St. Croix, whose bones lie on the north coast of the island (story below).

William Kidd

Red States, Blue States, and No Manner of Luck at All

Kidd was a Scot who went to sea as a boy. He became a captain and enjoyed a successful career as a privateer operating out of Barbados. David Cordingly says that as captain of the *Blessed William*, Kidd attached his ship to a British squadron that successfully won a battle with a French fleet off the island of St. Martin. His crew was angry, as it was not a battle for profit, and his first mate Robert Culliford (whom he would meet again) and crew sailed off with the ship to go pirating after they put Kidd ashore in Nevis. A grateful governor of Nevis rewarded Kidd, however, and gave him a captured French vessel as his own. Kidd retired to New York, married a wealthy widow, produced two daughters, and enjoyed very good social standing (Cordingly, ch.10). In 1695, Kidd owned some prime real estate in Manhattan, and also 'rented' a pew at Trinity Episcopal Church, helping finance Trinity's construction. (Harris, also Trinity Church Records). G

Each of the colonies had been making their laws for a long time. American ships traded with whom they wanted and paid no duties. English merchants wanted no competition. They had representation in Parliament, and the colonies did not. Parliament passed the Navigation Acts between the years 1651-63, which gave them what they wanted. British colonies could only trade with British markets, using British ships, with British crews. Letters of marque (privateer licenses) could only be issued in London. Merchandise originating from anywhere other than England had to be shipped to London for inspection and taxing before being shipped to the colonies. These laws made everything in the colonies more expensive. American merchants and ships ignored the laws, taking cargoes to the best markets, and purchasing from markets with the best prices, directly. They were smuggling, and it made outlaws out of most colonial merchants and ship captains. Colonial governors like Benjamin Fletcher in New York continued to issue letters of marque. The British government refused to accept his letters and called them 'pirates.' New York and Philadelphia vied with one another for luring the most 'smugglers' and 'pirates' to bring their cargoes into their cities. Thomas Tew, John Ireland, and others with Fletcher's letters of marque sailed into the Indian Ocean and plundered treasure-laden ships with jewels sailing from India to the Red Sea, bringing the treasure back to New York. Since their letters of marque were to operate against French vessels only, they were pirates, but Fletcher did not mind since they brought him profit (Harris).

With the "Glorious Revolution" of 1688, Catholic King James II was deposed by his own daughter, Mary, and her husband, his cousin Dutch Protestant King William. New colonial Governors were appointed. Fletcher, a member of the Tory (conservative) party, was out, and Richard Coote, aka "Lord Bellomont", a Whig (liberal) party member, was appointed the new Governor of Massachusetts, New Hampshire, and (soon) New York. For whatever reason, Kidd left his family and sailed to London. It seems he had the itch for adventure, and wanted to go back to privateering, but wanted a 'legal' letter. Bellomont approached Kidd about a voyage to intercept the 'pirate' ships of Tew and England, of which Fletcher owned shares, to capture their loot. Intrigued, Kidd agreed. The expedition was financed by four wealthy English lords, all of them from the Whig party. Shareholders also included some New York merchants, Kidd himself, Bellomont, one of the Directors of the East India Company, and King William III himself, who was in for a 10 percent cut. Kidd was given a letter of marque to take French ships (England's enemy once again) as well as 'pirates'. Kidd's letter of marque was signed by King William himself (Cordingly, ch.10).

The venture met with trouble from the beginning. Starting with a hand-picked crew from London, an English man-of-war stopped the brand new 34-gun *Adventure Galley* and pressed many of her men before she had even left British waters. Kidd sailed on to New York with a skeleton crew, but once there was able to fill the ship's complement only by accepting criminals and some who were believed to have been former pirates. This defined his whole life from that point. "No plunder, no pay": Kidd's crew signed on for no pay, only a cut in prize money, the normal arrangement for Privateers, Pirates, and Buccaneers. The *Adventure Galley* sailed from New York with 152 crew in September 1696. A year later, September 1697, found the *Galley* in the Indian Ocean, leaking badly. One-third of the crew was dead of cholera, and no ships had been taken; the crew had had enough. Coming on a Dutch ship, the gunner, William Moore, backed by much of the crew, threatened mutiny if Kidd did not attack. Moore started a fight, and Kidd knocked him out with a bucket that he threw (William III was King of England and also 'Stadtholder' -"leader of the state"- of the Dutch, and would not have been happy with that capture). The blow caused a concussion and was fatal. They let the Dutch ship go, and the crew temporarily settled down.

Kidd promised his crew rich prizes among ships carrying Muslim pilgrims sailing for Arabia. A few weeks later, Kidd was forced to choose between losing his command and taking a British ship. Flying a red flag, he attacked a British East India convoy but was driven off by the escort vessel. While that is what the escort vessels captain said in his log, it is also possible that Kidd broke off the attack when he realized that he was attacking British ships, as he claimed. Next, he stopped a British ship, the *Mary*, to ask her captain what other ships she had seen. While Kidd was questioning him down below, the men of the *Adventure Galley* strung up several members of the captive vessel's crew in the rigging and were torturing them. Kidd held the captain prisoner for a few weeks as a pilot before letting the ship and its captain go, with its cargo (Cordingly, Ch.10).

The *Adventure Galley* finally stopped a ship they kept, the *Quedagh Merchant*. While Armenian, and with an English captain, she was sailing with letters of safe passage guaranteed by the French East India Company, allowing a tenuous claim that she was a 'French' prize. It was a great haul. A lot of the merchandise belonged to a Moghul (chief from northern India) ally of Britain, however. Tories in Parliament, eager to embarrass Kidd's Whig backers, pushed official buttons to have Kidd tried inabstentia as a murderer (William Moore) and a pirate. The court heard testimony from the captain of the *Quedagh Merchant*, a captain from the East India Company convoy, and the captain of the *Mary*, and the king issued an order for the navy to pursue and capture the "Notorious pirate Captain Kidd." Kidd had no clue. He felt himself a world away and did not realize that word from the Indian Ocean had made it to London. The convoy and the *Mary* put into the Red Sea. Caravans carried merchandise and letters a few short miles to ships waiting in the Mediterranean, and thence home to England quickly.

In Madagascar, the *Adventure Galley* put in for provisions and met famous pirate Robert Culliford, who had been an officer on one of Kidd's earlier privateers. Some reports say that Kidd had a drink with Culliford and talked about old times. Others insist that Kidd ordered his men to attack but the men by now considered themselves pirates, and Culliford to be 'one of their own.' At any rate, many of Kidd's crew deserted to Culliford. Without enough men to work the now worm-eaten and leaking *Adventure Galley*, Kidd took the *Quedagh Merchant* as his own, renaming her the *Adventure Prize*, and left the *Adventure Galley* in Ste. Marie harbor. She sat there for the next 30 years, decomposing slowly into the beach sand. Kidd sailed for home. He had only 20 crew left.

Kidd finally captured his only legitimate prize, a small French sloop, which the *Adventure Prize* needed desperately for food. Kidd next stopped in St. Thomas to refit, sell his cargo, and re-provision, where he was genuinely surprised to learn that he was a wanted man. Despite the offer of a bribe, Governor Johan Lorensen denied him the right to use St. Thomas to refit, provision, or sell his cargo (CSP, 1700, v. 18). Nonetheless, somehow Kidd was able to turn most of his booty into cash. Governor Archibald Hamilton in Jamaica wrote a letter to Lorensen accusing him of complicity, as Kidd's crew, including quartermaster Hendrick Quintar, were seen hanging out in Charlotte Amalie bars by sailors who reported back to Hamilton. Lorensen answered that he had also heard this 'unsubstantiated rumor,' but that he did not know where Kidd had anchored or sold his loot (CSP, 1700, v.18). Kidd traded ships and the last of his cargo with a merchant named Bolton at little Mona Island, located in the Mona Passage between Puerto Rico and Hispaniola, and sailed up to New York to see his family and clear his name.

Arriving in New York, Kidd visited his wife and two daughters, buried some treasure on Long Island, and, after a couple of months, paid a visit to Lord Bellomont in Boston. Kidd paid him his share of the profits (though later the governor denied it), and asked for his help in clearing his name. Promising a pardon to get Kidd to his office, the governor --a consummate politician-- had him arrested at the door, to distance himself from the affair. Kidd sailed to England in chains.

Kidd's is the only known pirate trial ever to have been before Parliament. The Tories were out for Whig blood, and he was their tool. Embarrassed, and hoping to minimalize the political damage, Whigs washed their hands of him. The French papers from the *Quedagh Merchant* that Kidd turned in to his defense team disappeared. They let him rot in jail for a year in poor conditions before setting a date for his execution. Before hanging, the prison Parson badgered him to repent of his sins, to which he incessantly plead his innocence. The Parson then adjured him to repent for lying, which he would not do, either. Instead of a final meal, he asked for a bottle of rum and showed up to the scaffold quite drunk. Kidd was hanged at Execution Dock on May 23, 1701. Somehow, the rope broke. Falling to the beach alive, the Parson rushed to his prone body, still nagging for a confession. Kidd refused to give one, and he was quickly strung up again. His tarred body hung in chains for two years over the harbor as a warning to anyone who would ever consider trusting politicians again (Harris, epilogue).

Sam Bellamy

'Robin Hood'

"Damn ye, you are a sneaking puppy, and so are all those who will submit to be governed by laws which rich men have made for their own security, for the cowardly whelps have not the courage otherwise to defend what they get by their knavery. Damn ye altogether! Damn them, as a pack of crafty rascals. And you who serve them, a parcel of hen-hearted numbskulls! They vilify us, the scoundrels do, when there is only this difference: they rob the poor under the cover of law, and we plunder the rich under the cover of our own courage. ... I am a free Prince, and I have as much authority to make war on the whole world as he who has a hundred ships at sea, and an army of 100,000 men in the field." –Bellamy to Captain Beer (4)

According to Colin Woodard, Sam was born on March 18, 1689, in Hittisleigh, Devon. His mother died in childbirth, but his father made enough of a living to have him educated, apparently including learning some French. Friends called him "Black Sam" for his black hair and olive complexion, in a land of fair hair and freckles. His father may have died leaving him alone, but at any rate, Sam signed on as a 13-year-old cabin boy and sailed for Massachusetts. A few years later, having risen to become a mate, he parted company with his ship. Sam wandered into the village of Eastham on Cape Cod, where he met 15-year-old Mary Hallett and fell in love. Her family were solid farming folk, and would not have their daughter marrying a penniless sailor. Sam also met Paulsgrave Williams, son of a former attorney general of Rhode Island, a married man with two small children, and they quickly became friends. Woodard says that one of Williams' sisters had married a personal friend of Captain Kidd, and another, possibly the niece-in-law of pirate Thomas Paine, was implicated in trying to help Kidd; pirates were in his family. When the Spanish treasure fleet slammed into the coast of Florida, Sam and Paulsgrave became partners. Sam would be the captain, perhaps returning after making his fortune to claim Mary and the child they had on the way. Williams, always with his powdered wig (was he bald?) bought them a seaworthy sloop, and served as the quartermaster. They recruited a crew and sailed for Florida to 'fish the wrecks.' It was the 1715 equivalent of a gold rush (Woodard, pp. 28-9).

After plundering only a small amount ‑competition and the Spanish defense were fierce-- they sailed to Nassau. Paulsgrave ‑ Paul-- still had a wife and children to go home to, and Sam wanted to go back to Mary and, he thought, their child. Their object in treasure hunting was to be able to support those they loved. After trying to 'fish', they put into Nassau as the closest port before going anywhere else. When they did, a British spy recorded their names onto the list of pirates trying to loot the Spanish treasure. Not knowing this, Bellamy's little gang sailed to Mexico to harvest logwood. On the coast of Mexico they found a small reef and lost their ship. Ashore, they asked for food from a logging camp, and were refused. Desperate, they stole a couple of Indian pirogues and sailed them back to Nassau, where they heard that their names had been sent to England along with the others who were 'fishing'. If they returned home, they would be sent to England, tried as pirates, and hung. What choice did they have? They were cut off from their loved ones.

Bellamy took a page from Henry Morgan's book. They were, after all, in Indian pirogues… his men tied their hair into ponytails and rubbed them with charcoal, shaved their beards, and painted their naked (probably with breechcloths?) bodies with primitive symbols. When they approached a victim, Bellamy and Williams, probably the only two still dressed as Europeans, informed the target that they had a deal with their 'cannibal' crewmembers: if the victim surrendered without a fight, they could not eat them, but if not, they could not be held responsible for what happened. Later, when they got a nice sloop to use and discarded the pirogues, they continued the masquerade (Woodard, p. 30).

As with all pirates, they used terror to dissuade resistance, thereby reducing the chance of bloodshed. Once taken, prisoners always heard embellished, gruesome (tall) tales of sailors who had resisted them in previous captures, only to be tortured gruesomely. As word got around, more prey surrendered peacefully. What would you have done? Confronted by a dangerous band of murderous pirates who would let you live if you surrendered, would you have risked your life for the furniture or hardware in the hold? Who wants to die for Wal-Mart?

Pirates were above the law, however, and some of them had a bone to pick. Captains were given purses from which to buy food for their crew and pay them after the cruise. A big percentage of captains could not resist temptation to enrich themselves, so many sailors were given mere dog food, and not paid what they had been promised. Charles Vane, Thomas Anstis, and Ned Low had very bad experiences with such captains. When they captured a ship, they asked the crew if their captains were fair men. If they heard bad stories, they tortured and murdered the captains. This explains why, though they all took the pardon for crimes of piracy when offered later, they returned to piracy as soon as they learned they were indicted for a different crime: murder.

Bellamy and Williams first partnered with Captain Henry Jennings and his lieutenant, Charles Lane (*Lark*), but later double-crossed them and joined with Captain Hornigold and his lieutenant, Edward Thatch, who had been double-crossed by Jennings and Lane a short time before. Hornigold soon gave Bellamy and Williams a big blue French sloop they captured, the *Marianne*, with 50 men. Olivier LaBouse joined the flotilla with his sloop, *Postillion*.

Hornigold's men voted him out as Captain for his refusal to attack English ships. He and Thatch were given a small sloop with 23 men, and the rest sailed off with Bellamy, Williams, and LaBouse. Hornigold and Thatch returned to Nassau. Hornigold took many prizes (CSP 1716, #240, i), and eventually had a change of heart. The governor of St. Kitts sent a sloop of war, HMS *Barsheba*, and a smaller sloop, HMS *Eagle*, after him. In self-defense, Hornigold captured Jennings' old command *Barsheba* in battle and opted to begin plundering English ships, after all, remaining on good terms with his former protégés (CSP 1716, #180). Henry Jennings and Charles Lane split up later when Jennings decided to take the Kings pardon [H], and Lane declared war on the Bahamas with his sloop, *Lark*.

Bellamy and LaBouse headed south, plundering as they went. They put into St. Croix to distribute plunder, careen, and have a hole to duck into for the 1716 hurricane season. Almost there, they passed a French 40-gun frigate which the crew voted to attack. They were beaten off and damaged, but escaped. By the time they sailed into Salt River, they had looted goods to fence and repairs to make. Haitian pirate Jean Martel and his gang were already there, and the crews enjoyed a period of epic debauchery together (Johnson). As usual with the Flying Gang, alcohol flowed wherever it was available, and gambling and women followed loose money. One reason that 'pirate treasure' did not exist as we know it (except rarely, as with LaBouse in the Seychelles later, or Owen Lloyd in 1750) is that captains only got two shares where men got one. Unless the ship was lost before they could make shore, it disappeared quickly. As soon as the cargo was sold to the Walker's agents (Nassau) or the Danish West India Company agents (St. Croix) and the proceeds divided, the crew spent their shares immediately. "Treasure chests" could exist only briefly, until an opportunity to divide it arrived.

> *"Deposition of Abijah Savage, Commander of the sloop Bonetta of Antigua. Antigua, 30th Nov., 1716. On 9th Nov. between St. Thomas and St. Cruix he was over-hauled and plundered by two pirate sloops, who also took a French ship and six sail of small vessels, keeping the French ship etc. One, called the Mary Anne, was commanded by Samuel Bellamy who declared himself to be an Englishman born in London, and the other, Postillion, by Louis de Bouse a Frenchman, who had his sloop chiefly navigated with men of that Nation. Each sloop was mounted with 8 guns, and had betwixt 80 or 90 men. The Mary Anne was chiefly navigated with Englishmen. Deponent was detained at St. Cruix. The pirates only wanted provisions and a ship to make a voyage. Gives names of some of the pirates etc. Signed, Habbijah Savage. Same endorsement, Copy. 2pp. (CSP 1716, #425, iii)"*

In October of 1716, Bellamy and LaBouse operated out of St. Croix, darting into the other Virgin Islands to take prizes, and carrying the merchandise back to be fenced (CSP 1716). Bellamy's men enjoyed especially high morale. He made them think that they were on high moral ground; they referred to themselves in front of captives as "Robin Hood's Men." On November 9, they took a sloop out of Antigua, the *Bonetta*. On board was a nine-year-old boy in satin clothes, John King, sailing with his mother, an Antiguan plantation owner, in the company of his 10-year-old personal Indian slave boy. Little John begged the pirates to take him. When his mother objected, he threatened her, and the *Marianne* sailed off with two new cabin boys (Woodard). They were now equal, though John may not have realized it at the time. To Bellamy, Williams, LaBouse, Thatch, and many others, black men were brothers, equal crew members. This was not always the case with pirates. On Howell Davis' ships, the black crew did not receive equal wages. With Jean Martel's gang, black men who spoke a European language were crew; African people who did not were merchandise. Twenty of Martel's crew were black, and as many more were mulattos, but they sold some slaves they captured as plunder (Johnson).

Bellamy and LaBouse took what they needed, what they wanted, and then usually let the ships continue on their way. Bellamy expected Governor William Hamilton in St. Kitts to react to the taking of the *Bonetta* with force (unfortunately for Martel's gang, he did) (CSP 1716, #204), so he and La Bouse headed down island, plundering dozens of ships. As soon as they left St. Croix, they captured a French 26-gun ship, *Sultana*, of which Bellamy assumed command, giving Williams the *Marianne*. When the Northeast trades began kicking up in late January, they returned to St. Croix and Salt River. There was a surprise waiting for them; the charred remains of the *John and Martha*, Martel's ship, on the reef guarding the harbor entrance, and another large sloop half submerged just inside the entrance channel, destroyed in an encounter with Captain Hume and HMS *Scarborough*. Captain Hume had stripped the spars and rigging off of the sloop for the *Scarborough*. Bellamy noted the dismounted guns of the shore battery which had lain behind the earthworks of Fort de Sales. One hundred or so survivors from Martel's gang, a mix of white, black, and mulatto, came out of the bush. All were welcomed as equal members of Bellamy's and LaBouse's crews; having added the *Sultana* to the fleet, they needed more men. To avenge the raid on St. Croix, Bellamy and company sailed across to Virgin Gorda, putting into Spanish Town Harbor for a week. While there, some of their forced men unsuccessfully sought sanctuary. However, indentured servants in Spanish Town who asked were allowed to join the ship. Bellamy and LaBouse made the governor pay a ransom for them to leave. They then returned to St. Croix for a while longer, waiting for high winds to subside. When the wind backed down, LaBouse continued operating out of St. Croix for eight more months, periodically going down island (Johnson; CSP 1716).

Bellamy and Williams sailed up to Nassau and the Straits of Florida, looking for a more powerful ship to acquire while in the main shipping lane. Arriving in the Gulf Stream, they met the *Whydah*, whose captain was an old acquaintance of Bellamy's. After a three-day chase, Bellamy and Williams captured the *Whydah*. They swapped ships with him, giving him the *Sultana*, unwanted looted cargo from other vessels, and a little bit of gold. The *Whydah* was homeward bound with the profits of a voyage slaving, carrying a fortune in gold and silver coins. Bellamy and Williams then sailed *Whydah* and *Marianne* home to New England and those they had left behind, plundering with great success as they went (CSP 1716, #317, #318). Off the Carolinas they split up, planning a rendezvous in Maine.

Unfortunately for Bellamy, Williams, and crew, they never got to enjoy their loot. Williams put into Rhode Island and briefly visited his family. Bellamy, on the way up to Maine and their rendezvous, first steered for Cape Cod to find Mary. He got very close. In the night of April 26, 1717, Off Eastham, Cape Cod, the *Whydah* was destroyed when a fierce nor'easter drove her ashore. Reports agree that Bellamy perished that night, with all but two of the crew on board. According to Barry Clifford, who found the Whydah shipwreck after a huge effort,

> *"The Whydah began a slow turn toward the wind, taking thousands of tons of water over the gunwales as she was swept by forty-foot waves. Many of the 148 men on board must have been swept over the side at this point. The ones who weren't had probably taken refuge in the hold,*

or were clinging desperately to the rigging, where the wind was colder than the forty-degree water.

Still the ship turned... then came the fateful bump that meant the stern had run aground and the ship could turn no more. More water swept the deck, filling the holds and slowly rolling the ship. Within fifteen minutes of striking, the mainmast was snapped off and floated free. The ship rolled upside down. Pirates were crushed as cannons and goods stored below came crashing through the decks. Those who could, swam, but in water so cold, there were few who could make it the five hundred feet to shore. Those who did froze to death trying to climb the steep sand cliffs of Eastham." (Clifford, The Black Ship, p. 265)

One hundred thirty pirates lost their lives that night off the coast of Cape Cod on 26 April 1717, including Bellamy. Clifford and his party discovered what is probably the remains of young John King when they excavated the ship; a fragment of a child's leg bone wrapped in a silk stocking, and a small leather shoe still fastened with its buckle (Clifford, Black Ship, p. 265).

Bellamy ended where his journey began, almost back in the arms of his Mary, who was sleeping in her hut on top of the cliff (Johnson; CSP 1716, #677).

Five of Bellamy's crew who were on a small prize sloop were exhausted after sailing through the storm. A man and a boy who had been captured with the ship steered her straight into a beach the night after, while the pirates slept (CSP 1716, Preface xiv, #360, #677.). The five pirates were hung along with one of the Whydah's survivors (the half-Indian, now 16-old John Julien either escaped or was sold into slavery to future President John Adams' grandfather Quincy, depending on what you read). Interestingly, one of the hanged men was Hendrick Quintar, and unless two men had this unusual name, according to the Calendar of State Papers 1700 (v.18), he was Captain William Kidd's last quartermaster. Quintar ended up in New York at the end of Kidd's adventures in 1700.

Whether he hooked up with Bellamy and Williams on Cape Cod, or at sea on a taken vessel, is a matter of speculation, but on November 15, 1717, he was hung in Charlestown, outside of Boston.

Paulsgrave Williams sailed back to Nassau, where many of his crew took the king's pardon and returned home. Williams ended up sailing off to Africa with LaBouse. When he kissed his wife and small children goodbye, he was only going on a treasure hunting adventure. Williams returned to Rhode Island as one of the most notorious pirates in the world. Since he did not take the pardon, it is safe to say that when he visited with his family, he did not find himself welcomed home. It's a pretty safe bet that he never saw his children again, but who knows what life he made for himself from the treasure of the *Cabo* in the Indian Ocean, or if he ever returned to New England?

Olivier Levasseur (LaBouse)

A Riddle from the Buzzard

A French family of the minor nobility sired Olivier Levasseur. Shortly after Olivier graduated from a private primary school, his mother died, and he was placed into the navy as a midshipman. After the requisite service he became a lieutenant, and then commander. A young man with no immediate prospects of command, he accepted an offer to be second captain (first mate) on a French privateer, *Postillion*, on the opposite side of the War of Spanish Succession from the rest of the future "Flying Gang." Louis XIV was putting his manpower into the army and had few left to man his navy, except the ships of the line. By royal decree, Louis allowed private investors to lease warships carrying less than 44 guns, to be outfitted at private expense, but reserved the right to appoint French officers to their command. The *Postillion* was probably one such vessel (Bromley, Ch. 10).

During the war, Levasseur saw action and received a wound that resulted in his often wearing the iconic pirate eye patch for the rest of his life. With the end of the war, the *Postillion* sat at her mooring, idle by order of her captain. As usual, privateer crew were paid a share of the plunder, but no salary. Out of supplies and with no prospects for pay, Levasseur and the crew took over the ship. Levasseur had just learned of the death of his father, and with it his only influence at court for advancement; he had no reason to return to France. Leaving the "1ˢᵗ Captain" ashore, the *Postillion's* crew sailed off with his majesty's ship to 'fish the wrecks' around Vero Beach, alongside all of the Englishmen. Meeting with little success, the *Postillion* put into Nassau for supplies and recreation. While there they learned that their attempted 'fishing' expedition got them on the list of sailors judged to be pirates by the sovereigns of Europe (Benaben).

Levasseur met Benjamin Hornigold, and after consulting his crew, they decided that they were now pirates, like it or not. Bellamy was with the group, and they sailed in tandem. Levasseur's men took to calling him "LaBouse," which some have taken to mean "The Buzzard." It translates from French as "The Shit." Other accounts call him "LaBuse," which translates as 'the nozzle', a derogatory French nickname for someone with a large nose, or "LaBouche," which means "the mouth." Barry Clifford thinks it was just Booz, short for buzzard –pronounced booze-ard in French. Some accounts say that, while Hornigold did not speak French nor LaBouse much English, Bellamy was the interpreter who made the partnership possible. LaBouse and Bellamy split off from Hornigold to attack English ships, which LaBouse had done during the war anyway, and they stayed close partners, plundering in the Lesser Antilles together while operating out of St. Croix, until Bellamy headed up North in the *Sultana*.

LaBouse continued operating out of St. Croix for some months after the *Sultana* and the *Marianne* headed north. There are tales of LaBouse being wounded in a bar fight in a saloon in the village of Bassin during this time. In early July, Leeward Islands Governor William Hamilton finally dared leave St. Kitts to make a tour of British possessions in his territory. He wrote that he could not perform this duty with just the sloop-of-war at his disposal until he learned that Bellamy and Williams had left the Caribbean. Hamilton took advantage of their exit to visit St. Thomas, where he threatened Governor Erich Bredal with an invasion, telling the

Governor that Britain was not going to continue 'putting up' with the 'illegal' Danish occupation of St. Thomas and St. John, if pirated plunder from "that French settlement" continued to surface in Charlotte Amalie. As he was returning to his ship, a pirate sloop came zooming from out of nowhere, cannons firing and forcing Gov. Hamilton's sloop to cut her cable to try and escape. The British sloop did not get a shot off in return. As the pirate went by, Governor Hamilton noted her "huge white flag with a dead body spread upon it." It was LaBouse, still operating out of St. Croix at this time, flying his version of the 'pavilion blanc ' (CSP 1717-18, p. 57, #134). Sometime in late July, LaBouse headed back down island, plundering as he went, where he was to meet Captain Hume and the *Scarborough* after all:

> "Eight months after the end of the *John and Martha*, Hume surprised the infamous pirate commodore Olivier La Buse and his 77-man gang at Isla La Blanquilla, a popular hideaway off the coast of what is now Venezuela. Seeing the *Scarborough* bearing down on their six-gun sloop, La Bouse's men made a mad scramble onto a small merchant vessel they had been plundering, which was better prepared for a speedy departure. Cutting her anchor lines, La Buse fled out of the harbor with most of his men and their treasure. "I gave chase, but with night coming on, [he was] gaining to windward [so we] stood away again for the [harbor]," Captain Hume, HMS *Scarborough*. He would return to Barbados with just 17 captives (Johnson) (CSP 1716)."

[8] Reproduction of sloop "Katy", aka "Providence", 110' 12-gun sloop, similar to many pirate vessels of the Golden Age, including LaBouse's *Postillion*, Bonnet's and Thatch's *Revenge*, also Bellamy's and Williams' *Marianne*.

The *Postillion* had been emptied for careening. All plunder, cannon, supplies, and ballast had been transferred to the smaller sloop, which would have soon been used as the lean-against vessel while the *Postillion* was careened. Emptied of all ballast and therefore unseaworthy, they could only use *Postillion* as a decoy. Seventeen sailors on the beach preparing the tackle to haul the *Postillion* ashore had to be left behind. LaBouse took a few months to recover, eventually finding a more suitable sloop, then a large ship of force, the *Queen of the Indies*, a 26-gunner. He sailed it back to St. Croix and raided around the Virgin Islands once again. At this time, he took some prizes off of St. Thomas. A witness said LaBouse was flying "A huge white flag with a dead man spread on it" (CSP 1717-18, Jan. 6, 1718). From St. Croix, LaBouse headed back up to Nassau after hurricane season.

In 1719, LaBouse took his new ship and operated together with Howell Davis and Thomas Cocklyn for a time off the West Coast of Africa. Paulsgrave Williams is reported to have been with him (CSP 1717-18). In 1720, they attacked the slave port of Whydah, reducing the local fortress to ruins. Later that year, LaBouse headed for the Indian Ocean (Johnson). The *Queen of the Indies* passed around the

Cape of Good Hope and headed north between the island of Madagascar and the African continent.

During a storm, the *Queen of the Indies* wrecked on rocky shores of the Island of Mayotte in the Mozambique Channel, and he and the survivors of his crew were stranded on the island of Anjouan, one of the Comoros Islands. Fellow pirate and friend, John Taylor, stopped at the island and found LaBouse there. He had just taken a sloop and not yet placed a captain on her. He gave the sloop to LaBouse and his survivors, and from 1720 onwards they launched their raids from a base on the island of Sainte-Marie, just off the Madagascar coast. Together with Taylor and Edward England, he cruised the Western Indian Ocean until he and Taylor parted company with England for being 'too timid'.

On the 26th day of April 1721, Taylor and LaBouse took one of the richest prizes in pirate history; the seventy-two-gun Portuguese *Nossa Senhora do Cabo*. A brush with a cyclone had left the *Cabo* damaged, leaking, and missing her main mast. She limped into Saint Denis Harbor on Reunion Island for repairs. It is quite likely that is why Taylor and LaBouse put into the harbor, as well. Moored fore and aft in the, most of her cannon and crew ashore, the *Cabo* was easy prey. LaBouse took the Portuguese Viceroy of India, Count Ericeira, captive, holding him for ransom. He then took the *Cabo* as his own, renaming her *Le Victorieux* (*The Victorious*) (Benaben, chapter "*Nossa Senhora do Cabo*"). I believe this to be the largest pirate ship of the age. He would not have kept her long, however. Careening a vessel of this size would have been impossible, and he would have had to have an extremely large crew fed and paid.

Each member of Taylor's and LaBouse's crew received 50,000 golden guineas and 42 diamonds (Johnson). On September 23, 1724, King Louis XIV offered amnesty to pirates in the Indian Ocean through the governor of Reunion Island. LaBouse and his crew were ready to retire but wary. They sent already pardoned pirate Captain John Clayton to petition the Governor of Reunion,

Desforges Boucher, to test the waters. They were told to come in; the pardon was theirs. When the time came to turn their ship over and sign the papers, LaBouse learned that for the crew it was no problem, but for himself, it would only be possible to receive the pardon if he returned all sacred vases that belonged to the Catholic Church in Portugal that had been on the *Cabo*. He was also required to turn in all of the loot from the *Cabo* to Governor Boucher (a former French pirate himself, known then as 'Captain Dumas'). Plunder having been already split up and much of it spent over the previous four years; this was of course not possible. LaBouse sailed off in a small vessel. LaBouse disappeared from history for five years, until he offered to pilot a British East Indiaman, *Medusa*, into the harbor of Antongil, Madagascar. The captain recognized him, as LaBouse had once captured his ship, and took him prisoner, turning him over to Governor Boucher (Dumas) (Benaben). The Governor ordered that LaBouse be hung.

LaBouse wrote a famous riddle telling where he hid his treasure on a medallion that he tossed to the crowd as he climbed the scaffold, saying, "Find my treasure, the one who may understand it!" What became of this medallion is unknown, but it was copied before disappearing. Many treasure hunters have since tried to decode the cryptogram hoping its solution will lead to this treasure. That riddle (below) remains unsolved to this day. Are you ready? You could be the one to find the treasure!

"Blackbeard"

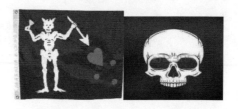

The king of 'brand.'
Never killed a man till the day he died

Though historians can't agree whether his real name was "Teach" or "Thatch", most historians agree that "Blackbeard" was born about 1680 in Bristol, at that time England's second largest city and center of the transatlantic trade. However, historian Baylus Brooks offers a good argument for Jamaica. Brooks says that a farm owned by a family named Thatch, with a son listed in census records, was burned when French Buccaneer Jean Baptiste du Casse looted Port Royal in 1691. For a boy of 10 or 11 years old, it would have been traumatic. The legend goes that he was then sent to sea as a midshipman, passed for Lieutenant, but found himself on the beach in Jamaica with no ship until he signed on with Benjamin Hornigold in the War of Spanish Succession. Regardless of where he was born, all agree that he was of middle-class stock, and one of the lucky kids to receive an education, as he could read, write, and navigate using trigonometry. Acquaintances reported him to be tall, thin, athletic, intelligent, capable, literate, and charismatic, with a remarkable long, full black beard. After the war, Thatch sailed with Hornigold to fish the wreck of Ubilla's fleet. When King George declared them all pirates, Thatch canoed with Hornigold to Nassau, where they quickly traded their canoes for a prize sloop they called *The Happy*

Return, seizing ships in the waters of the Gulf Stream as they sailed north to catch the Westerly trade winds.

Stede Bonnet and his *Revenge* limped into Nassau after a narrow escape from a battle with a French frigate, thanks to a clean bottom and the sloop's superior ability to point closer to the wind. Hornigold relieved Bonnet of command with the approval of the crew and made Thatch captain of the *Revenge*. The arrangement seems to have been amicable. Bonnet continued on board as a gentleman apprentice and got to keep his cabin (which included his extensive library). This is the only example that I have found of a captain's cabin that was not for the use of all of the crew, but Bonnet had, after all, paid to have his ship built.

Leaving Nassau, Hornigold and Thatch first sailed up to the Eastern Seaboard and had a stellar cruise. It was on this cruise that Thatch adopted the nickname "Blackbeard", and began lighting matches in his beard to frighten victims. After selling their plunder in Nassau, they headed to the Lesser Antilles (some accounts say that Hornigold stayed behind and that Thatch and Bonnet went south on their own). They took several prizes on the way down, and on November 17, 1717, in the Grenadine Islands, captured the large French slaver *La Concorde*. She was pierced for 40 guns, all but 26 had been left in France to make space for 516 African captives. When the pirates took her, 461 were still alive. Out of *La Concorde's* crew of 75, 16 had died, and 36 more were ill with dysentery (Ernaut, Folio 90). Surprisingly, statistics from the seventeenth and eighteenth centuries show that as a percentage, 25 percent of white sailors serving on slavers died making the middle passage, compared to an average 20 percent of African captives (Fort Frederick Museum, St. Croix). Equally surprising, despite chains, and despite being naked with no weapons, one in ten slave voyages would experience a revolt on board. While most were brutally suppressed, the courage and resourcefulness of the African captives left a mark on history which must be admired.

Thatch took *La Concorde* for his own, and a now trained Bonnet got his *Revenge* back. *La Concorde* cabin boys Louis Arnaut, 15, and Julien Joseph Moisant, 16, asked to join the pirates and showed them where gold dust was stored on the ship. Three more crew also signed the articles, and Thatch forced another ten --carpenters, surgeons, cook, and sailors-- to join. He accepted 70 of the Africans on board as crew but had to put the rest ashore on Bequia, a beautiful Grenadine island that had no slavery (They, and the men who followed Thatch from Hornigold's commands, would be his most loyal crew). French Captain Donnet was left to sail off with 10 healthy men and 36 sick ones, in a small prize sloop they were given by Thatch. Unfortunately for the Africans, once Thatch sailed off, Donnet started making round trips, recapturing the Africans on Bequia a few at a time and taking them to Martinique where they were sold (Haring, chapter "Blackbeard").

Thatch renamed his new ship the *Queen Anne's Revenge* and began his first solo cruise. At this time, Thatch took to calling himself 'Blackbeard,' tying pieces of slow-burning waxed cord in his hair when going into battle to frighten his enemies. Taking a cue from his friend Bellamy, terror was his tool, by which he avoided bloodshed as much as possible. Before freeing captives, his men made sure to tell horrible stories of murder perpetrated by "Blackbeard" and his men on crews of prizes that had resisted capture. Thatch was popular with the men as quartermaster under Hornigold and as Captain of the *Revenge*. He was their mentor and coach, fond of staying in shape by working out and practicing swordplay with them, but also for drinking them under the table.

Thatch and Bonnet put into Bequia to drop the Africans off, cruised off of St. Lucia, and sailed past Martinique. Like Hornigold and Bellamy, there is no verifiable account of Blackbeard killing a captive, or anyone for that matter (until his final battle), and he rarely abused captives. He initially let ships go after plundering them, but after his Bellamy's surviving crew were hung in Boston, he threw the cargos of New England ships into the sea and burned them.

At Basse Terre, Guadalupe, they sailed right into the harbor in the middle of the night with guns blazing. The cannonade upset a lantern, setting fire to the town (no wooden ship fired red-hot shot); they cut several ships anchor lines and sailed away with them. After looting St. Kitts and cruising off of Montserrat, Nevis, and Antigua, Thatch got a fever. The two ships and their prizes headed over to St. Croix to careen, rest, recover and distribute their plunder.

On December 2, 1717, the *Queen Anne's Revenge* and Bonnet's *Revenge* passed the HMS *Seaford*, a frigate carrying Governor Walter Hamilton on a tour of the islands. The *QAR* had advantages in broadside weight of metal and men, and they voted on whether or not to attack, but decided it would be too costly. No Royal Navy frigate would be easy prey; men would die, and ships would be damaged. The Governor and the Captain of the *Seaford* thought they were just passing a group of slave ships. Taking two sloops as prizes off of St. Thomas, Thatch took them into Salt River Bay, St. Croix, where he quickly learned that pirates did not take Danish ships in the Lesser Antilles, and the Dane was released. The Pirates added 12 cannons to the *Queen*, bringing her armament up to her intended 40; they possibly got them from the *John and Martha*. While the guns could have come from various smaller prizes, it makes more sense to get them from one source, all of one size. The English ship was run into the reef right beside the *John and Martha*, possibly for use as a bridge to swing the cannon over to a carefully anchored *Queen*. After looting her, they burned the English one for recreation, adding her bones to those of Martel's two ships already there from a year before. Using St. Croix as a base, they plundered off the coast of Puerto Rico for a few weeks before heading further west to cruise off of Hispaniola and Cuba (Johnson).

"The Queen Anne's Revenge passed the HMS Seaford, a frigate carrying Governor Walter Hamilton on a tour of the islands. Teach and

his crew voted on whether or not to attack her, but decided it would be too costly. As for Seaford, they just thought they were passing a group of slave ships. Taking two sloops, English and a Dane, as prizes, Thatch took them into St. Croix's harbor, where they let the Dane go. After looting, they burned the English one for recreation, adding her bones to those of Martel's two ships already there (Two collaborating references in the Calendar of State Papers *1717-18: "Letter of Captain Rose to Admiralty, Dec. 23, 1717"; also, "Depositions of Henry Bostock and Jonathan Rose as given to Captain Francis Hume", letters to the Admiralty, 16 and 18 February, 1718)"* (Note, at the National Archives in Kew I found the first reference to the deposition in CSP 1716, p. 231, #425iii. I'm not sure who stuck the deposition into the previous year's file, but that is an example of how dates got confused in the Calendar of State Papers.).

Blackbeard and Bonnet initially decided to reject the king's pardon and look for another ship of force to take. They went looking for an English frigate off of Honduras they heard had lost most of its crew to malaria but did not find her. Instead, they ran out of rum. *Queen Anne's Revenge* was a big ship and had a big crew. Thatch had taken 40 of Hornigold's men with him, and had the 70 mostly grateful Africans, but had accumulated 140 more men that had no bond with him. Apparently, an experienced lieutenant of Thatch's, a friend who let his ego destroy their relationship, was put up as a rival candidate. With the vote split right down the middle, Thatch was almost voted out as captain; it got ugly and personal. Thatch finally found a prize with cases of rum on board which settled the crew down, but he was no longer on his honeymoon as a captain.

Thatch and Bonnet sailed back to Nassau, and probably met Hornigold to attend the stillbirth of the "Republic of Pirates". According to A General History (Johnson), Hume and the *HMS Scarborough* encountered the 40-gun *Queen Anne's Revenge* while on her way up, when Thatch was at his zenith. The *Scarborough* lost the fight and had to let the Queen Anne's Revenge sail away (Johnson). Historian Colin Woodard went to England and checked the log books of the *Scarborough*. He did not find any entry of such a battle. Is it possible that Captain Hume and his officers just forgot to make a log entry, that day? Would they want their superiors to know? More likely it was just a tale, exaggerated over a glass of rum by one of Blackbeard's old crew, inaccurately recalling when they had passed the *Seaford*.

Queen Anne's Revenge had an abysmal cruise sailing up the coast of North America. Their plunder off of South Carolina was meager; the *Queen* couldn't catch anything but a cold. All Thatch asked for while besieging Charleston was a stocked medicine chest. The crew began talking of voting for a new captain, again. Thatch had enough. Giving up his dreams of a better ship of force and more ambitious exploits, Thatch double-crossed his crew before they could double-cross him. Off Beaufort, North Carolina, Thatch ran the *Queen Anne's Revenge* aground on purpose, stripped her of her loot, and sailed away on the little *Adventure Galley*, stranding all but 100 of his crew on a barrier island. Possibly out of rum again, and maybe anticipating a call for a vote, he could not have continued to be responsible for feeding and paying 250 souls. For Ocracoke inlet, he just needed a nimble sloop and a few men; marooned sailor David Herriot later told authorities that Thatch kept forty white and sixty black sailors. Thatch and his 100 took the pardon from Governor Eden in Bath, North Carolina (CSP 1717-18, #430).

A Sailor's Two Cents:

Eyewitnesses said that the Concorde (Queen Anne's Revenge) was 'Dutch-built'. Dutch ships of this age were fatter, and bluff (fat, again) bowed. This spread their weight out more, meaning that they could draw less water, to enable them to get over the sand bars that surround Dutch ports. Admiral De Ruyter defeated the combined English and French navies in the Battle of the Schoenefeld by luring their deeper draft vessels onto sand bars while his fleet sailed over them. Sailors know that sharper-bowed, deeper drafted vessels can point closer to the wind than bluff-bowed vessels with less draft, and have less leeway (sideways slippage). When the Revenge sailed to Honduras, it was because Thatch was not happy with her, and wanted to upgrade to a better sailing ship. A large ship like the Queen Anne's Revenge would have still drawn too much for Ocracoke Inlet, however. She also needed a large crew that would have to be fed and paid, and with the flukey winds off the North American coast, she would have been an awful ship to sail the area. A smaller fore and aft rigged vessel would be able to point much closer to the wind and, with much less effort, more easily adjust to wind shifts and oscillations, catch more prey, have a better chance of escaping police vessels, need less crew, and be easier to maintain and careen.

[9] An example of a Dutch-built, bluff-bowed ship.

When he ran out of money, Thatch put to sea on the little *Adventure Galley* and captured one more prize, a French sloop. He bribed Governor Eden and the state attorney general to help him sell his loot and keep quiet, even storing plundered merchandise in their barns (Cordingly). According to "Johnson", Thatch drank too much ashore and, for entertainment, took to bullying the planters between Ocracoke Inlet and Bath, the then capital. He still had crew he was responsible for feeding, and he would show up at farms drunk and demand food. A report to the Admiralty says that he forced the fifteen-year-old daughter of local planter William Ormand, Mary, to become his wife; other accounts say she fancied him, but that her parents were horrified.

Thatch and his men met their doom when some North Carolina planters convinced Governor Spotswood of Virginia to send a force down to destroy them. Despite having accepted the pardon from Governor Eden and so being a legal citizen, Thatch may have been the victim of his own propaganda campaign; planters may have been more afraid of him than they needed to be. Some of his double-crossed men may have spread his murderous reputation over mugs of rum, out of spite. Too, Spotswood may have been eager to distract attention from complaints of widespread corruption made to the crown by Virginia planters; as Governor, he had transferred sixteen *thousand* acres of Virginia land to his name (CSP 1717-18, #430).

The planters told Governor Spotswood that Thatch would either be staying at a house in Bath with his wife or on his ship in Ocracoke Inlet. Spotswood sent soldiers by land to Bath, and sixty men from the crews of two British warships, *Pearl* and *Lyme*, under a 34-year-old experienced lieutenant named Maynard, to Ocracoke Inlet. Maynard's men were picked for their combat ability from among the many who volunteered. The two small sloops had no cannons, so

Maynard depended on the element of surprise, with the men hidden below decks. Maynard caught Thatch with only nineteen pirates aboard (teenagers Louis and Julien were not), all of them tremendously hungover from a big party the night before. One of Thatch's men awakened the rest when he realized that the little sloops were coming straight for them. Thatch suspected the truth immediately. When the sloops ran aground, Thatch sailed over to Maynard's, the *Ranger*.

"Damn you for villains, who are you? And from whence are you?

"You may see by our colours we are no pyrates," Maynard answered.

"Send your boat over and come aboard that I might see who you are."

"I cannot spare my boat, but I will come over with my sloop, as soon as I can."

Blackbeard took up a glass of rum and drank to Maynard with these words:

"Damnation seize my soul if I give you quarters, or take any from you."

Maynard answered, "I expect none, and will give none" (Johnson; CSP 1717-18, #800).

The *Adventure Galley* then gave Maynard's ship a broadside, killing ten men and wounding six, and boarded her in the smoke. Maynard's men poured up from below where they had been hiding. In the furious melee which followed, Thatch is said to have been shot four times and cut twenty. He and Maynard dueled on the stern. Maynard stabbed Thatch's cartridge box, and his sword bent at the hilt. Thatch countered, and Maynard was only able to block in such a way that Thatch cut off the tips of some of Maynard's fingers. Maynard ignored the wounds and shot Thatch when he drew back for a killing blow. Thatch kept fighting. One young Scot swinging a claymore sword nicked Thatch's neck; Thatch glanced over to him, nodded, and said, "Well done, lad." Turning back to his duel with

Maynard, Thatch never saw the Scot move behind him and swing again. This cut severed Thatch's head, "laying it down upon his shoulder, hinged on just a piece of skin (Johnson; CSP 1717-18, #800)." When an artery is severed, blood shoots four feet in a plume, the fountain gradually going down as blood pressure drops. Maynard cut the skin to finish beheading Thatch.

Maynard took the *Adventure Galley* back up to Williamsburg, with Thatch's captain's log in hand and his severed head tied to the bowsprit. Most of *Adventure Galley's* crew were quickly dispatched on the gallows, but as his Quartermaster Howard was about to be hung, another chance at pardon came from the King. He took it but watched as black members of the crew were taken to be sold (except for Caesar). Howard first officially petitioned the Virginia court for the pardon to extend to them, but the petition was denied. He then filed another petition, arguing that the black crew were his plunder and that as per the pardon he was allowed to keep his plunder. That, too, was denied (CSP 1717-18, #800).

There are today many who carry blood in their veins from the crew of the *Queen Anne's Revenge*. Apparently, a child was born to Mary Ormand, and there seem to be living relatives. There are of course many living relatives of his crew; Stede Bonnet would not have been able to accept the marooned men onto his already crewed sloop, and so would have put them ashore. Also, Thatch only had nineteen with him in the final battle. Two survived the battle and were pardoned; the other 81 *Adventure Galley* crew were somewhere on shore during the fight.

Black Caesar
Key Largo's best tourist attraction

Black Caesar, according to Florida legend, was a prominent African tribal war chieftain, widely known for his huge size, immense strength, and keen intelligence. Tricked into boarding a slave ship as a guest, he was captured. Nearing the Florida Keys, a hurricane began to blow. A member of the crew he had befriended set him free as the ship was about to founder and the two of them escaped in the ship's launch and made it to Elliot Key. The two used the boat to raid passing ships, taking food, plunder, and women. Fighting over one of the women, Caesar killed his friend and went on to amass 'a harem of captured women', as he recruited a small crew and continued raiding using the launch. He kept other prisoners to ransom, most of whom the legend says died of starvation. He is also said to have held children as prisoners. Once, while he was off raiding, they supposedly escaped, living for years on the Key off of shellfish and berries (their ghosts are said to haunt the island still). If you vacation in the Keys today, you will be able to buy paraphernalia with his name on it at the tourist stores. Hats, plastic swords, mugs, flags. Maps show places like "Ceasar's Rock", a small island nearby. The legend says that he left Elliot's Key to sail with Blackbeard. There is no footnote here, because this entire legend is unsubstantiated, though interesting and profitable.

We do find in 'Johnson's' *Notorious* that "Black Caesar" was indeed a sailor on the Queen Anne's Revenge, one of the hundred that Blackbeard decided to keep around after marooning most of his crew, and Caesar was one of the men who fought in the final battle. After Blackbeard was killed, Caesar went below to light the fuse and blow them all to kingdom come, but was tripped and subdued before he could accomplish his mission. Making an exception because of his ferocity and intelligence, authorities decided he could not be sold.

Caesar was hanged in Williamsburg, Virginia, with the rest of the white crew members of the *Adventure Galley* (Johnson, CSP 1717-18, #800).

Why were there no other black pirate captains? Pirates wanted experienced sailors for their captains, not just brave warriors. Captive Africans were seldom sailors any more than white indentures were, and no one from either group is recorded as having been trained in trigonometry for navigation. History does record some mulatto pirates of note, but they had been raised on ships, not in Africa.

Possibly the greatest Buccaneer of all –after Morgan-- was Laurens de Graaf, a "quadroon" (one-quarter African) genius who operated out of Petit Goave, Haiti. Originally from the Netherlands and free, he was enslaved when his ship was captured by a Spanish privateer. He escaped and later captured that very ship, using it for a while as his own. As a slave, De Graaf had married. Once free, Spanish authorities imprisoned his wife, and though De Graaf wrote letters and tried to make deals, he would never be able to free her, or see her, again. After many years he finally remarried, maybe hoping that Spain would release his first wife. Buccaneers often allied with others to make temporary fleets, and de Graaf was elected commodore for some remarkable raids, but De Graaf was also perhaps the Buccaneer kindest to his captives. De Graaf, the Chevalier Michel de Grammont (with Buccaneers from St. Croix) and Nicholas van Hoorne sacked Veracruz together in May of 1683. While De Graaf was away on an errand, van Hoorn ordered the beheadings of a dozen prisoners and had their heads sent to the town council as a warning against following them. Enraged at the senseless murders upon his return, de Graaf killed van Hoorne in a duel, saying, "It is not right to behead any surrendered man who has been granted quarter." (Ayers, chapter "Vera Cruz"). De Graaf was granted a privateering commission by Louis XIV and participated in friendly correspondence with Sir Thomas Lynch, Governor of

Jamaica. To get him to calm down, he was given a commission as Major in command of militia for San Domingue. He invaded Jamaica, then tried to defend San Domingue when the British and Spanish united for a reprisal invasion. Though they did not stay long, they did take the capital of Cap Francois and burned a lot of farms. Many planters wrote letters blaming him, and he was removed from his position. He lived to a ripe old age, retiring to Petit Goave on his plunder.

Hendrick Quintar (van der Huel) was a Dutch mulatto (half African) who served as William Kidd's last quartermaster. He was reported partying in Charlotte Amalie with some of Kidd's crew while Kidd and their ship were in St. Croix (CSP 1700, v.18). He was also quartermaster for Sam Bellamy. He survived the wreck, only to be hung. Mulatto Diego Grilo commanded a ship with Morgan when they sacked Panama, and another mulatto, Francisco Fernando of Jamaica, commanded a ship in 1715 which took just one good prize, after which the crew and captain retired. There were Hispanic pirate captains of partial African descent as well, but that must be the subject of another book.

Stede Bonnet

Poor little rich boy

A wealthy planter on Barbados with a wife and kids, and a major in the local militia, Stede Bonnet paid to have a well-armed sloop built on the island, the *Revenge*, then shocked the island by – supposedly-- sailing off to Port Royal to be a 'privateer'. Bonnet was pudgy, too well dressed, and no sailor. Bonnet had paid for the *Revenge*; he had his cabin and his well-stocked library (Boston News-Letter, Nov. 11, 1717). He hired a navigator named Richards actually to sail the ship. Colin Woodard says that Bonnet paid his crew and officers a contracted salary, the only pirate vessel known to ever have that peculiar arrangement. Bonnet intended to keep his anonymity so that he could return home periodically to visit his wife and children.

To pull off the double life he had planned, he sailed right past the Caribbean islands to begin his career as a pirate off of Charleston, South Carolina. As the captives of his first prize arrived aboard the *Revenge*, he introduced himself as "Captain Edwards." That ruse failed immediately, as the vessel was from Barbados, and the captain an acquaintance. Faced with the choice of either murder or losing his anonymity, Bonnet let the crew go (Johnson), along with his chance of ever reuniting with his wife and children.

Soon after, Bonnet almost got his ship and crew destroyed when he attacked a French frigate, thinking it a merchantman. Thanks to a clean bottom and the sloop's superior ability to point closer to the wind, they escaped and limped into Nassau, where Hornigold relieved Bonnet of command with the approval of the crew and put Thatch to captain the *Revenge*. Richards was made first mate under Thatch. The arrangement seems to have been amicable. Bonnet continued on board as a gentleman apprentice and got to keep his cabin.

Later, when Hornigold gave Thatch *La Concorde*, Bonnet was considered ready for command. The crew, with the approval of Hornigold and Thatch, voted Bonnet back in as captain of the *Revenge*. The *Revenge* and the *Queen Anne's Revenge* raised a lot of Hell together in the Lesser Antilles, took many prizes, enjoyed operating out of St. Croix for a while, sailed over to the islands of Honduras, sailed back to Nassau for the pirate convocation (the aborted 'republic of pirates'), and moved on up to the Carolinas. Both Thatch and Bonnet took the King's pardon at the hands of Governor Eden of North Carolina and then split up. Bonnet took more prizes, however, and lost his protection.

Stede Bonnet's *Revenge* happened by the sand bar just in time and rescued Blackbeard's crew from the barrier island. Most were put ashore in North Carolina, the *Revenge* not having room for 150 more men. It is possible that to get even, these men spread the old murderous tales of Thatch which made the planters of Bath afraid of him.

After finding nothing of value to capture for weeks, the *Revenge* was surprised at Cape Fear, North Carolina, by a flotilla sent by the Governor of South Carolina after Charles Vane, who had only days before been capturing ships in the area. Bonnet plead that he was a gentleman, and above hanging. He argued for extradition to Barbados, where he might hope for clemency from old friends. He also plead that had been given a pardon, to no avail whatsoever.

Bonnet and his crew hanged in Charleston, South Carolina.
Authorities had a test they applied to men captured on pirate ships.
It was known that most pirates had volunteered from captured
vessels and signed articles, but others –skilled craftsmen, musicians,
and surgeons-- were often 'forced men'. The test was whether or not
they had signed the articles, accepted any of the plunder, or whether
witnesses had seen them fight in any of the captures. There were
generally crew from plundered ships in the area that could be called
upon to testify; if not, authorities sometimes offered clemency to the
first pirate who would testify against their brothers. The more
notorious were hung first, and their corpses tarred and put into cages
–gibbets-- or chains, and hung out over the water of the harbors as a
gruesome lesson to would-be pirates. That was the lot of Major
Stede Bonnet (CSP 1718).

St. Croix's Pirate Shipwreck

Jean Martel

Boston News-Letter, _Monday November 12, 1716:_

Rhode Island, Novemb. 8. Arrived here Thomas Pemberton from Antigua, Daniel Waire from Connecticut both for Boston, Ford & Whitfield from Boston the first for New York, Col. John Cranston from New London, gives an account that in his Passage from Philadelphia to Jamaica in August last off Portorico, he met about the 21st of September with one Capt. John Martell a French Pyrate of 135 Men, being most of them French, who took his Ship and Cargo, made him and his Company Prisoners, but afterwards was so civil as to make an Exchange in giving him his Pyrate Sloop, and otherwise was very kind to him & his Men. He also gave him a New London Sloop to come home in, one Butels Master, and at his Arrival he return'd her again to the right Owners.

According to Highfield (Sainte Croix, p. 520), Buccaneer Captain Charles Martel (born in Petit Goâve, San Domingue) was given land on St. Croix. Names of families appear on a map made in Amsterdam in 1660 by Gerard van Keulen, and the Martel estate is clearly marked on land that included part of what is now part of the Gallows Bay development and the Buccaneer Hotel. What is now called Gallows Bay was called "Baie La Martel", and the little bay directly in front of the present Hotel, "Anse Martel" in 1660, is today officially "Bay Martel". Charles, his wife, and two sons (Jean-Roux and Francois Goron) appear in census records for St. Croix,1681-1687 (by 1681, older brother Charles, Jr. was already away at sea). Census records were by militia company district, and the Martels were enrolled under "Compagnie de Quarter de la Majore" (Archives Nationale Outre Mer, cote: 5DPPC/52).

In 1678 Martel probably sailed with Grammont and the other Crucians to join de Estrees ill-fated expedition. From 1688 Charles does not appear on the census records, though his estate and his wife do. It is probable that he sailed with the other Crucian Buccaneers as a privateer in the War of the League of Augsburg, and his sons, now of age, probably sailed with him. The Martel estate stayed intact through the war, with his wife running it. Ordered to abandon Sainte Croix in 1695, the Martels ducked out of being landed at Cap Francois, managing to be put ashore in Petit Goave where they had family, along with Laurens de Graaf and Jean de Casse. Captain Charles Martel appears in several accounts as having been present at the raid on Cartagena.

From author Baylus C. Brooks, "French Pirate Jean Martel: A Deception in History":

"Jean Martel was a French pirate of the early Golden Age of Piracy. He was probably born or closely related to the Martels' in Hispaniola (The Martels' grew sugar there since the 1550s - there is a town near Petit Goâve named "Martel" and the family borrowed money from Spain to invest in sugar cane, making a connection with earlier (1708) Spanish privateer Lewis Martel seem plausible)."

From the Calendar of State Papers, 1717:

"John Martel, with a sloop of 8 guns, began pirating after operating as a privateer in the War of Spanish Succession, cruising mostly in the

Mona Passage between Puerto Rico and Hispaniola. He took several prizes, including the John and Martha, Captain Wilson, with 20 guns, loaded with lumber. The top deck was dismantled, two more guns added, and Martel's mate, Kennedy, given the sloop."

Jean-Roux Martel was the middle son of Buccaneer Captain Charles Martel. He was raised on Sainte Croix where the Buccaneer Hotel now stands. Jean, his older brother Charles, Jr., and his little brother, Francois Goron Martel, went to sea with their father when they reached twelve years of age, and at least the two younger boys were present at the sacking of Cartegena. Jean became a privateer captain, sailing the 8-gun sloop *Renown* in the War of Spanish Succession. Though French, he spoke excellent English. During the war, he operated out of Jamaica. He got intel by hanging out in harborside bars with sailors where he learned which ships sailed, and when. Jean then chased the English ships down. With peace declared, Jean and his crew continued as pirates. They began plundering out of Petit Goâve where the Martel family had settled after Sainte Croix was abandoned, sailing mostly in the Mona Passage between Hispaniola and Puerto Rico.

The most often read and quoted book on the pirate age is <u>A General History of the Robberies and Murders of the Most Notorious Pyrates</u>, by 'Captain Charles Johnson', published in 1728. 'Johnson' is universally considered to be a pseudonym, with the real author up to speculation. A few earlier historians had named Daniel Dafoe as the author, but most now agree on Nathanial Mist. We can substantiate a lot of what is in this book, other things we cannot, and some research refutes; however, it is impossible to get away from the fact that it is a hugely important primary source of English pirate history. 'Johnson' apparently got some of his material from interviews with pardoned pirates, tales probably embellished over time and a glass or more of rum. A General History also quotes extensively and verbatim from the Calendar of State Papers, so "Johnson" had connections; he was privy to correspondence between British colonial governors, spies, and the Admiralty in London.

Martel took two 20-gun ships and several sloops in the Mona Passage in August of 1716. The first was the lumber ship *John and Martha*, which he converted to be the flagship.

Real sailors sail fast:

Pirate ships did not look like what you see in movies. Pirates were sailors. They tore off the upper decks, thereby lightening the ship (increasing the 'power to weight' ratio), making them less top heavy and therefore more seaworthy, and decreasing the surface area that wind could push on to send them sideways instead of forward (leeway). This made the ships 'flush', or with one clean deck line from the bow to the stern. They often added more cannon, adding some of the weight back, but lower. They also rigged to use fore and aft sails between the masts, 'topmast staysails', which, when they needed to steer closer to the wind, gave them an advantage. According to "Johnson", Martel's men did this to the *John and Martha*, adding two more guns.

After taking a few more prizes, the crew voted to have a crewmember named Kennedy made overall captain. "Johnson" says that the crew was fed up with Martel's cruelty to prisoners, but given the quote above from the <u>Boston Newsletter</u>, that seems unlikely; more likely, they got mad at his generosity. According to 'Johnson':

> *"They concluded now, that 'twas high Time to get into Harbour and refit, as well as to get Refreshments themselves, and wait an Opportunity to dispose of their Cargo; therefore 'twas resolved to make the best of their*

Way to Santa Crux, a small Island in the Latitude of 18, 30, N. ten Mile long, and two broad, lying South-East of Porto Rico, belonging to the French Settlements. Here they thought they might lye privately enough for some Time, and fit themselves for further Mischief. They met with a Sloop by the Way, which they took along with them, and in the Beginning of the Year 1716-17, they arrived at their Port, having a Ship of 20 Guns, a Sloop of eight, and three Prizes, viz. another Ship of 20 Guns, a Sloop of four Guns, and another Sloop last taken; with this little Fleet, they got into a small Harbour, or Road, the N. W. Part of the Island, and warp'd up two Creeks, which were made by a little Island lying within the Bay; They had here bare 16 Foot Water, at the deepest, and but 13 or 14, at the shallowest, and nothing but Rocks and Sands without, which secured them from Wind and Sea, and likewise from any considerable Force coming against them.

When they had all got in, the first Thing they had to do, was to Guard themselves in the best Manner they could; they made a Battery of four Guns upon the Island, and another Battery of two Guns on the North Point of the Road, and warp'd in one of the Sloops with eight Guns, at the Mouth of the Channel, to hinder any Vessels from coming in; when this was done they went to Work on their Ship, unrigging, and unloading, in order to Clean, where I shall leave them a while, till I bring other Company to 'em. (Johnson) (CSP 1716).

While whoever he was interviewing over a glass of rum did not remember the exact latitude, this was Salt River Bay, St. Croix. Many wreck hunters, including Jacques Cousteau and Bob Marx, have looked for the remains of the *John and Martha* in Christiansted harbor. The logbook of the *Scarborough* says she found the *John and Martha* in "Bassin", but that is not the NW of the island, and "Bassin" (Christiansted, now) is *not* a hurricane hole. 'Johnson' says that they looked for an anchorage, "which secured them from wind and sea" –a hurricane hole. Sailors know what September and October, even November, can bring. Other ships, like the Spanish

Treasure Fleet, may be ordered to sail in these months, but pirates were not bound to follow the schedules laid down by companies in London, or the Admiralty. They obeyed the law of self-preservation instead. For pirates, their ships were their homes, their livelihood, their everything.

They careened the *John and Martha* and the *Renown* and began transferring loot off of the two captured sloops and the second 20-gun ship they had brought with them. 'Johnson' says that this loot included 1000 pounds in silver, 20 African captives, sugar, molasses, and bolts of cloth. They had taken a ship loaded with Africans and ivory, but 'Johnson' says that they 'let the elephant's teeth go' when they allowed captured sailors to take a small prize sloop and sail home to Boston. According to "Johnson", one-third of Martel's gang was white, one-third were mulatto, and one-third were black. It was a different age; The captives chained below had been sold into slavery by Africans, and to Martel's crew, they were plunder.

Signs of a dangerous weather system appeared, as Bellamy and La Bouse arrived in Salt River Bay shortly after (Johnson).

A Sailor Knows:

There was no early warning system, but nature lets you know a couple of days ahead when a storm is coming. With only a little warning possible, all sailors want to be close to some sheltered place where they can disappear into the mangroves during hurricane season. In 1716, this was 'marine insurance' (the barometer was not yet available for ships). A tall and strong low-pressure system rotates at different speeds, at different altitudes. The result is every type of cloud is in the sky at once, at all different altitudes, all moving in different directions. The swells are affected as well, and though they may not look very different, sailors watch the direction they move in and can feel the wild power they possess. The wind blows from the storm, instead of blowing in the direction the trade wind should. Flags point to where the storm is, while it is two to three days out, and at one day out, the counter-clockwise circulation of the storm itself changes the wind direction, so that you can tell exactly where the storm center is. I've experienced this many times, living on St. Croix. Once you get in the wind affected by the storm, your senses come alive, and there is electricity in the air. Adrenaline keeps you paranoid. You KNOW it is out there, and it is coming soon.

Preparing for the Storm

On arriving in St. Croix, 'Johnson' says that the Martel gang put two cannons on the Northeastern side of the harbor (Judith's Fancy point, now part of Salt River National Park), and four on the Western side (de Ruyter's and Morgan's old earthen fort, also part of the park, very close to the original Taino ball court). In 1716 the eastern side of Salt River was a mangrove covered sand spit tipped by a small sand island, with red mangrove swamps behind it.

According to Johnson, Salt River Bay was at that time 13-feet deep at the least, deep enough for the *John and Martha* but too shallow for an English frigate (Christiansted is deep enough for a frigate, another argument for Salt River). If Marines landed, the pirates could defend themselves among the twisted mangroves in the swamps. The first line of defense: protect your ships. The second line of defense: don't get hung. These defensive arrangements showed that they planned on staying for some weeks. That is another argument for November as the time of battle, as you are more likely to plan on staying for a while during hurricane season. The *John and Martha* was pressed into the larger, southerly of two 'creeks' that form a small mangrove island on the west side of the bay (the sea wall of the marina, now), and their original 8-gun sloop, *Renown,* on the Northern side (by what is now Gold Coast Yachts) (Johnson).

This Sailor's Been There:

Contorting yourself to pick through the web of mangrove roots that bend under your feet and often slipping into the mud, you tie as many lines around the trunks as you can. Back on the boat, you put chaff gear on and grease it, so ropes don't wear through when working in a storm. Anchors are run into the channel ahead and set, to keep the boat from being pushed backward. Martel's gang would have unbent all of their sails, and taken the yards and topmasts down. After all this work, you may as well enjoy the pleasures ashore for a few weeks in case another storm comes, as they often do. A democracy does not operate the same way as the Admiralty, nor a merchant for whom every day costs money in terms of salary, food, and lost profits. What is the point of being free men, if you can't stop and have fun? "A short life, but a merry one," as 'Bartholomew' Roberts said.

Just north of St. Croix, Bellamy and LaBouse had taken some prizes on the way into Salt River. Their crew was looking forward to a good time. They were on St. Croix, a French island, 'a malaria island'; it was hurricane season, and they were a force to be reckoned with. They did not expect molestation from the British Navy. While hurricane season was in full swing, they were correct in their assumption. At some point, though, Bellamy realized they had made a mistake.

Sailors lime:

Let's take a moment to enjoy their stay. "Taking a Lime," or "Limin'," is hanging out. British sailors ashore would often stand around on street corners sucking on limes. According to records kept at Execution Dock in London, the average age of a pirate was mid-twenties. Think Spring Break. In regattas in the Northern Caribbean over the years, I have often had a college-aged crew.

During the day, when not at work on the ships, the young men would have been doing exactly what my sailors did: swimming, spear fishing, jumping off of the masts into the crystal blue Caribbean water, swinging from halyards as high as they dare before letting go, and snaring lobsters from the reef. Pirates would have added games like marksmanship, boxing, deer hunting, and cockfighting. The young boys —John, his former servant, and John Julien, a half Indian boy of 15, would have especially enjoyed these activities, and there were probably other local children to play with, as well. In the evenings, there would have been cards, dice, drinking games, smoking meat on the boucan, music (musicians were often pressed on pirate ships), rum, female laughter and companionship, and tall tales from the old-timers. Tobacco grew wild around Salt River (it continued to do so into the 1990's).

Trips to Bassin would have provided some variety, and they arranged in shifts to get over to St. Thomas on the trading sloops, dressed in their finest, to enjoy a new set of bars and meet different young women (CSP 1716, #340). Captain Thomas Candler, of HMS *Winchelsea*, reported on May 12, 1717, that Charlotte Amalie was filled with many rogues and pirates of all nations (but he did not say pirate *ships*). See also the passage above about Captain Kidd's visit. Kidd's crew was seen partying in Charlotte Amalie, but the Governor had not allowed Kidd or his ship to stay in Danish waters. I have been to many sailing parties that were probably not too different; testosterone is still the same, although, with the constraints of civilization left behind, a darker intensity pervaded the revelry. It would make a big difference to know that the whole world was against you. It also added to the comradery that the pirates enjoyed. In the Golden Age, Pirates would never fail to look after each other where possible and even wreak revenge on those who had hurt their brethren.

Tragedy

According to 'Johnson', Captain Hume of the British frigate *Scarborough*, 32 guns, was sent from her base in Barbados at the request of Governor William Hamilton, who had reports of a couple of pirate sloops that had taken the *Bonetta* and several other ships. Many pirates were operating in the Lesser Antilles at this time, and many ships were captured. Bellamy learned too late that John King's mother had some influence with Governor Hamilton, and he expected trouble to come; he and LaBouse took off down island. If he shared his fear with Martel, it was ignored. The *Scarborough* put into Spanish Town, Virgin Gorda, just as a boat arrived from St. Croix, probably one of the small sloops that were bringing portions of the stolen cargo to sell. A sailor from the boat -probably over a tot of rum- told a member of the *Scarborough*'s crew about a party of pirates in St. Croix. Hume was informed. The *Scarborough* recalled her crew and left immediately, sailing at night and arriving off of Salt River Bay at dawn.

The *Scarborough* anchored in Easterly winds and fell back parallel to the reef. Her log book notes one navigable channel into the bay that was too shallow for her to enter (Christiansted, where most historians mistakenly thought the battle took place, has two navigable channels, not one, and was deep enough for a frigate). It also records the cannon that the pirates had placed in the old sand fort on the west side of the bay, the cannon on eastern side, and an 8-gun sloop that had been anchored just inside the cut in the reef to command the entrance. This was almost certainly *Renown*, which had 8 guns, Martel's privateer in the War of Spanish Secession and his pirate ship until taking the *John and Martha* only recently. She was probably moved out of the swamp after the most dangerous time for hurricanes, September, was past.

HMS Scarborough systematically destroyed both batteries and sunk the sloop in the channel (*Renown* is still there. So close to the beach, her cannons have long since been looted, but even now her pile of ballast stones—water-smoothed river rock, not coral or local stone-- mark where she sank). *HMS Scarborough* then began cannonading the *John and Martha* "Through the mangrove island." The mangroves would have absorbed most of the shot, but more and more would have gone through (You can't fire through Protestant Cay in Christiansted harbor; Captain Hume could see the *John and Martha*'s masts and was firing into the mangroves. This was Salt River, not Christiansted.). When the evening calm set in, 'Johnson' continues, the wind died away, and the *Scarborough* began swinging into the reef. Captain Hume weighed anchor and stood off and on for a few days, blockading the harbor. 'Johnson' continues,

> "On the 20*th*, in the evening, they observed the man of war standing off to sea, and took the opportunity to warp out, in order to slip away from the island; but at 12:00 they ran aground, and seeing the Scarborough stand in again, as their case was so desperate, so they were put into the utmost confusion; they quitted their ship, and set fire to her, with 20 negroes in her, shackled in the hold, who were all burnt; 19 of the pyrates made their escape with Kennedy (and Martel) in a small sloop, but the rest, 20 of them being negroes, betook the woods, where 'twas probable they might starve, for we never heard what became of them afterwards: Captain Hume released the prisoners on the ships that remained, and then went after the two sloops he had been sent after in the first place." (Johnson) (CSP 1716, #204, #351, Gov. Lowther)."

Forensics

What time of year did this battle take place? Johnson" first says January, and then contradicts himself saying November 15-20. The 'official' account says January 15-20 (Colonial Records, 22 #204, letter from Governor William Hamilton to the Council of Trade and Plantations). Another source suggests June 8, but that would mean southeast winds, which doesn't fit at all. Governors can change dates. Saving successes to use them to offset setbacks or accusations of corruption later can be useful. At any rate, any sailor will tell you it was most likely November 15-20, 1716. First, 'Johnson's' account is the closest to the original source material. Second, he states that the Martel gang were looking for a place "that secured them from wind and sea" –they were going into a hurricane hole. Bellamy and La Bouse went in at virtually the same time; it would have most likely been for the same reason. They would not have stayed two months to sell plunder and careen. To this day, when a storm is coming, sailors end up in the best mangrove bays at the same time, tying in beside each other; Salt River Bay is still very popular. *John and Martha* tied into the mangroves, which is what I have done for many hurricanes. For 13 years while living on my sailboat, I tied in next to the mangrove island in Salt River, exactly where Martel and Kennedy put their sloop, *Renown*.

It is a lot of work climbing into the mangroves to tie 20 lines, running your anchors out and setting them, wrapping rope with leather or cloth (chaff gear) and greasing it, and getting the sails down below. Once nested, no sailor unties until the season is over unless they have to. As soon as they do feel safe, however, they get out; the mosquitoes by that mangrove island are horrible. I got dengue fever there after hurricane Marilyn in 1995. As soon as the storm season was over, typically the middle of November, I would move out into the bay or sail east to another bay, for fresh air and fewer bugs. In November, and the pirates were already getting ready for sea. Topmasts had been swayed back up by the time the *Scarborough* arrived, as she could see them sticking out above the mangroves.

While the *Scarborough* was cannonading the *John and Martha*, the wind shifted to the NE, because 'Johnson' says that the *Scarborough* began to swing into the reef, which is the only explanation for why Hume had to pull the anchor up. He blockaded the pirates by reaching back and forth off the harbor entrance, perpendicular to the wind direction until the wind might shift back and he could resume his cannonade. Every sailor in the Caribbean knows that the wind starts swinging back and forth between the Northeast and East just before the arrival of the "Christmas Winds," the North East trades that blast in at the end of November or early December.

Martel, Kennedy, and crew would not have wanted to wait around for the wind to veer back to the East, bringing the *Scarborough* back to anchor. 'Johnson' says that they had to warp the *John and Martha* out; this is true. The current runs in a circle, into the mangroves on the South side of the island where the John and Martha was, and out on the North (where the sloop was), through a neck which is too shallow and narrow to be navigable. You can drift in on the south side, but you can't sail out, the current and breeze funneling right on your nose. I never had an engine on my sailboat; I took my sails down in the outer bay for those many years and drifted into my spot in the mangroves with the current. I had to have a tow out, however. To come out of the mangroves, the pirates would have taken two anchors to the east and pulled to one, then taken it out further while they pulled to the second, etc. until they could catch the breeze ('kedging'). Another anchor would be out to the North and tied off amidships. The *John and Martha* would swing like a pendulum on that line as she came out, therefore not having her stern pushed into the mangroves by the northeast wind ("warping"). Raising sails when on the east side of the bay, they would have people from the village with lanterns, on the east side of the cut in the reef, and another on the half-sunk sloop on the west side of the cut, and steered between them on the way out.

If you want to get technical, get your compass out (see diagram, below). In the fall, trade winds are usually from @90 degrees (E). With the Salt River Bay reef running east to west, the *Scarborough* anchored parallel to it and begin cannonading the John and Martha. In November, however, the wind begins to swing back and forth from 90 degrees (E) to 45 degrees (NE), in anticipation of changing to NE for the winter months (the "Christmas Winds"). Such a shift to the NE would have swung the *Scarborough* in towards the reef. Johnson says that when the wind shifted, the *Scarborough* had to pull up her anchor and sail back and forth off of the harbor entrance like a cat outside a mouse hole.

Captain Hume would have chosen reaching legs of about 80 degrees to the wind (allowing for 10 degrees of leeway, meaning 90 degrees actually) to sail legs perpendicular to the harbor entrance. Thus, his courses would have been something like 325 degrees (NNW) on starboard tack away from the island, and 125 degrees (SSE) on the port tack back towards the island

The pirates would have been watching the *Scarborough* do this for a few days. They timed their move so they could slip out when the *Scarborough* was as far away as possible on her starboard tack, and the moon had set so that the *Scarborough* could not see her sails. Astropixels.com shows that the moon would have been between new and the first quarter on November 20, 1716. Cornell University's moon phase chart for the same night shows the moon rising about 10:00 a.m. and setting about 10:00 p.m. If this took place two months later, the wind would have been the same, from the NE, but the moon would have risen about noon and set about midnight, which doesn't fit with the times "Johnson" reports.

The *Scarborough* was nearly 1/3 of her compliment short due to malaria and had only filled enough spots to fire her cannon by bringing soldiers on board the week before. Without a veteran crew, and in the dark, she would have gybed to change course -turned by putting her stern to the wind- and it would have taken around a half hour to do so.

John & Martha sailed faster than the *Scarborough*, as she had a clean bottom. Also, Martel and his crew had sailed a sloop for years. The *John and Martha* would have set her fore and aft sails to head 60 degrees to the wind, for a course of 345 degrees, 20 degrees farther upwind than the *Scarborough*, but that is still too close to the Scarborough's path for comfort.

Off the coast of Salt River Bay, the ocean shoals from 1,000 feet deep to 50 feet deep almost instantly. That makes for some big, steep waves, which are shoving you backward as you sail out of Salt River Bay on starboard tack (wind coming from the right side of the boat). It is very frustrating; you seem to be going nowhere. The Pirates needed to tack over to port (the wind coming from the left side of the ship) as soon as possible, so they were neither headed towards the *Scarborough*, nor trying to push into the waves. They were eager to tack, using a 110-degree angle as a lay line. Once on port tack, she would have picked up good hull speed and been getting to windward of the Scarborough quickly, which would have ensured her escape.

John and Martha tacked too soon. Coming out of Salt River, you make good hull speed once you go over onto the port tack, but those steep waves, now from the beam, push you sideways toward shore ('leeway'); the pirates did not allow for this.

The *John and Martha's* course would let them sail by the land closest ahead, the point at Judith's Fancy. Their fatal mistake was to forget that there was a small reef 80 yards offshore, right in their path. The wind had to be around 12 knots, with small swells. Much more wind or bigger swells, and the pirates would have seen and

heard the waves breaking on White Horse Reef. Much less wind
and they would not have been able to sail out against the swells.
White Horse Reef slopes quickly up to two feet deep at its shallowest.
In light and medium light air, it is invisible and quiet. The pirates
would have seen and heard the waves breaking on the barrier reef to
starboard --only inches from the surface-- but they could not detect
White Horse Reef, lying silently in the darkness ahead.

The *John and Martha* struck the reef on its northern edge near
Black Rock at midnight, and stuck fast, according to 'Johnson.' The
crew worked to kedge her off for hours until the sun came up. They
took anchors astern and tried to reel the lines in on the windlass. I
have kedged off of reefs in the middle of the night more than once
and done what they did. Grinding towards the anchors (there are
two old anchors there, still) off of the SW corner of White Horse
Reef, the ship would have hopefully been pulled backwards off of the
reef and ended up catching the breeze to go forward again on a
starboard tack, so that they could resume sailing away from the
shore. I bet they took an anchor out to the NW as well, to make sure
that, once off, the swells could not carry them backward towards
shore before their sails filled. They would have cut the cables to the
SW anchors once the sails drew, and pulled the NW anchor out as
they sailed off.

They waited until the moon set to try to escape so that they
would be invisible to the *Scarborough*. However, with the moon in the
west, the tide was falling, and they had less water under them with
each passing minute. They tried for hours, with no success. On the
bow they tried to lighten the ship, tossing some cannons and ballast
stones overboard. Keeping the cannons on the stern would have
served to create a 'see-saw', raising the bow off of the coral. The bow
cannons are still there on White Horse reef, along with the ballast
pile.

Daybreak showed the *Scarborough* on port tack, heading straight
for them. She opened fire with her bow chasers. Exhausted and

hopeless, the crew panicked. Trying too quickly to get the silver offloaded to a small sloop, the *John and Martha* was set on fire by an accidentally overset lamp. Martel, Kennedy, and 19 men took off on the sloop, while screams from twenty African captives chained below pierced the morning. The remaining hundred pirates swam to shore and ran into the mangroves. Captain Hume sent the boats into the bay, but could not get near the *John and Martha*. They were able to come away with only eight African captives, two vessels, and salvageable cargo worth £450 (Johnson) (CSP 1717).

John and Martha lightened as she burned. With easterly winds, the fire would have charred the stern of the ship, but not spread forward. Periodically in the winter large swells come from the northeast, sweeping across White Horse Reef. Some months after the battle, they lifted the *John and Martha*'s remains, carrying her over to rest at Judith's Fancy, where she is today.

I knew the *John and Martha* had hit White Horse Reef. I went looking for her and even dove the site with Phillipe Cousteau and his wife (Travel Channel, Pirate Caribbean Gold, "The Buzzard's Treasure"). We found a swivel cannon, but not the ship. Later, talking with my friend Lee Morris, he was shocked. Lee looked for *John and Martha* with Jacques Cousteau and Bob Marx in the 1960s, but they were unable to find her (they were looking around Christiansted). He knew of my wreck, though. He had photographs (below). Brian Bishop had shown him the site 40 years before, in 1977, exactly where I said it would be.

On October 15, 1977, a 110' steel freighter from Santo Domingo, the *Cumulus*, went aground on the eastern edge of White Horse reef. The wind and seas were unusually calm; salvors were able to get a barge to the side of the ship and got some heavy deck cargo off. They could not get the ship herself off, though they were able to lighten her. When the winter swells came in, waves lifted the hull off of White Horse Reef and carried it across to Judith's Fancy, where she lies, today (St. Croix Avis, October 16, 1977, front page article with photographs showing the *Cumulus* on White Horse Reef; in my possession, gift of Lee Morris).

In 1977, standing on White Horse Reef while working in waist-deep water with the salvage crew, a wave came in over Brian Bishop's head. He instinctively grabbed part of the reef to hold on to. After the wave passed, he looked down. He was holding onto a cannon. He saw more, and ballast stones. Seven weeks later, working on the *Cumulus* but now walking on Judith's Fancy Reef, A big wave tried to smash him into the coral. Once more, he grabbed on to part of the reef. When he looked down, he saw that he was once again holding onto a cannon, an exact twin of the ones on White Horse.

Brian was excited to learn the story of the wreck he had found so many years before and took me straight to the spot. I had been within 50 feet. With an 8 second window between dangerous breakers, I measured them, and sent the information to Mr. Charles Trollope in London, a leading authority on antique cannons (Just like Brian, I had to hold onto them when the waves hit.). According to Mr. Trollope, they are eight 4-pounder minions, two six-pound sakers, and three mortars. The 4-pound minions probably manufactured between 1680 and 1716 (the only period of manufacture for five-foot-long cannons). There may have been many wrecks on White Horse reef over five centuries, but this narrows the circle. I sent my hypothesis to the National Park Service in December. The NPS had a team on the wreck site in March. They are not divulging anything they found, even to me. While the story the story of the *John and Martha* is poignant and deserves to be heard, they fear that looters would be out trying to pry relics off to sell on the black market, if the location or possible identity of the wreck were made public. This fear is well-founded, based on recent history around the world, but not practical, due to the cannons advanced stage of decomposition. Despite their reluctance to open this site up to the world, it may be that under the cannons will one day be found manacles, possibly with some carbon remaining, still holding the bones of the doomed.

[10] Reproduction of a 17th-century merchant ship. Martel and his gang tore off all superstructure above the level of the main deck. The ship was pierced for 20 guns; two more were added.

[11] Salt River Bay, St. Croix. East is up. The narrow "V" in the lower right-hand side pointing down is where Martel and Kennedy put their ships. The *John and Martha* was on the right, or southern, side; the *Renown* was on the left of the "V". They were on either side of the dark patch in the middle, which is the mangrove island. In this picture, sailboats line the right, or southern, side of the "V".

The entrance to the bay on the bottom is the only navigable one, the eastern opening being too narrow, twisty, shallow, and treacherous. De Ruyter and Morgan built the sand fort on the point just opposite the cut, where Martel put four cannons. White Horse Reef is visible in the upper left-hand corner; it must have been blowing more than 12 knots when this picture was taken. (photo from the V.I. Dept. of Tourism).

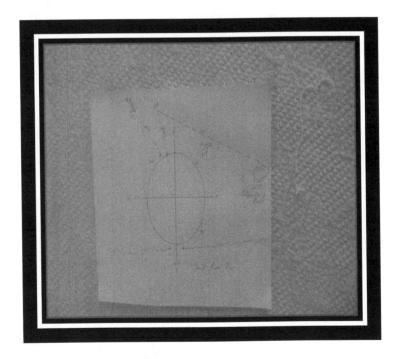

[12] Dots show the approximate reaching legs of the *Scarborough*. Dashes indicate the approximate courses of *John and Martha*.

[13] wreck photos of what is almost certainly the *John and Martha*, courtesy of Lee Morris.

THE MOTOR VESSEL M.V. CUMULUS, from Santo Domingo, aground on White Horse Reef by Salt River since Saturday evening, was submerged up to the decks by late yesterday afternoon. On board are several new pieces of earth-moving equipment bound for Venezuela.

From the Avis, October 16, 1977. "THE MOTOR VESSEL M.V. CUMULUS, from Santo Domingo, aground on White Horse Reef by Salt River since Saturday evening, was submerged up to the decks by late yesterday afternoon. On board are several new pieces of earth-moving equipment bound for Venezuela." The Cumulus can be seen today, by snorkeling the Judith's Fancy Reef. John and Martha went aground on the west side, the Cumulus on the east side. Today, they lie on Judith's Fancy reef, the length of White Horse Reef apart.

There are no other ships with this many cannon recorded as being sunk around St. Croix; I have checked British, French, and Danish colonial records, and also the Lloyds list of shipwrecks in the Virgin Islands (Towle). Both White Horse and the main site are very dangerous, with ripping currents and smashing breakers. The cannons themselves have taken a beating over 300 years. They are concreted into the coral and extremely fragile, riddled with holes and rust. Any attempt to excavate the cannons would destroy them.

Returning from their cruise down-island, LaBouse and Bellamy found the 'burned-out bones' of the *John and Martha* piled on top of 'the reef that guards the harbor entrance.' They did not write that they found it on the reef at the entrance to the bay. Further, Bellamy and LaBouse were able to sail their ships into Salt River Bay through the channel, which would have been very difficult, as small as it is, if the *John and Martha* had run aground on the entrance cut, her stern reaching back towards the sunken sloop.

Martel appears in the <u>Calendar of State Papers 1717-18</u> writing a letter to warn the Governor of Petit Goave of an impending pirate attack but asking to be kept anonymous. Baylus Brooks says,

> *Martel perhaps operated between Hispaniola and Puerto Rico by fall of 1716. He took a boat of Saint Domingue with English pirates near Cape Tiburon (Hispaniola) in late 1716 and had a sister-in-law who lived at Petit Goâve, Saint Domingue, Hispaniola, also late in 1717.*

The "sister-in-law" would make sense with St. Croix census records, which showed that Charles Martel had two sons. Martel became an informant about a pirate attack planned for Christmas 1717 on Petit Goâve, and asked French officials to not to mention his name "because it would risk his life if the English [pirates] learned the secret of his French heritage." (CSP 1717-18).

I have found no mention of him afterward. Martel's partner Kennedy, a "hunter, who was raised in Cuba," seems to have disappeared as well. One author says he may have been the Walter Kennedy who ended up with Captain Howell Davis in 1718, sailed with Bartholomew Roberts, betrayed Roberts, made off on his own, and ended up hung when he tried to return to normal life in England. This is unlikely, as Walter Kennedy was raised in England).

More sails are on the horizon; open the bars. There were many pirates whose names no one remembers today, who sailed Caribbean waters. Let's meet a few, as they sail into Salt River. ☠

Pirates of ST  : Part 2

'Bartholomew' Roberts

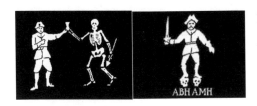

War Hero

From bad-ass, rock-star war-hero to …nothing. John Roberts was from a middle-class family in Pembrokeshire, where he attended school and learned math and his letters before going to sea at the age of 13. Twenty-four years later, John Roberts was worshipped by sailors throughout the British Navy. He was such a sailor's sailor, such a warrior, that every man in the British navy knew of him. Tars admired him, but his officers were jealous and took credit for his heroism for themselves. They got promoted and made no mention of him whatsoever in their dispatches. He had no connections. As a commoner but a good navigator, Roberts would have risen to be a Masters Mate in the wartime navy, as high as he could ever get with no influence. When the war was over, he was left on the beach along with 30,000 other sailors. With so many sailors looking for work, the only job he could get was a poor paying job as third-mate on a disease-ridden slave ship, the *Princess*.

Roberts was 37 years old when the *Princess* was captured by Captain Howell Davis, who had the *Royal Rover* and the *Royal James*. Davis had sailed to West Africa to loot ships and forts in company with LaBouse and Robert Conklyn, which pirates had just left him for the Indian Ocean. Davis was a veteran privateer from the war. Turning pirate with Hornigold and Jennings and operating out of Nassau, he had afterward taken the King's pardon, accepted a ship to go capture pirates, seized that vessel, and turned to piracy again. He was also from Pembrokeshire and had met Roberts before, at which time Davis had already tried to talk him into joining his crew.

As Davis' prisoner, Roberts was forced to join the pirates against his will. They knew who he was, and they wanted him. He refused. He would not sign their articles. He demanded to be released. Davis did not give up. Speaking their native Welsh language together in the evenings, Davis no doubt pointed out that in the first two weeks Roberts was aboard, each of the pirates had earned more money than Roberts would make in a year on the *Princess*.

Six weeks later, in an attempt to capture a Governor and hold him for ransom, Davis and a party ashore were ambushed and killed. The crew came to Roberts. They were divided into two groups: the 'Lords,' who had sailed with Davis from the beginning, and the 'Commons,' who had volunteered down the line. The Admiralty in London may not have known who John Roberts was, but they did. They voted Roberts to be their new captain. He stood up,

...

And accepted. "Since I've dipped my hands in muddy waters and must be a pirate, it is better to be a commander than a common man. In honest service, you cannot win; there is only hard labor, poor food, and low wages. I've seen your side in the last weeks. Good food, equal shares, liberty, and power. What man would not balance the creditor on this side, when the only hazard run for it is a sour look at choking? No. A merry life and a short one shall be my motto." (Johnson)

Roberts had experienced for the first time a society of equals, in which you were respected and promoted if you deserved it, regardless of birth.

For a veteran pirate crew to elect a newcomer to be their captain, one who had not yet even signed the articles, means that he had a reputation that the pirates greatly admired. Pirates were not going to trust their lives to some stranger with no experience, who was not even one of them. They had to have solid reasons to expect that Roberts was an excellent sailor and an aggressive, intelligent warrior. I have no citation and do not need one. There were capable men among the Lords who expected to be elected, but were not. Walter Kennedy and Thomas Anstis, anticipating their own election to the position, had to be bitterly disappointed; the time would come when they would get even.

Roberts took "Bartholomew" as his alias and signed the articles. With his black hair and olive complexion, his men referred to him as "Black Bart." Captain Roberts' first action was to destroy the fort where Davis was ambushed. He then led his men in plundering ships off the African coast. They abandoned the *Royal James* due to torredo worm holes, and after a vote, the crew decided to head to Brazil on the *Royal Rover*.

In Baia de Todos Santos, Brazil, Roberts performed one of the most amazing piratical feats in history. The *Royal Rover*, fresh from the trans-Atlantic crossing, found before them a fleet of 42 heavily armed Portuguese galleons, waiting for two battleships to escort them to Portugal. Roberts sailed the *Royal Rover* right into the fleet of ships, pretending to ask for directions. Roberts headed for the smallest one, and when abeam of her ordered her master to row over to the *Rover* or be blown out of the water. Once aboard, Roberts told him he and his ship would go free if he pointed out the richest ship in the fleet. He pointed out the *Sagrada Familia*, which had 40 guns and a crew of 170. Roberts and his men sailed over to the *Sagrada* and asked her captain to come over as their guest. The captain of the

Sagrada was no fool; he cleared for action. Merchantmen were never known for doing this quickly; regardless, Roberts' ruse was up --it was time to fight. In the middle of this large fleet, and before the *Sagrada* could fire her cannons, Roberts took the helm and laid the *Royal Rover* right alongside. Grappling on, he and his men boarded her and won a fierce pitched battle. They took 40,000 gold moidores and jewelry designed for the King of Portugal (a king's ransom in loot). With one of the battleships sailing towards the *Rover*, Roberts cast off from the *Sagrada* and sailed directly at her, to fight her before her consort could come up. Cowed, the ship hove to and waited for the other warship to join her. In the meantime, the *Rover* turned and sailed away with her prize.

Twelve hundred miles later, they put into the Devil's Islands off the coast of Guyana to divide the plunder. When a brigantine said to have a valuable cargo sailed by, Roberts took off in a small prize sloop with forty men after her, sailing downwind. They could not catch her and had to turn back, but the wind died, and it took a couple of weeks to return to where they had left the *Royal Rover*. They found an empty harbor. Quartermaster Walter Kennedy had seen his chance to be Captain, and with the 160 men Roberts had left behind took off in the *Royal Rover*, with all the accumulated loot (Johnson). --Pirates! Regardless, this was only the *beginning* of the most successful piratical career in history.

Making the best of a bad situation, Roberts and his men began plundering in the Windward Islands in the little sloop, which they named The *Fortune*. They drew up articles, which were only unusual in that they specifically barred women and boys from the ship. Discouraged by the desertion of the *Rover* and blaming Roberts, the crew voted him out as captain, replaced by Thomas Anstis. They partnered with French pirate Montagne la Palisse in another sloop, the *Sea King*. After plundering together for weeks, the governors of Barbados and Martinique sent sloops of war after them.

The Governors' warships trapped the pirates in a small, isolated bay. It could have been a fair fight, but the *Sea King*, more favorably positioned for an escape, took off, leaving the *Rover* to her fate. After a brief, heated battle against the two warships, the *Fortune* was just barely able to escape, with 20 of her crew dead and the little sloop badly shot up. Roberts was re-elected as captain. This battle led to the second flag above, with Roberts standing on a Barbadian's head (ABH), and a Martinican's head (AMH), to let them know he was going to get even one day very soon.

Licking their wounds, the *Fortune* sailed to sell their plunder, refit, and regroup. There was only one island in the Lesser Antilles where all of this could be accomplished safely: St. Croix. They rebuilt, recuperated, and enjoyed the island for three months, before getting back to work (Johnson).

From St. Croix, the *Fortune* sailed up to Newfoundland where they captured dozens of small ships, recruited crew (fishing vessels at this time were notorious for paying little and treating their men terribly), and took two brigs they renamed the *Good Fortune* and the *Royal Fortune*. Quartermaster Thomas Anstis was appointed the captain of the *Good Fortune*. Returning to the Caribbean, they were rejoined by the *Sea King*, which was full of apologies (Sanders).

In late September 1720, the little fleet entered the anchorage of Basseterre at St. Kitts, black flags flying, with drummers and trumpets playing, and every ship in the harbor surrendered without a shot. Sailing up to Gustavia, St. Barts, the French governor allowed the pirates ashore for a few days of recreation. Off St. Lucia, they captured 15 French and English ships in three days! Roberts learned from captives that the British navy was sending warships in response. The crew voted to sail back over to West Africa, but first, they disappeared for three weeks to dispose of their plunder, careen, and refit −St. Croix, again. There was not another island in the Lesser Antilles that fit the bill. They had just entered the Atlantic heading east when, on April 17, 1721, Thomas Anstis and his men sailed off on their own under cover of the night in the *Good Fortune* to continue plundering in the Caribbean.

The *Royal Fortune* began sinking as they neared the Cape Verdes Islands; torredo worms were in her hull. The crew worked the pumps ceaselessly, the carpenter doing all he could. As soon as they made an island with a beach, they ran her aground and transferred what they could into the little *Sea King* (Sanders). On the West African coast, Roberts and his crew took several prizes including a Danish frigate, the *Onslow*, which he made his own, renaming her the new *Royal Fortune*; a brig, which they named the *Ranger* and armed as a consort; and a sloop they called the *Little Ranger*, used as a tender.

The Royal Navy sent two frigates after them. On February 5, 1722, Captain Ogle of the HMS *Swallow* finally caught up to Roberts at Cape Lopez, and Roberts' luck ran out. The *Swallow*, with a dirty bottom, slow and not very maneuverable, decided to divide and conquer. Ogle lured the *Ranger* away first, by making the *Swallow* appear to be a slaver coming into the bay which, upon seeing the pirates, turned to flee. Roberts' protégé on the *Ranger* did not alert anyone on the *Royal Fortune*, probably hoping to impress Roberts. The *Ranger* left her anchor and gave chase. The *Swallow* was unable to out-sail the nimble *Ranger*, and did not have to; she lured the *Ranger* close, then turned and destroyed her.

The day before, the *Royal Fortune* had captured the *Neptune*, a ship loaded with rum, and the crew had drunk themselves into oblivion. Roberts rarely drank, but could not deny his men their fun. He had the right ship to fight with, but the men were in no condition to fight, and besides were caught completely off guard, everyone being asleep. At the last moment, someone noticed the Swallow, and the pirates stumbled to quarters.

Roberts had just enough time to throw on the brilliant silk scarlet suit he wore into battle. Broadsides shattered the air while pirates still struggled to their guns. Roberts died at the helm when grapeshot ripped his throat apart and was tossed overboard by his crew, per his wishes.

The articles demanded that their ship be blown to kingdom come rather than surrender, but the drunken crew was prevented from doing so by a couple of the forced men who knew the drill and posted themselves by the powder magazine, where they tackled anyone who came down the stairs with a match. At the trial, presided over by the Governor of the Royal Africa Company at the Cape Coast Castle, the crew were disposed of in the following way: fifty-two were hung, two reprieved, 20 sold into indenture with the Royal Africa Company, 17 given the benefit of the doubt and sent to London for trial, and 65 African crew members were sold into slavery. Roberts is said to have taken a tremendous amount of plunder and more than 400 ships in his five-year career. Ogle plundered Roberts' chest, securing for himself a fortune in gold dust which he did not report to authorities, and was knighted by the King when the Swallow returned home (Sanders). Roberts' luck seems to have transferred to Ogle; Ogle is the only naval captain recorded to have become both wealthy and knighted for destroying a pirate. Others, like Capt. Francis Hume and Lt. Maynard, would not be recognized, and experienced terrible luck for the rest of their short lives.

Famous sayings of Captain Roberts:

"A merry life and a short one shall be my motto."

"Since I've dipped my hands in muddy waters, I may as well be a Captain."

"Damn to him who ever lived to wear a Halter!"

Thomas Anstis

Died in his sleep

Thomas Anstis and Howell Davis were Flying Gang members who took the king's pardon in 1718. Out of work, they accepted positions as crew on the *Buck*, an armed sloop sent by Governor Woodes Rogers of Nassau to destroy pirates who had not taken the pardon. They mutinied, turned pirate again, and elected Davis to be their captain. When Davis died in an attack on a Portuguese fort on the West African coast, the recently forced 'Bartholomew' Roberts was elected to take his place, instead of "lords" Walter Kennedy or Anstis. Anstis was with Roberts when they were betrayed by Walter Kennedy, but Anstis separated from 'Bartholomew' Roberts on the night of April 18, 1721, in the brigantine *Good Fortune*. Returning to the Caribbean after only sailing a few days into the Atlantic, he and his crew began plundering ships off Hispaniola. On their way to plunder in the Leeward Islands, they stopped briefly to careen and sell their cargo, probably at St. Croix. Returning to the 'game', they plundered a dozen ships from Jamaica to Martinique, after which they put into "an island off the beaten track, where men of war were not likely to happen along" for hurricane season, and to sell their plunder --St. Croix. They continued to operate from St. Croix for a month, and then sailed north to Bermuda (Johnson).

On their way up to Bermuda, they captured the *Morning Star*, which they fitted out with 32 guns and 100 men. Anstis allowed John Fenn to captain the vessel so that Anstis could remain with the *Good Fortune* as he favored its handling. At this time, a petition was drawn up to request a pardon from the English crown which they sent via a merchant ship. The crew then retired to an unnamed island off the South West end of Cuba, where they felt safe from the Royal Navy. Here they lived for the next nine months surviving on the bounty of the island and sea, spending the days in dancing, drinking rum, sport, drinking rum, boxing, drinking rum, shooting, drinking rum, and other diversions (Johnson).

In August of 1722, a merchant vessel passed the word that their petition had drawn no interest. At last, they were forced to return to work, but almost immediately they wrecked the *Morning Star* on a reef in the Cayman Islands, and while anchored to recover the crew of the wreck, the *Good Fortune* was set upon by two men of war, the *Hector* and *Adventure*. The pirates were able to escape by cutting their anchor cable and ran from the two men of war for some time, finally escaping by rowing their ship during a calm. They then sailed far to the west to the Bay of Honduras to clean and refit (Johnson).

Early December 1722 found the pirates back in the Antilles, where they again took a sizable ship and mounted her with 24 guns. Despite having only one hand and having wrecked the *Morning Star*, Fenn was given command of the ship, a brigantine. Together, the two pirates took a dozen prizes between the Bahamas and Trinidad, then put into Tobago to clean and refit. In April 1723, the pirates were surprised by the arrival of HMS *Winchelsea*, which destroyed all of the pirates' ships except the brigantine, which escaped (Johnson).

Anstis forced too many honest men to join his crew. They missed their homes, and they had watched while the pirates, with Anstis' encouragement, raped and murdered young women they captured. After being chased by Admiral Flowers of the *HMS Winchelsea* for months all over the Caribbean, the forced men of the crew got an opportunity and murdered Anstis in his sleep, took over the *Good Fortune*, sailed her to Curacao, and accepted amnesty from the governor, to whom they turned over their pirate prisoners. The pirates were quickly hung (Johnson).

George Lowther

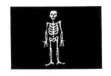

Popular with His Crew

George Lowther took a job as the first mate of a crew hired to bring a 16-gun slave ship, the *Gambia Castle*, from England to Gambia for the West Africa Company. Upon arrival, the company refused to pay and left them to starve. The crew had a better idea: they put their captain ashore, elected first mate George Lowther as Captain, and went pirating. They renamed their ship the *Happy Delivery*, and after pillaging off of Africa for a few months, crossed the Atlantic to the West Indies. Here they cruised off of Hispaniola and Puerto Rico. After taking a small sloop off of Fajardo, they were of a mind to careen, divide the plunder, and look for a hurricane hole safe from the British and Spanish navies.

> They put into St. Croix, "a small island where they cleaned, and stay'd some time to take their diversions, which consisted in unheard of debaucheries, with drinking, swearing and rioting, in which there seemed to be a kind of emulation among the pirates then on that island, resembling rather devils than men, striving who should out-do one another in new invented oaths and execrations... then they all got aboard about Christmas, and sailed for the bay of Honduras, stopping at the Grand Caimans for water (Johnson)".

From St. Croix, the *Happy Delivery* sailed to the bay islands off of
Guatemala, where, while careening her, Indians surprised the crew
and burned the ship. Lowther and crew transferred what they could
save to a captured sloop they renamed the *Revenge*. They then sailed
for the island of La Blanquilla, off of Venezuela, where Captain
Walter Moore and the HMS *Eagle* found them. Caught by surprise,
the *Eagle's* men were boarding when Lowther and twelve of his men
–including two teenaged boys and a small boy-- climbed out a cabin
window in the stern and tried swimming to shore. The marines
opened fire. Only four –Lowther, the boys, and one other adult,
made it ashore alive. The marines landed and searched for them.
The captain's log says that 'Lowther's' body was identified, that he
had shot himself rather than be captured and hung. The <u>London
Post-Boy</u> (May 2, 1724), however, based on letters from a reporter in
St. Kitts, says that he escaped into the jungle with some of his crew.

The log entry seems to have come from the captured boys'
testimony, which could have been fabricated to protect their captain.
By being captured, the boys may have saved Lowther's life; as boys,
they were not themselves in danger of being hung (Rediker). The
body was perhaps a swimmer who was fatally wounded.

Edward "Ned" Low

Merry Christmas!

When his wife died in childbirth, a heartbroken Ned Low deserted his infant daughter and went to sea as a rigger on a sloop that sailed to Honduras for timber. The captain made himself hated by his crew on the voyage, and once ashore in Honduras, the captain refused to allow the men to eat until all of the logs were loaded. Furious, Low shot at him, missed and killed another. Low and twelve men then took the ship's boat and sailed off. Taking to sea in a small open boat took guts, but it paid off. They met pirate captain Lowther and joined the *Happy Delivery* in May of 1722. This union lasted until the pirates took a brigantine, the *Fortune*. Lowther gave her to Low and 44 men, who took off cruising alone.

Ned Low flew different flags from the usual skull and bones: a red skeleton on a black field from the mainmast and a yellow trumpet player on a green field from the mizzen. Ships that saw these flags and heard Ned blaring his trumpet knew they had better surrender quickly.

Low began his career refusing to harm married men or any women, setting them free with money, but he also had to cultivate a murderous reputation to encourage a quick and bloodless surrender. Tales often involved a bluff, which sometimes really turned into torture: for example, slow match would be put between a captain's fingers and lit, to encourage him to tell where he hid the money. Low also asked the prisoners if their captain was a fair man or a tyrant? Low tortured tyrannical captains, sending a clear message: treat your men fairly, or you may be next.

Plundering in the Leeward Islands, the *Fortune* ran into the edge of a hurricane. She survived, pumps working hard, to "A small island of the Caribbees, where they refitted their vessels; they got provisions from the natives, in exchange for goods of their own (Johnson)." Low and his men left a schooner in the harbor and went for a short cruise, after which they returned for the prize.

St. Croix was the pirate base serving the Leeward Islands. It wasn't just provisioning they needed, but spars and hardware. Retired pirates in Salt River stripped prizes left in the harbor and sold parts to pirates in need. On leaving St. Croix, Low and his men sailed north and captured a sloop which Low gave to his quartermaster and good friend Charles Harris. HMS *Greyhound* caught the pirates off of Long Island, and after a ferocious battle, captured the sloop. Harris and crew soon met the hangman at Execution Dock in London.

Low began drinking more and lost touch with his humanity. Witnesses told harrowing tales, which suggested that he became one of the most murderous pirates in history. As their consumption of rum grew out of control even for pirates, Low and his men tortured captives horribly, taking great pleasure in it, according to Edward Leslie. Low's men captured many vessels and took a good haul. Low joined Lowther again, then Low transferred his trumpet and flags to a prize, the *Merry Christmas* of 34 guns, giving quartermaster Spriggs the *Fortune*.

Low sailed back to the Caribbean but soon disappeared from history. According to 'Johnson,' no one ever saw the *Merry Christmas* again after the hurricane season of 1723.

Many have debated the end of Captain Ned Low. Some say the *Merry Christmas* and all hands perished in a hurricane near the Virgin Islands. Others say they survived it, limped into St. Croix, and retired there. Another account says that Low sailed to Brazil and retired there. "Johnson" says that Low's crew deposed him and set him adrift and that he was 'rescued' by a French ship which took him to Martinique, where he was identified and hanged. Massachusetts claims to have hanged and gibbeted Ned Low at Nick's Mate Island on July 12, 1726 (Boston News-Letter, same day).

This holiday season, if you hear a trumpet blowing in the 'Christmas Winds,' trim your sails and make a run for it, but suck up to your crew by passing out coquito, just in case. It may be the Caribbean's version of the Flying Dutchman, the *Merry Christmas*.

William Moody

Identity Crises

Governor William Hamilton of Barbados wrote, *"Captain John Brown, of the ship* John and Thomas, *of Road Town, Antigua, was taken off of Carolina Bay by a pirate ship of 36 guns and 130 men, white and black, called the* Rising Sun, *Captain William Moody. They came to St. Thomas at the end of November (1718), where they stayed two or three days, and took three more vessels, from Martinique. They held the vessels and their crew hostage, demanding a ransom of the Governor of St. Thomas in beef, flour, and wine. The pirates then sailed to St. Croix for water, taking three or four more prizes along the way"* (CSP 1717-18, p 410-11, #797).

"The man of war that is on this station is not capable of doing any service to that vermin, for I have now lately received an account of three pirate vessels, that are cruising amongst those (Virgin) islands, to wit a ship of 24 guns, commanded by one William Moody, a brigantine of eight guns, commanded by Captain Frowd, and a sloop of six or eight guns. They have taken, stranded, and burnt several vessels, between this island and Santa Cruix. They were several days anchored off the harbor of Charlotte Amalie, from whence it was said they secured provisions, and it must be so, for that is a nest that harbors all villains, and vagabonds" (CSP 1717-18, p 409, #797).

More entries in the <u>Calendar of State Papers</u> indicate that a Captain Charles Moody and a Captain Thomas Moody were among pirates known to have been operating in the Caribbean at this time. Either Captain Moody had a lot of first names, or Moody was a popular name for a pirate captain. Captain 'Charles' Moody took the pardon along with Hornigold and Jennings at Nassau, from Governor Woodes Rogers, and no pirate Captain Moody was mentioned in dispatches again.

Richard Worley

"You are, without a doubt, the *worst* pirate I have ever heard of."

Young Richard Worley and his eight buddies wanted to be pirates. They bought a small sailboat, packed groceries and pistols, and sailed out of New York harbor without telling their parents good-bye. That morning, they captured a small coastal craft loaded with kitchen utensils.

Two family-owned sloops carrying household merchandise stopped to see if Worley's warriors needed help, and the brave pirates took them, too. One was large enough to sail offshore, so they let their victims take the small vessels. With a compass and a chart, they left Ellis Island behind and sailed for the Bahamas.

Reaching the islands, the warriors took a brigantine and a half-rotten sloop. They kept food and water and added more men to their team, letting the brigantine go and sinking the sloop. Worley's now twenty-five-man crew drew up pirate articles and adopted the flag below. They vowed to fight to the death --no surrender. Arrrrrrr, again!

Our heroes sailed down to the Caribbean but found ships to be better armed, and not so charitable. The warriors spent what little they had in bars and decided after only a month that there were easier pickings off the coast of Carolina.

Worley's crew of desperadoes, flying the British ensign, hoisted tattered sails and called for help from all craft that happened by. With this ruse, they took several small coasting vessels and made such a nuisance of themselves that the Governor of South Carolina, Robert Johnson, put together a posse to go after them.

Flying the British ensign outside of Charleston harbor, Worley chased and boarded an unarmed merchant vessel loaded with twenty-five male and thirty female convicts Johnson had sold to the Governor of the Bahamas. The prisoners signed the pirate articles, swelling Worley's crew of warriors to eighty.

Only two hours later, a small fleet of ships sailed out of Charleston harbor. The approaching vessels raised the black flag, hailing Worley's crew as brothers. Worley's men struck their British flag and hoisted their own black one proudly, welcoming their new friends. Below decks, Charleston's militia crouched silently, waiting for their chance.

As the fleet approached, fake black flags were replaced by the British ensign. Cannons appeared and blasted Worley's ship. Worley's warriors ran below decks, leaving just their captain and one other to fight, and Militia killed the two pirates quickly.

Though they never had a chance to participate in taking a prize and did not fight, the male convicts had signed the articles, and so were quickly hung. It was against Carolina law to hang a female, so Governor Johnson sent the thirty female convicts to the Bahamas in chains, with orders that they not be fed. They starved to death on the voyage as planned, and fed the fish.
(Johnson).

Emanuel Wynne

"... but you *have* heard of me..."

Emanuel Wynne began his career operating off of Charleston, South Carolina, before moving his operations to the Caribbean and the Lesser Antilles. "Johnson" speaks of his pirating in the vicinity of the Virgin Islands, but with no elaboration on captures or activity. He is often considered the first pirate to fly the Jolly Roger. His design incorporated an hourglass beneath the bones to represent that time was running out. Not much is known about Wynne, except his flag, which was described by Captain John Cranby of the HMS *Poole*, after Wynne escaped his grasp (Johnson).

Owen Lloyd
"Captain Flint"

From Lapouge:

"One of the most celebrated historical accounts of piracy involved Owen Lloyd, who was part of the crew on a Spanish treasure galleon named Nuestra Señora de Guadalupe. In 1750, thirty years after the "Golden Age of Pirates", the ship was forced to seek shelter from a storm on the North Carolina coast when, at the instigation of the first mate, the crew mutinied and escaped with the galleon's valuable cargo. Part of the cargo was loaded into two bilanders, one of which was commanded by Owen Lloyd. Lloyd and his associates then proceeded to St. Croix, where they off loaded part of their plunder."

When the hurricane damaged *Nuestra Senora de Guadalupe* was forced to seek shelter on the North Carolina coast in 1750, Captain Juan Manuel Bonilla enlisted the aid of two Englishmen, Owen Lloyd and his brother John, to carry the cargo to the West Indies. Lloyd knew what to do—he persuaded the crew to turn pirate. They came straight to St. Croix, where they sold the silks, porcelain, and spices to the Danish West India and Guinea Company in Christiansted. Lloyd then sailed to Norman Island, put the chests – loaded with 250,000 pieces of eight- in the caves on the southwest coast just outside the Bight, and sailed to St. Eustatius, where the Dutch apprehended him.

Sailors drink, and sailors talk. Word got out, and the good citizens of Tortola, led by their "President", sailed over and looted the treasure. More sailors drank, and more sailors talked. The Lt.

Governor of the Leeward Islands, Gilbert Flemming, sent a warship. Flemming didn't know if the rumors were true or not, so he wrote a letter to Chalwill pretending to know, and offering him one-third of the treasure to keep if he fessed up (or else). Chalwill posted the letter publicly, and the good citizens of Tortola collected and sent "2/3" (at least as far as Flemming knew) to Antigua.

Many see this as the inspiration for Treasure Island. At any rate, as late as 1750, two years after the Crown had taken control of St. Croix from the Danish West India Company, the Company on St. Croix was still fencing stolen merchandise for pirates. Later the same year, and possibly because of the notoriety of this incident, the Danish government had had enough. A frigate was sent to clean out Salt River and, according to legend, the last known pirate ship operating out of St. Croix was flushed out. She made it out of the harbor, but could not get away, and was destroyed somewhere off the North shore (see below). While the Danes would help undermine the British Navigation Acts, they would no longer be business partners with pirates. Wealth now poured into Danish royal coffers from taxes on sugar, made profitable on the backs of slave labor. Ironically, the 'civilized' world considered pirates to be verminous outlaws, but allowed slavery, destroying the lives of millions.

Have Caribbean pirates vanished in the fog of history? Sail to Saint Croix and find out.

End of the Line

Not surprisingly, once piracy was suppressed, the DWIGC ceased to show a profit. From 1721 to 1733, the Danish West India Company paid no dividends at all (Rigarkivet). The sham was up; the company was not making profits from agriculture on St. Thomas and St. John, but from trade, and that trade was dependent on a supply of underpriced merchandise. The directors saw the only possibility to save the company was to purchase St. Croix, an island known to have many acres of good soil, and leap into the sugar industry along with the British and French who were doing so well with it.

The DWIGC purchased St. Croix from the French West India Company in 1733, though the first attempt to colonize the island did not happen until 1735. Too slow to start up, it was too little, too late for the company. The DWIGC went bankrupt in 1755; it could not survive without the profit from selling pirated cargoes of merchandise, and the government of Denmark took over management of St. Croix. A few years later the corporation was reorganized as a slave and molasses company and re-chartered. Over the next century, the island would become one of the most profitable of all the sugar islands. Through the draining of wetlands for agricultural purposes, and a growing appreciation for the use of the cinchona bark, malaria lost its stranglehold on St. Croix. Deaths from the disease quickly went down to 10 percent of the population and continued to drop from there over the next century.

When King George I declared sailors who 'fished the wrecks' to be pirates, he created "The Golden Age of Piracy", which reached its high-water mark in 1718. By his high-handed, arrogant decree ("Off with their Heads!") he put them "At War Against the World."

European navies were stretched too thin to be able to challenge them, and with the social conditions of the time, piracy quickly spiraled out of control.

The sailors who went to war against their world changed it. By asking crew about their captain's behavior, and punishing captains that had been cruel, merchant skippers all over the world received notice that they were not above the law.

To rein in piracy, George I was forced to introduce measures that eased the lives of his citizens. The Board of Trade convinced the King to exempt merchant sailors in the Caribbean from impressment by the Royal Navy.

Laws were passed so that agents for Caribbean plantations could no longer purchase indentures of men and boys unless they had papers proving a court conviction or a legal document proving self-indenture in exchange for transportation to the colonies.

Lloyd's of London was bankrupt, and, with it, the retirement plans of many in Parliament. The odds that ships and cargoes would reach their destinations had to be improved. Immediately.

Jennings and Hornigold had written letters to friends in London explaining that the pirates longed to return home, and if given a chance, would give up piracy --if allowed to keep their plunder. Woodes Rogers managed to convince King George I to do exactly that. The first draft was rejected in Nassau; it offered pardon in exchange for surrendering all ships and loot the pirates had seized. The second allowed them to keep everything they had taken. That had to gall the merchant houses of England, but the king, in desperation, went for it (CSP, May 31, 1717, #3596). The King offered a pardon, giving time for those at sea to make port, hear of it, and make their way to Woodes Rogers in Nassau (or to any Colonial Royal Governor) to accept it. The pardon was signed on September 5, 1717, and expired on January 5, 1718. The original Proclamation can be read in appendix [H], below

Rogers was sent with this carrot and a stick –the offer of pardon and a powerful naval force-- to Nassau. He came close to failure. A superior Spanish fleet threatened to invade the Bahamas, and Charles Lane and his ship *Lark* promised to invade Nassau and execute Rogers. The British frigates sent with Rodgers deserted him to sell merchandise to Spanish settlements and then sailed to New York. The captains were more interested in using their ships for private profit than in protecting Rogers and the Bahamas (CSP 1716). The Bahamas were spared when the large Spanish invasion force headed for Nassau was diverted at the last minute to stop an English invasion of Florida (once again, the fledgling British settlement at what is now Jacksonville was wiped off the map).

Before Captains Hornigold and Jennings signed the pardon, they called a grand meeting of all pirates at Nassau. If Pirates could come together, they could beat Rogers' force, and establish a 'pirate republic' in the Bahamas. A grand vision, but alas, they could not. Most of the Flying Gang met in Nassau in January of 1718. The pirates could agree on nothing. Men used to total freedom could not accept the rule of law or civil responsibility. Hornigold and Jennings gave up the idea of a Pirate Republic, and when Rogers arrived, he was unopposed. Hornigold and Jennings took the pardon.

Like the majority of pirates, the young men from Marblehead who sailed with Jennings made their way home, either quietly or after accepting the pardon. They used their share of the loot to build cod schooners, and their bones are mingled with the sand of Cape Cod, thrown ashore in various nor'easters and post-tropical cyclones. Their children captained infamous privateers in the American Revolution. Philip LeCraw was captured with his brig *Raven* in a joint operation with the young United States Navy and spent the rest of the war on a prison hulk in New York harbor. William LeCraw had the schooner *Necessity* (according to the Boston Newsletter, "the fastest ship on the Atlantic seaboard), then the brig *Black Snake*, and later the schooner *Morning Star*. When the *Black Snake* was cornered by a British frigate in Drakes Passage, Virgin Islands, LeCraw got his crew into the boats and cut them free. They rowed to different small Islands. He sailed the ship by himself down the passage, plowed her into the east end of St. John (Privateers Bay), and ran off into the rocks, where British marines captured him. He was sent to the Old Mill Prison in England, from which he escaped with Captain Joshua Barney of the U. S. Navy (Admiralty records). They made their way to France on a fishing vessel to Canada, and home to new ships, Joshua to a naval vessel and LeCraw to the *Morning Star*. Joseph Pitman had the schooner *Centipede*, and later the V*iper*. John Conway captained the brig *Terrible*. Peter Martin captained the schooner *Civil Usage*, and William Ross the brigantine *Active*. Nathan Goodale and James Laskey, too old to fight, financed a dozen privateers between them. Young George Girdler never got the chance, being pressed aboard an English ship of the line and serving in the battle of Ushant against the French.

Out of some 4500 pirates estimated to be operating in the Caribbean at the height of the Golden Age of Piracy (British estimates, CSP 1716), only some four hundred took the official pardon, and some of those like Blackbeard and Howell Davis went back to pirating, but the high-water mark had passed. Slightly over four hundred met the gallows, and the rest just disappeared. The great captains had retired, died at sea, or died in battle, and the tide inexorably turned against the remaining pirates. English and French authorities put a plan to end piracy in place: anyone accused of doing business with, or even fraternizing with pirates, was hung quickly, and publicly. Sailors of ships that did not resist when attacked by pirates were thrown into prison (Boot, p. 88).

Profit from sugar was more than the DWIGC could make by dealing with pirates. Moreover, France was gradually rebuilding its navy, and adding more ships to police the Caribbean.

St. Croix's pirate operations were winding down, as well. On October 2, 1729, the armed transport *Le Portefaix* was ordered to look into Salt River in response to reports that pirates were operating out of the harbor. Lt. Jeremie de Maschin wrote that he found three pirate sloops in the anchorage. They pulled in close and ranged their guns against him when he approached. Outgunned, he chose discretion and sailed off (Highfield, St. Croix, p. 542-3).

The last pirate is surprised in Salt River. Making a run for it, the ship is 'destroyed'. Walk the decks one last time. ☠

The Last Pirate Ship in St. Croix

Crucian legend says the last pirate ship on St. Croix was flushed out of Salt River when the Danish King sent a frigate in 1750. That makes sense; the King of Denmark would have been embarrassed. He needed to respond to international outrage over Owen Lloyd's selling his plunder openly in Christiansted to the Danish West India and Guinea Company. The old custom was no longer acceptable; the Danes now owned St. Croix, and taxes were starting to come in from *'legitimate'* slave-run sugar plantations (stealing people's lives; different piracy, but piracy, nonetheless).

Running west down the north shore from Christiansted, the great square sails of the frigate and her longer waterline length would have enabled her to catch up to the pirates. The legend says that the pirate ship was destroyed. The Pirates could choose: be blown to kingdom come, drown, or surrender and hang at Gallows Bay. Sailing west along the coast from Salt River, there is a pretty stretch of beach, with jungle behind. What would *you* have done?

Heading west from Salt River, the reef is never far from shore. I started thinking about the place I would pick to run my ship aground. It would be the first beach west of Salt River, and I would turn a tight corner around the reef and go straight in. One Sunday soon after, I was at the probable spot looking around when I saw my friend Barry. He said, "Hey, Stan, you ever notice these pieces of wood?" Glancing down, I saw brief glimpses of wood in the sand, which seemed to have a pattern. Excited, I looked closer. They seemed to be deck beams, 18'-20' long, perpendicular to the beach, 2 1/2 feet apart, 5" to 6" wide. In some places under the sand, there is driftwood on top of the beams; you have to look under it.

Barry dug a little and picked up bronze spikes, which were obviously fasteners. Our friend EJ walked over, stubbed his toe on a bit of coral, picked it up, and it looked to my imagination like a swivel cannon, encrusted with coral and rocks (see photo, below).

Mr. David Brewer, the territorial archaeologist, identified it immediately as an iron breech-loading swivel cannon from the late 17th century. Snorkeling the area, I found another swivel cannon, the doubled-barreled windlass (broken into two large pieces), the pile of ballast stones, the stove, various bits of iron hardware, a small concretion of cannonballs, and a dozen or so wrapped bundles of pig iron. With deck beams at 18-20 feet and the ballast pile in 7' of water, the hull would have been 70 feet long and about 110 tons.

This vessel was deliberately run into the reef. After breaking the keel, the waves naturally turned the ship broadside on and washed her into the beach. The swivel cannons are at DPNR to awaiting restoration. The order from DPNR is that nothing else in the sea be touched until a professional team can come down and explore the site. The relics, Mr. Brewer pointed out, are stable electro-chemically. Disturbing them will start the full electrolytic process up again.

I have searched British colonial records, Lloyds of London, and the colonial records of France and Denmark. There is no wreck reported at this site. The Danish legend says the pirate ship was 'destroyed' off the North Shore. If I were the frigate captain, I could say that I had sunk the ship, or captured it, but if I said I 'destroyed' it, I would mean that there was no point in anyone worrying about finding it; in other words, after the ship went on the reef by the beach, he sent in the boats and looted it. This wreck on the north shore could be any ship, or it could well be the final resting place of the last pirate ship to sail from St. Croix. Lying here for years as she disintegrated into the beach, she was stripped of anything valuable, but the *legend* is our treasure today.

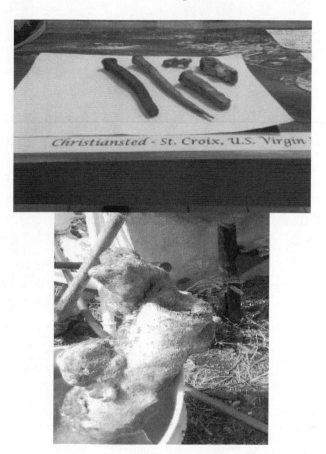

[14] Bronze ship fasteners, part of the windlass, and two swivel cannons from the other north shore wreck.

Don Roberto Cofresi
The Last Pirate of the Caribbean, *"El Mosquito"*

One hundred years after the end of the "Golden Age of Piracy", the "insurgent privateers" (Spanish: corsarios insurgentes) were private armed vessels recruited by revolutionary governments during the Spanish American wars of independence to destroy Spanish trade and capture Spanish merchant vessels. Pirates took advantage of the situation to sail without authorization under the new flags. Roberto Cofresi was one such pirate, but probably the most famous of these was Jean Laffite. He and his brother Pierre began as smugglers operating out of New Orleans, with Pierre running the office ashore. Jean then began capturing Spanish ships headed for Mexico. The Laffite brothers helped the United States win the Battle of New Orleans, and Jean again turned to taking Spanish ships while calling himself a privateer working for Mexican freedom, operating out of Galveston Bay. The American Navy ran him out of the area, and he sailed down to cruise off of Columbia. On February 4, 1823, Laffite was captain of the small pirate sloop *General Santander* (43 tons) under the new flag of Columbia when he attacked a schooner and a brigantine sailing together. The sun fell, and in the night the fight continued. When Laffite was mortally wounded, he handed command to his quartermaster, but he was also wounded and soon died. The bosun, Francisco Similien, took charge and fought on until 1:00 a.m. when, unable to continue the fight, *General Santander* sailed away (Gaceta de Columbia, April 20, 1823).

Other 'privateers' joined the operations against the Spanish, and from 1821 to 1829 dozens of privateers operating in the Gulf of Mexico and the Caribbean sailed under the flags of Mexico and Colombia.

When the governor of Puerto Rico invited wealthy nobles fleeing European revolutions to settle in Puerto Rico, they brought fabulous wealth, which they threw around, resulting in incredible inflation. Normal people could not afford a decent living. The economy of Puerto Rico collapsed in 1821, and many of the poor turned into highwaymen or pirates. Puerto Rican pirates often flew the flag of Columbia, to pretend to be legitimate privateers. The boldest and most successful of these, Don Roberto Cofresi, was extremely well connected politically through cousins on his mother's side. A real Don, Cofresi was the son of a noble of the Austrian Empire, Franz Joseph von Kupferschein, who fled to Puerto Rico after a duel, and María Germana Ramírez de Arellano, who was from a noble Spanish family. Born June 12, 1791, in Cabo Rojo, Puerto Rico, Cofresi was well educated, but the family fell on hard times. He became a highwayman first, then under family pressure became a legitimate sailor. The temptation was too much, and he combined his two skills to begin pirating.

Cofresi had an astonishing career, taking an estimated seventy ships of many nations and escaping from prison or captivity dozens of times. Cofresi's home territory was southwest Puerto Rico, but he operated between Santo Domingo and the Virgin Islands. When cruising out of Vieques and Culebra, he captured two ships off of Christiansted, St. Croix, was next seen off of Ponce, and then sent his quartermaster with a small sloop to rob a bank on St. Thomas in broad daylight. He went through a dozen ships; when trapped, he ran them ashore, and he and his men would run into the bush. It was never long before they would be back out again, either by capturing or just buying a new ship. In one exploit, he raided a shipyard where a gunboat was being built to pursue him and stole the largest cannon from the unfinished ship for his own. In another, he took on eight ships at a time in the Mona Passage, with only his one sloop. He was a Robin Hood figure in Mayaguez and Cabo Rojo. He sold his plunder cheaply in the markets, kind of an early, piratical version of "Big Lots". The people loved him; he was their Robin Hood, and a resort town near Puerto Plata in the Dominican Republic was even named for him. Tradition has it that Cofresi used the caves along the banks of the Rio Yuma in southeastern Santo Domingo to hide and bury his treasure. Today, relics purported to be from his treasure trove are on display in Cabo Yuma.

His last ship, the sloop *Anne*, was destroyed by an unlikely warship from St. Croix. Built in America around 1790 as a privateer for the false war between the United States and France, the *Vigilant* was a beautiful little sixty-five-foot schooner that had been carrying the mail between her home port of St. Croix and St. Thomas for years. With Cofresi as the last of the major 'insurgent privateers', a combined naval force consisting of five warships from the United States, two from France, two from Columbia, several from Puerto Rico, and one from Denmark was put together to destroy him. Four of these cornered him near Ponce in a shallow bay, but most could do nothing as their ships drew too much water. The shallow drafted *Vigilant* was sent in much as Maynard's *Ranger* had attacked Blackbeard, with no cannons but a large group of soldiers hiding below deck. Cofresi allowed her to come too close before realizing his mistake, at which time Cofresi's outnumbered men leaped overboard and swam into the bush as usual. This time though, after a long chase, they were caught and executed (Cardona-Bonet). The governor of Puerto Rico, embarrassed by the corruption of his island that had enabled Cofresi, claimed that one of their own Guardia Costas vessels had been the one to destroy the *Anne*, but log books of other ships in the squadron name *Vigilant*. Thus, ironically, St. Croix provided the means to end the career of the last pirate of the Caribbean.

Isolated power boats operating out of Venezuela will occasionally capture elderly couples cruising on their sailboats, but it is not quite the same.

Above: [15] contemporary pencil drawing of the battle between the *Vigilant* and the *Anne*. This is more than a little romantic; first, the battle occurred in sheltered Guayama Bay. Next, the *Vigilant* was only a tiny schooner, not a ship, and the little *Anne* was just a sloop. Embarrassed before Spain and the world by the entire episode, in which many public officials enabled or outright supported Cofresi, the Puerto Rican governor reported that one of his guardia costa vessels had won the day, and did not even mention the little *Vigilant*. In the Virgin Islands, however, we remember the truth. Middle: [16] the people of Puerto Rico still revere Cofresi (statue in Cabo Rojo bay). Below: [17] *Vigilant*, launched in the American colonies around the year 1798 as a privateer for operating against the French, which was still serving the Virgin Islands when she drove ashore during a hurricane in September 1928.

Pirate Sunset
Once and forever free

British colonial governors estimated the number of pirates active in the Caribbean during different periods. Their estimates for the years 1715-26 range from 2500 to 4000 (CSP, 1726). They may have exaggerated to encourage reinforcements; none gave any basis for their estimates. A little more than 400 pirates took the king's pardon, and a little over four hundred hanged. That would suggest that some 1700 to 3200 pirates simply disappeared back into normal life. Most of the pirates used aliases in front of captives that were to be released. Stede Bonnet claimed to be "Mr. Edwards"; no one knows Blackbeard's real name to this day; John Roberts was born "Bartholomew"; etc. Former pirates could have taken berths on any merchant ship desperate to fill positions lost to malaria. We know some moved ashore. There were no passports; people were emigrating from Europe to the Americas every day, and sailors could blend in easily. Wherever the sailors originated from, their new neighbors probably thought they were just merchant sailors' home from the sea. In only a few cases were pirates recognized by former victims, and hung.

Some European pirates tried to go back home. Of these, there were those who went ashore, flashed gold, and talked too much, like Walter Kennedy. They met the noose quickly. Smart pirates would have quietly blended in. There are rumors of former pirates buying Inns or taverns in England, and of French pirates returning to privateering or smuggling, sailing out of Dunkirk or the Channel Islands. Notorious pirate Christopher Condent became a wealthy merchant in Brittany. Dutch pirates returned to trading.

Madagascar provided a whimsical, fantasy retirement home for pirates. It was their way station for staging raids on ships loaded with jewels and riches sailing the Indian Ocean, and for some, a safe retirement far from Execution Dock in London. Henry Avery and his crew sailed the Indian Ocean and took the Great Moguls' ship of jewels, and every pirate dreamed of doing the same. Rumors of the rich life they led on Madagascar were, however, untrue. The pirates who settled there were constantly pulled into tribal wars and lived in muddy squaller. They took many wives and fathered a race called 'Zana-mulata,' a mix of Indonesian, African, and Caucasian heritage which still claims pirate lineage. Originally joining a group of his own and some Dutch pirates who retired on the island of Reunion, La Bouse moved to a small island just off the coast of Madagascar, Isle Saint Marie, where he worked as a harbor pilot until being captured. Captain Thomas Tew's quartermaster and 23 of his crew retired on Madagascar, the rest returning home to New York or settling on the island of Bermuda. As for Henry Avery, most historians believe that he became homesick and returned to England, dying on the streets without a penny to his name.

Some of Thomas Tew's men were from New York, as were the crews of Captains William Want and Thomas Wake. Many of them ended up blending back into their hometown. Newport and Providence, Rhode Island, were common ports for pirate recruitment, and Boston was home to pirate Captain Daniel Plowman, who sailed with Quartermasters John Holding and John Quelch, and Captain George Wall. Holding made it home to settle back down, and most of the rest of the crew did, as well.

A few of Blackbeard's men managed to get themselves hung by splashing gold everywhere and bragging drunkenly in taverns, but pirates with sense would have had no real problem; the 150 mostly white pirates he stranded probably became working citizens of North Carolina. Some of the African in his crew, most of whom he had retained after marooning the 150 on the sandbar, were sold by the State of North Carolina, and their descendants are probably still in the area. Others settled in the marshes of eastern Carolina, and lived free.

In the American South, unless you were a certified guild master who the local officials knew well, it was illegal to be black and free. There is no way former free men and women were subjecting themselves to this. Used to a life as an outlaw and not afraid to fight, black pirates would have escaped as quickly as possible. Others were never sold but came ashore to retire quietly, out of sight. On the coasts of South Carolina and Georgia, communities of free black people existed in the swamps from the early years of the 18th century. They grew crops, fished, and raided plantations for powder, shot, guns, pots, plows, etc. The governors wrote each other often and spoke with wonder about the military tactics the raiders often used. Militia occasionally cleaned out these 'maroon' camps, but the Maroons would melt into the bush and build another. Maroon societies were never eradicated.

Many pirates in the islands went under the radar to more 'legitimate' pursuits, such as smuggling. The British and French Navigation acts made it illegal for ships from America to carry merchandise to or from the colonies. American ship owners and sailors could not obey, so smuggling was the natural way to go, even though Britain and France termed it 'piracy'. Inter-island schooners and sloops captained and crewed by West Indians of African lineage also sailed the islands carrying merchandise for centuries, rarely troubling themselves with Customs offices.

Sailors see pirates still:

Smuggling continues. I've seen small boats carrying boxes of merchandise like insect repellant and sunscreen between islands of different nations. There are more sinister operations too, of course. I was ashore on St. Martin when a rusty freighter anchored offshore at dawn and started sending large rubber inflatables filled with Chinese immigrants into a deserted beach. I've sailed many times in Drake's Passage at night as large 'cigarette boats' with no lights blast by in the wee hours of the morning; any sailor in the islands can tell you of that. Three years ago, a local DPNR chief was caught using government boats to run cocaine from St. Martin to the Virgin Islands. I had sailed to Buck Island for the night some years back when the sound of powerful outboards awoke me at about 3:00 a.m. The cigarrette boat anchored right beside me. A few minutes later a trawler showed up, rafted up with it, and cargo was transferred. I stayed down below with my flare gun pointed at the companionway in case anyone decided that they did not like witnesses, but they both just left.

The DEA tries harder sometimes, and not as hard at others, to stop this traffic. Once while sailing to St. Martin from St. Croix I looked up and saw that Orion's belt had four stars in it. Four. I thought I had gone crazy until I noticed that one was just a little too blue. As dawn broke, I saw a rusty freighter with a giant winch on deck pulling the balloon down. When I sailed into Marigot a couple of hours later, the ship was in the harbor. I assume the balloon had a night vision camera and radar.

As for descendants of pirates who did not go into smuggling, some apparently found that government jobs provide interesting opportunities. U. S. Government money disappears like water on sand in the VI.

IV. EPILOGUE:

Sugar

Jean Frédéric Phélypeaux, the *Compte de Maurepas* (representing the French foreign office), Louis Robert Hypolite de Brehan, the *Compte de Plelo*-- French Ambassador to Denmark and brother-in-law to Maurepas--and Frederich Holmsted, representing the Danish West India and Gunea Company negotiated the sale of Sainte Croix to Denmark to the DWIGC, which became final in 1733.

In 1734, the DWIGC sent the ship *Unity*, Captain Moth, to scout St. Croix. Moth visited two villages, Bassin and Salt River, and travelled between them. According to Moravian Missionary Oldendorp, who arrived on September 11, 1734, Governor Moth told him that on arrival he found the island largelly gone back to bush. Moth said he found 150 white men capable of bearing arms (many heads of households) around Salt River, most of whom spoke English (retired pirates) and 200-230 slaves (Moth and Oldendorp would have assummed that all people of color were, of course, slaves) between Salt River and Bassin, plus a small camp of 120 English loggers harvesting lignum vitae --the world's hardest wood, and the only wood that sinks in water-- at Limetree Bay (Haring, p. 66). Women, children, and old people were not in the count.

Were there only 500 people on Saint Croix when the Danes arrived? I do not believe so. When Louis XIV ordered the island abandoned in 1695, property deeds for Sainte Croix were surrendered and deeds to land in San Domingue issued in return, so that the island had no legal property owners when the Danes arrived. The free mulatto children who had been led to believe that they were legal heirs to the estates were cut out. French white people and their 'property' relocated to San Domingue, but mulattoes had nowhere to go. Historians ignored them entirely and, at first, so did Moth.

When Captain Moth became "Governor Moth" of the Danish Island of Saint Croix, he staged a ceremony and gave a speech. The French warship *Saint Antoine* arrived with the royal notary Pierre Borde, and the official transfer ceremony took place at 9:00 a.m. on January 8, 1735. The ceremony was all translated into French, as that is what most people on the island spoke, as well as the official delegation from Martinique, though Governor Moth declared in his speech that, "There are no Frenchmen on the island, only Danes." He may have meant, "from this moment, only Danes." Borde's report of the ceremony stated that "approximately 2000 French-speaking people attended the ceremony."

Dr. Arnold Highfield wrote that 175 plantations were in operation during the French period. French census records showed only the names of the estate owners within each of the districts, not the names of indentures, mulattoes, craftsmen, merchants, or sailors, much less women and children. French tax accountant Diverger estimated 6000 souls were on the island in 1692. History says that the DWIGC had the 'uninhabited' island surveyed, divided it up into 250 estate plots, and sold them. This is not the real story. How do I dare say this? The first map from the Danish period, the 'Beck Map,' shows @fifty estates in the same location and with the same names written on them as appear in French census records from 1680-95. French names. In the exact same places (see appendix, Sang des Francaise). Moth was instructed by the DEIGC to get the island profitable as soon as possible. To do that, he needed estates working and paying taxes. What better way to do that than to work with the people already farming them? I am convinced he allowed mulatto families to stay where they were and buy the estates on time. That is why so many estates on Saint Croix carry French names to this day (no, Mon Bijou is *not* a Danish name), estates like:

Anguilla, Belvedere (Rattan), Belvedere (Northshore), Tuites (Corn Hill), Bellevue, Bonne Esperance, LaGrainge, La Grange, La Retriate (Boetzburg), Fountain, Catherine's Hope, Catherine's Rest, Cane Bay, Clairemont, Concordia, Contentment, Granard, Grange, Grove, Hermitage, Jealousy, La Grande Princess, La Reine, La Valee, La Pres Valois, La Princess, Cane Garden Bay, Libannon Hill, Jerusalem, Little LaGrange, Little Princess, Bethlehem, Mon Bijou, Moirs, Mint, Mamme Tres, Montpellier, Mount Pleasant, Parara, Parasol, Petronella, Pleasant Prospect, Pleasant Valee, Mount Misery, Plessens, Moors, Rust Op Twist, Menagerie, Sorgenfri, Sainte Johns, Sainte Peters, Sainte Georges, Tiparera, Die Lifede, Maison de Poincy (Beeston Hill), Pointe de Sable (Sandy Point), Judith's Fancy, and River Salee (Salt River).

Over twenty-eight years of teaching at St. Croix Central High School, I have entered many names in my roll books that also appear in old French census records, names like Richards, Vialet, Martin, Gautier, Renard, Bastien, Girard (mixed with Salomon), Gilbert, Duval, Griffin, DuBois, Boucher, Bernier, Bernard, Christopher, Cornelius, Daniels, Danielson, Daniel, Garret, Roger, Durand, Rousseau, Cullen, Salomon, Legrand, La Grande, Vigne, Gaignet, Baron, Monfort, Langlois, Claude, Lenoux, Renard, LaFontaine, Thierry, Massicotte, Andrew, Bernard, Estienne, Etienne, La Croix, Lefebure, La Roux, Royer, Maturin, Laurent, Duval, La Clerq, Roziere, Picard, Salomon, and Neuville. Some of these families may have relocated from other islands after the French period, and it may be a coincidence that they have reappeared on Saint Croix, but families such as Girard and Richards can tell you that they never left.

317

Another piece of evidence: Most Danes were Lutheran, and most of the estate owners in the Danish period were English and therefore Anglican, but the Catholic Churches had the largest congregations on St. Croix, even before corporations began hiring poor Irishmen to come manage their estates.

The Danes

Hell On Earth

Planters in Barbados taught the world that sugar was the way to a fortune. All you needed was an island with some relatively flat land, some rain, some young cane shoots, and a lot of labor. Free labor. Free to the ones holding the whips, that is. In exchange for a pile of glass beads and a few muskets given to African war lords, European slavers filled their ships with people, chained them in the hold like sardines, and sailed for the Caribbean.

The horrors of the middle passsage are recorded elsewhere. So are accounts of what it was like in the blistering hot cane fields, working for no money while enjoying the legal rights of a dog. It is hard to imagine now that people could have enslaved other human beings, yet the very institutions that made it possible are still with us. People who owned shares of stock in candy and rum corporations probably knew little about how the company operated. Teachers, policemen, doctors, seamstresses, they bought shares in a company to provide for their retirement. Those Corporations were run by

CEO's who knew that the opposition was producing a less expensive alternative. How could that be? Because they were paying very little for labor. The choice was simple: buy estates and produce sugar the same way, or go bankrupt. European corporations and limited partnerships hired plantation managers to purchase slaves and manage them. Typically, managers were poor Irishmen with no prospects for employment at home. By taking the job as a manager, they hoped to make enough money in a few years to go back home and buy a small farm. O'Reilly, O'Neil, O'Neal, Bough, McGregor… many of them settled down with African ladies instead and never made it back home.

Having your life stolen is worse than anything imaginable, but for what it is worth, being a manager was not a job anyone would want for long, either. The Whim Great House Museum on St. Croix is an example of an eighteenth-century plantation house. It is surrounded by a moat that at night was once the realm of big dogs — the only bridge across leads to a massive three-inch-thick hardwood door. Windows are wider on the outside but smaller in, to allow for a rifleman to cover a larger field of fire while limiting space for projectiles to come in. Most moats were filled in long ago, but many houses in Frederiksted still have bookcases with secret handles to swing open, revealing a tunnel down to a small, secret basement room. The people running the plantations were afraid to go to sleep at night and lived in constant fear of rebellion.

The only ones enjoying themselves were shareholders who, dividends in hand, never met the beast they were responsible for. In case the story got out, a narrative was indoctrinated into white children that people with dark skin needed 'to be looked after'--"The White Man's Burden." This narrative of superiority crushed self-esteem among many people of color; this fuels social and economic inequality to this day. Without self-esteem it is very hard to realize your potential.

Phillip Gardelin, Governor of the Danish West Indies, insisted that Fort Christiansvaarn be built on the hill to the east of town. His vision was to prevent an invasion force from landing troops in Martel Bay while also covering the Christiansted harbor entrance. The European people on the island insisted that the fort be built in town instead, so they would have somewhere to run in case of insurrection. They petitioned the King, and Gardelin was recalled. Both arguments later proved to be valid. During the Napoleonic Wars, the British fleet merely anchored off of Martel Bay, sent in marines, took a mortar up to the hill, looked down on the fort, and waved. The fort surrendered without a shot. On the other hand, there were several times when insurrections were actual, and people rushed to the fort to stay alive.

The Danish government understood the basic human need for hope. Market squares were built, and laws allowed slaves to sell products they had made or grown in their allotted garden space or to perform skilled work for hire on Sundays. If a slave could set aside enough to match his purchase price, he could buy his freedom. "Free Gut" was a village on the outer edge of each town where they could build a cottage.

SMUGGLER'S PARADISE

On Saint Croix, hundreds of retired pirates met the Danes when they arrived in 1733. The Danes immediately plunged into the business of molasses. Pirates turned to smuggling.

Planters were supposed to send their molasses to either the Christiansted warehouse or the Frederiksted warehouse, both of which were far too small to hold even a fraction of what was produced on the island. Danish customs officers weighed the molasses. As ships arrived, the first hogsheads brought in sold first. If a planter brought his late, he might not be able to sell it before it spoiled, and if it did sell, he paid heavy taxes on it. On an island with as many bays and inlets as St. Croix, planters had a simple answer. Ships, mostly American, anchored offshore at night. In New England at the time, longboats were designed to hold one hogshead of molasses each. Planters sent enough to the warehouses to satisfy Danish authorities but mostly sold to smugglers. Weather can change quickly, and ships anchored close to lee shores sometimes have to move fast. Anchors litter the reefs of St. Croix. For each anchor cut loose in a hurry, many more were safely retrieved. The Smithsonian Institution sent a boat with a magnetometer around the coast of St. Croix in 2016 which found 114 wrecks, not counting any in harbors. For each ship that wrecked, far more sailed away safely.

In 1780, customs records from St. Eustatius show that the island exported more than one million hogsheads of molasses (Museum of St. Eustatius in Oranjestad). *One Million.* Oddly, official agricultural reports in the same museum for the same year show the island produced barely a thousand hogsheads. Where did that molasses *come from?* It represented a *huge* amount of money in sales and taxes. It must have come from an island producing a tremendous volume that had no customs vessels patrolling its coast. Dominican Father Raynal visited St. Croix in the 1780s and did the math. He wrote that Denmark charged astronomical per-capita and land taxes, many times that of English and French islands at the time; when he added the official excise taxes, the math showed him no plantation on St. Croix could be solvent. Raynal also noted that, while the French and English navies patrolled their islands, there were no revenue cutters on St. Croix, and that the entire Danish naval presence in the Virgin Islands consisted of one Danish frigate that made only one brief visit per year, its arrival was not only punctual, but advertised in advance in the local newspaper. The only official local vessel was the tiny *Vigilant*, which was busily carrying mail between the islands every day, and did not bother with anything else. Smuggling was officially winked at, with only enough official threats to make sure at least *some* molasses made it to the customs houses.

English corporations and limited partnerships owned the majority of plantations on Saint Croix, and they had no patriotic desire to pay taxes to Denmark. Onsight managers had to show a profit to keep their jobs, and shareholders thousands of miles away did not care how. Denmark was pragmatic. High land and per-capita taxes saved Denmark the worry of customs enforcement.

Descendants of Pirates continued to fish, and some were smugglers well into the 20th century. Inter-island schooners and sloops captained and crewed by West Indians carried merchandise for centuries, rarely troubling themselves with Customs offices. During the 20th century, as merchandise traveled in ever larger motor-powered ships, their iconic island sloops and schooners escaped attention. Wine, cheese, Rum, machine parts, clothing, anything taxed represented a potential for a good profit. When Customs Agents were not present, they preferred to sail into Christiansted or Frederiksted, but if not, any beach would do. The smaller vessels could be pulled up on beaches like Cane Bay or the south shore, out of sight of Customs officials. During World War II, these same smugglers were heroes. Nazi U-Boats based in Martinique sunk any ships bringing supplies into or out of the Virgin Islands and Puerto Rico. Merchants quickly learned that U-Boats could hear ships motors. Sailboats traveled with impunity, so the old smugglers and their schooners became heroes, the lifeblood of the United States and British territories in the Caribbean. "Bomba" Allick, "No-No", and many others carried this trade through the war and on into the 1950s when the U. S. Coast guard finally put an end to it; they turned immediately to taking tourists to Buck Island for daytime excursions.

Smuggling still goes on. I've been anchored at Buck Island and had cigarette boats anchor next to me in the middle of the night. A boat inevitably comes from somewhere on St. Croix and collects contraband. Almost every night, cigarette boats zoom down Drake's passage with no lights on. Early one morning on St. Martin, I watched a rusty freighter ferry a few hundred Chinese people ashore. On a lighter note, less scary smugglers carry surprising things. A couple of years ago, while anchored at a deserted beach on a non-American island, a single-handing sailor arrived, anchored, and struggled to unload boxes in the surf. As a good Samaritan, I offered assistance, and he bought lunch afterward. Over lunch, I learned that I had helped unload a contraband cargo of Panama Jack sunscreen.

To customs officials, smugglers are pirates. Coming full circle, the seventeenth and early nineteenth centuries saw St. Eustatius become the smuggling and money laundering capital of the Caribbean. The descendants of the founders of St. Eustatius became more comfortable with piracy, and St. Croix, after all.

THE STRUGGLE FOR FREEDOM

. In St. Croix, the Danes had to make a deal with black pirates from the very beginning, respecting their freedom. Trouble arose when one of the free black sailors would fall in love with a lady who was considered 'property.' The two would then run off and join the maroon community on the northwest coast along with others who had run away. Danish attempts to eradicate this community were not successful.

Danish punishments for escape were harsh. The estate manager had a say in how severe the punishment would be. When John

Gottlieb's father escaped, his punishment was to be chained to the sugar mill. But punishment could be more severe: those caught escaping from slavery on Danish islands could be sentenced to have hands and feet cut off, one per incident if captured. In 1733 slaves at the Coral Bay plantation on St. John took over the island for over half a year. Free men recently sold and transported from Ghana temporarily won their freedom. France was in the process of selling St. Croix to the Danish West India and Guinea Company and did not want Denmark to get cold feet over their decision to get into the sugar business. Two hundred French soldiers were sent from Martinique to aid the Danes, and they retook the island when the freedom fighters ran out of bullets. Many of the last ones alive – men, women, and children-- leaped to their deaths from a cliff to avoid amputation or execution. Denmark went through with the purchase, and St. Croix plunged into the horror of Caribbean sugar for a century.

On Saint Croix the seeds of rebellion took root, as well. According to the *St. John's Historical Society* web page, John Gottlieb Bordeaux was born enslaved at Estate La Grange on March 19, 1820, to Maria Rosina. He was raised as a member of the Lutheran Church and worked in the fields as part of the 'big gang.' In 1841, his character was recorded as 'not too good. On April 12, 1842, he was arrested by order of Police Commissioner E. Didrichsen for 'theft and insolence.' At John's hearing, it came out that he took food to his father, who was chained to a sugar mill for trying to escape (George Tyson, "John Gottliff: The Man Behind Buddhoe," St. John Historical Society, June 7, 2006.). Being tied to the mill meant that his father was supposed to feed the cane into the rollers, a dangerous job that often led to crushed hands.

Ramsey, the manager, withheld food because John's father was not cooperating, and by feeding his father, John was ruining Ramsey's plan. John, known as 'Buddhoe,' (anyone who has lived on St. Croix will know this is exactly how 'Bordeaux' would be pronounced, and locals do not use first names) began to meet with Moses Roberts of Estate Sprat Hall and Martin 'Admiral' King of Estate Slob.

Crucians Blow the Conch Shell

18

Emancipation

On July 3, 1848, conch shells sounded all over St. Croix as eight thousand slaves trusted Buddhoe, Moses, and the Admiral, putting their lives on the line in a well-planned rebellion. Everyone had to act together; if one group rose first, they would be executed. Women brought sugar cane tops and torches into Frederiksted, ready to burn everything down. This time there would be no help for the Danes; other European countries had already outlawed slavery; this time, the Danes could expect no help. Danish Governor Peter von Scholten had no choice but to declare, "All unfree in the Danish West Indies are from today free." It is the only instance other than Haiti where slaves successfully rose and took their freedom.

Excitement, fear, and adrenaline raged after the declaration. Danish soldiers fired a cannon into a crowd at Bassin Triangle. In retaliation, rioters set fires in Christiansted. Buddhoe managed to quiet the rioters, at one point even using his own body to protect the life of Major Gyllich and helping the Danes restore order. But after things calmed down, Danish soldiers arrested Buddhoe and put him in Fort Christiansvaarn's dungeon. Outraged plantation owners tried to attack him, but a grateful Major Gyllich stayed in prison with Buddhoe to ensure his safety (Chas. Edwain Taylor, <u>Leaflets from the Danish West Indies</u>).

After six months, Buddhoe was exiled to Trinidad on the ship *Ornen*. Captain Irminger interrogated Buddhoe as to his accomplices, especially trying to get him to say that Governor von Scholten had plotted with the conspirators (Everyone knew that von Scholten's girlfriend, Anna Heegaard, was mulatto, and that he had a child with another mulatto woman on St. Thomas as well.). Buddhoe would not talk. Irminger left Buddhoe in Port of Spain, Trinidad, on January 8, 1849, with a warning never to return to Saint Croix.

Historian Deirdre Calley writes of a letter from Lewis Tappan Dated June 11, 1950. Tappan, a conductor on the Underground Railroad, wrote that John Gottlieb Bordeaux, a former leader of the revolt on Saint Croix, lived in New York City in 1850 and was assisted by a man who, as commander of the colored militia, had opposed him during the revolt. According to Ms. Calley, Buddhoe got a job as a shipping clerk and ran a boarding house in New York's Fifth Ward, where, according to the 1855 New York State census, John and his wife Hellena Bordeaux lived with a niece and two boarders at 9 Worth Street. The census also states that John was born in 1820 in the Caribbean and entered the United States in 1850. It's possible that Tappan owned the boarding house and that Buddhoe was helping house fugitives.

New York at this time was a dangerous place for black people. With the slave trade abolished, southern planters offered good prices for new laborers. 'Slave catchers' worked day and night, capturing free people and selling them to agents who were waiting to whisk them on board a ship headed south. Buddhoe had personal problems, as well. Calley reports that in 1856 Helena had an affair with one of their borders, John Dawson, and moved into his room. Buddhoe was arrested for assaulting Dawson but was soon released and disappeared from New York. Historian William Cissel says that Buddhoe moved back to the Caribbean, to Grenada.

Free, but Not Free

Denmark passed laws to keep the former slaves in bondage on the sugar plantations under the guise of freedom. Workers were allowed an opportunity to change plantations they worked on but one day a year, and then only if they owed no money. Food, tools, cloth, and other staples had to be purchased on credit from the plantation store at whatever price the manager set, so freedom from debt was rare, ensuring that wages and other employment conditions would not be competitive. The entire island rose once again in 1878 under the leadership of three women locally revered as "*Queens*" to this day: Mary Thomas, Axeline Elizabeth Salomon (Agnes), and Mathilda McBean, in what is now referred to as "The Fireburn." Many plantations and most of Frederiksted were incinerated. The Skeoch family on Centerline Road had a panicked Danish soldier appear banging at their front door, a mob behind him. "We have nothing to say against you, Mr. Skeoch, but this man is ours, and if you open your door, we'll have to come in to get him, and you and your family will be forfeit." The family huddled within as the soldier was torn limb from limb, screaming.

To restore order, Denmark rewrote the labor laws to be more favorable but severely punished the leaders. One hundred men and women were shot to death by Danish soldiers during the riots, and 12 were executed afterward. Thirty-nine were given a death sentence by the court and sent to Denmark for execution --among them the *Queens*-- but 34 of those, including the *Queens,* had their sentences commuted to life at hard labor. Freedom is never free.

Cheaper sugar made from beets doomed the sugar cane industry; corporations that owned the plantations left, the population shrunk, and St. Croix lapsed into sleepy and gentle poverty. St Thomas was a busy port, as steamships coming up from South America and the Panama Canal needed a coaling stop before making the jump across the Atlantic or up the coast of North America. Charlotte Amalie was even the Caribbean base of the British Royal Mail Service. Many poor, recently freed black people made their way to St. Thomas looking for work from different islands. Loading coal employed many on St. Thomas, but wages were poor and the labor hard.

Virgin Islanders were second-class citizens until a Crucian school teacher and writer named David Hamilton Jackson traveled to Denmark and successfully argued for the repeal of a law which prohibited independent newspapers and allowed strict censorship of publications in the islands. He returned home and founded the first free newspaper, The Herald, on November 1, 1913, now celebrated as 'Liberty Day.'

Since a newspaper was referred to as a "Bull," short for bulletin, and Jackson's other activities helped increase people's ability to feed their families, the holiday is known as "Bull and Bread Day." It is only coincidental that as the Virgin Islands are part of the United States, the holiday falls in election week when local politicians feed crowds lots of both.

Some Saint Croix estates still grew sugar, though not as much, paying low wages. Jackson and Ralph Bough created the first labor union in the Virgin Islands (Shortly afterward, George Moorehead on St. Thomas organized coal loaders into a second one), and pay increased for a short time, but then the remaining corporations pulled out. Paying a decent wage, they could not produce sugar from cane and make a profit.

Jackson approached the corporations with an idea. If the estates were to be abandoned, why not let the people who had worked it buy pieces for themselves on time? His idea was accepted, and many of the former slaves/sharecroppers/employees became owners of their own small cane farms. With new motorized machinery, the labor required was no longer as punishing, but small farmers could not afford to buy it. Jackson created the first farm co-ops in the Virgin Islands, organizing farmers of each estate to pool their resources to buy the machines and share them.

Jackson took an active part in convincing the Danish parliament that Denmark should sell the islands to the United States, even threatening the Danish government with rebellion if they did not. On March 31, 1917, the islands became a United States territory with 25 million dollars paid in gold to Denmark.

The United States Virgin Islands

In 1917, Germany wanted to buy the Virgin Islands for a U-Boat base within range of the Panama Canal. To keep it out of their hands, the United States purchased them instead. The flag of St. Croix today is the Stars and Stripes. Originally it was more of a colonial relationship, and the residents were not U. S. citizens, but now they are. Together with the islands of St. Thomas and St. John (and smaller adjunct islands), St. Croix makes up an "unincorporated territory" of the United States. Being part of a large nation serves well after hurricanes when huge amounts of aid come in quickly. It also means more educational and employment opportunities on the mainland. The islands are, however, autonomous, with an elected legislature and Governor, allowed to pass any laws they see fit so long as they do not violate the U. S. Constitution or federal law. While U. S. citizens, Virgin Islanders still living in the islands cannot vote in the Presidential election. The USVI is allowed one non-voting delegate the U. S. Congress, where membership on committees is the only power the delegate can wield. The principle of "No taxation without representation" is not an issue for Virgin Islanders, however, as all taxes paid in the territory stay here.

As a part of the United States, economic opportunities have pulled the Virgin Islands ahead of most other Caribbean islands, with better infrastructure and opportunities for young people. All taxes stay here in the islands, and federal money comes in for education, parks, road construction, etc.

In 1966 Hess Oil opened a large oil refinery on St. Croix. Governor Melvin Evans heralded it as the the end of one era and the beginning of another. To force Crucians out of agriculture and into industry, Evans ordered the last government-subsidized sugar factory at Bethlehem shut down. But Evans was from the drier side, from Christiansted. His decision did not set well with the west, and after only one term, he lost his reelection bid to Frederiksted's Cyril King. Regardless, it was too late: few grew cane by the time King took office. The days of sugar cane on St. Croix were over.

Hess filled many positions with people from the eastern Caribbean islands. At first, the influx overwhelmed local schools to the extent that the Department of Education refused to accept their children. Judge Almeric Christian, in Hosier v. Evans (1970), ordered that the schools admit all children whose parents or guardians were legally in the United States. After teaching nearly 30 years at St. Croix Central High School, I can say with authority that today most native Virgin Islanders live and work on the mainland as citizens of the United States. When I began teaching on St. Croix many of my students' parents were from eastern Caribbean islands. Now, most of my students' parents were born here, but only a minority of students have a grandparent who was born in the Virgin Islands.

Attempts to write a Constitution for the U.S. Virgin Islands have been unsuccessful so far, in part due to the question of whether people whose ancestry is from the eastern Caribbean or the mainland United States should have equal citizenship. Strong voices speak of decolonization, both from those with roots in the eastern Caribbean and from native Virgin Islanders. Emotions can run high and are often well articulated. Be that as it may, The Eighth Flag is a history concerned with the years 1493-1750, and this chapter merely an epilogue; I respectfully leave that debate to others.

Visitors complain that Crucians are not deferential, not effusively friendly as West Indians on other islands can be. Is that what tourists want? Hundreds of Buccaneers, Pirates, and free French mulatto landowners left their DNA in the blood of Saint Croix's people. Many more descend from the 8000 brave men and women who risked their lives for freedom. It's a safe bet that most Crucians have some pirate and freedom fighter blood in them. Children are raised to be friendly, but tough. Crucians are the most stubborn, independent, yet warm-hearted people you could ever meet. Crucians hate to be under anyone else's authority (especially anyone from St. Thomas), though they don't mind others under theirs. Pirate slang is still heard on the island; many Crucians 'talk like sailors'. Virgin Islands Senator Adelbert Bryan at one time introduced a bill in the V. I. Legislature to keep students who used such language from being punished, stating that it was part of local culture. Don't let this fool you; if you are polite with a "good morning", "good afternoon" or "good evening", you will get a friendly reception in return. If you are arrogant, impatient, demanding, or unfriendly, no Crucian will give you the time of day, and you may just get an ear full. Pirate blood is still here. Respect gets respect.

Walk the beaches of St. Croix today, and the sand between your toes is the same sand that was once between the toes of infamous pirates. Smell the salt in the air, and feel the rush of adrenalin as the thrill of adventure races through your veins.

Are there pirates in *your* blood?
Would you know?

19

V. Sources and More

Bibliography

1. Archives Nationale, Government of France Colonial Records, "His Majesty has taken the resolution not to allow any foreign nation to establish itself on Tobago or Sainte Croix Under any Condition", B-21, Minister to M. Bonreqaus, 29 July 1697.

2. Astropixels.com website, November 1716, http://astropixels.com/ephemeris/phasescat/phases1701.html

3. Ayers, Philip, The voyages and adventures of Capt. Barth. Sharp and others, in the South Sea: being a journal of the same, also Capt. Van Horn with his Buccanieres surprizing of la Vera Cruz to which is added the True Relation of Sir Henry Morgan, his Expedition against the Spaniards in the West-Indies, and his taking Panama. Together with The President of Panama's Account of the same Expedition: Translated out of Spanish. And Col. Beeston's adjustment of the Peace between the Spaniards and English in the West Indies, edited by Wm. Beeston and Juan Perez de Guzman as a supplement to Exquemelin's Bucaniers of America, 1684. Boston Public Library, digitized collection.

4. Bancroft, Edward, An Essay on the Natural history of Guiana, Printed for T. Becket and P. A. De Hondt in the Strand, London, 1769, reprinted by Amo Press, New York, 1971.

5. Benaben, Yannick, Sur les Traces du Trésor de La Buse Entre Histoire et Légendes Insulaires, http://ybphoto.free.fr/piste_la_buse_yb_1.html

6. Bonet, Walter Cardona, <u>Shipwrecks in Puerto Rico's History</u>, Model Offset Printing, 1989.
7. Boot, Max, "Pirates, Then and Now: How Piracy Was Defeated in the Past and Can Be Again", <u>Foreign Affairs</u>, 1 January 2009, pp. 94-107.
8. <u>The Boston Newsletter</u>, November 12, 1716.
9. Bromley, J.S., <u>Corsairs and Navies 1660-1760</u>, Hambledon Press, 1987.
10. Brooks, Baylus C., <u>French Pirate Jean Martel: A Deception in History</u>, pub. In "B.C. Brooks' Writer's Hiding Place", Oct. 12, 2016.
11. Burney, James, <u>History of the Buccaneers of America</u>, Luke Hansard & Sons, London, 1816.
12. <u>Calendar of State Papers, Colonial Series, America and the West Indies</u>, (CSP) Original source documents, Public Records Office, London, Vol. 1-18 (by year) 1574-1739.
13. Calley, Deirdre, "John Bordeaux's Time in New York," *Society of Virgin Islands Historians*, February 10, 2021; https://drive.google.com/file/d/1tarEmzpv2uEgURqStuhJS KZ5z7PqR49E/view?usp=sharing
14. Camus, Michel-Christian, "Le général de Poincy, Premier Capitaliste Sucrier des Antilles", in <u>Revue Française d'Histoire D'outremer</u>, tome 84, n°317, 4e trimestre 1997. pp. 119-125.
15. Carlile, Charles, "Journal of Captain Charles Carlile, HMS *Francis*", <u>Calendar of State Papers</u>, No. 1313, July-August, 1683.
16. Chanca, Dr. Diego Alvarez, <u>Letter of Dr. Diego Alvarez Chanca on the Second Voyage of Columbus</u>, Original source document, American Journeys Collection Document AJ-065, Wisconsin Historical Society.
17. Clifford, Barry, and Perry, Paul, <u>The Black Ship</u>, Headline Book Publishing, London, 1999.
18. Clifford, Barry, <u>The Lost Fleet</u>, William Morrow Inc., New York, 2002.

19. Columbus, Christopher, <u>Letter to King Ferdinand and Queen Isabella</u>, Original source document addressed to Luis Santangel, Barcelona, April 1493. March 15, The Gilder Lehrman Institute of American History Collection, New York, https://www.gilderlehrman.org/content/columbus-reports-his-first-voyage-1493.

20. Columbus, Ferdinand, translated by Benjamin Keen, <u>The Life of the Admiral Christopher Columbus</u>, Greenwood Press, Westport, CT, 1978.

21. Cornell University, Astronomy website for analyzing phases of the moon,

22. Cordingly, David, <u>Under the Black Flag</u>, Harvest Books, 1996.

23. Cardona-Bonet, Walter, "Pirata y Contrabandista Roberto Cofresí (1819–1825)", <u>Sociedad Puertorriqueña de Genealogía El Marinero</u>, Bandolero, 1991.

24. Cissel, William, "General Buddhoe, Liberator of the Virgin Islands," *Sierra Nevada World Music Festival Phorum 2019*, posted March 16, 2006.

25. Columbus, Ferdinand, translated by Benjamin Keen, The <u>Life of the Admiral Christopher Columbus</u>, Greenwood Press, Westport, CT, 1978.

26. de Cordova, Luis Carera, Filipe, <u>SEGUNDO REY DE ESPAÑA</u>, "The battle of San Juan de Ulúa", Madrid, 1619, p. 515. Translation online.

27. De Carrocera, Padre B., <u>Los Primeros Historiadores de las Messines Capuchinas en Venezuela</u>, Biblioteca de la Academia Nacional de la Historia, Vol. 69, Caracas, reprinted from Colonial letters in 1964.http://astrosun2.astro.cornell.edu/academics/courses/astro201/moon_phase_pict.htm

28. Creque, Darwin D., <u>The U. S. Virgins and the Eastern Caribbean</u>, Whitmore Publishing, Philadelphia, 1968.

29. Crouse, Nellis M., The French Struggle for the West Indies, 1665-1713, Columbia University Press, New York, 1943.

30. Cultru, P., "Colonisation d' Autrefois, Le Commandeur de Poincy a' Saint-Christophe", Revue de l'Histoire de Antilles Francais, Societe de l'Histoire des Colonies Francaises, Paris, 1915.

31. De Cuneo, Michelle, "Concerning the New Things of the Islands of the Western Ocean Discovered by Don Christoforo Columbo of Genoa", Letter on the Second Voyage, 28 October 1495, de Lollis text, http://www2.fiu.edu/~cookn/cuneo1.pdf . Also, another Letter was written to a friend, Hieronymo Annari, on October 15, 1495, "Concerning the New Things of the Islands of the Western Ocean Discovered by Don Cristoforo Columbo of Genoa", discovered in 1885 at the University of Bologna and found online at https://issuu.com/boricuababe723/docs/michele_de_cune o_s_letter_on_the_se

32. Dampier, William, A New Voyage Round the World, London, 1697; reprint by Adam and Charles Black & Co., 1937.

33. D'Anghiera, Pietro Martire (aka Peter Martyr), De Orbe Novo, Volume 1, (first edition by Antonio de Nebrija, Alcalá de Henares, 1516) MacNutt translation to English, Project Guttenburg digitalized collection, 2011.

34. De Courpon, M. Sieur, "Memorandum Concerning the Colonies", Archives Nationale, French Colonial Records, C8B-2 item 36, 1697.

35. "The slave trade in the Danish West Indies" display, Danish West Indian Society, Fort Frederick Museum, St. Croix.

36. De las Casas, Father Bartolome, Observations by Bartolome de las Casas, Original source documents in possession of the Gilder Lehrman Institute of American History, "Source Eight" and "Source Nine".

37. Dookhan, Isaac, <u>A History of the Virgin Islands of the United States</u>, Canoe Press, Trinidad, 1994.
38. Dube', Jean Claude, <u>The Chevalier de Montmagny, First Governor of New France</u>, Collection Antique Francaise, translated by Elizabeth Rapley, University of Ottawa Press, 2005.
39. Du Casse, Robert, <u>L'Amiral Du Casse, Chevalier de la Toison d'or (1646-1715)</u>, Berger-Levrault &Co., Paris, 1876.
40. DuTertre, Father Jean-Baptiste, trans. Caron and Highfield, <u>Jean-Baptiste DuTertre on the French in St. Croix and the Virgin Islands: A Translation with Introduction and Notes</u>, Translation by Highfield and Caron, College of the Virgin Islands, Occasional Paper #4, Bureau of Libraries, Museums, and Archaeological Services, Department of Conservation and Cultural Affairs, 1978.
41. DuTertre, Father Jean-Baptiste, Chez Thomas Lolly, <u>Historie Generale, des Antilles Habitees par les Francais</u>, au Palais, en la Salle des Merciers, a la Palme, & aux Armes d'Hollande, Paris, 1667.
42. Ernaut, Francois, "*La Concorde de Nantes Plundered and Taken by Pirates*", <u>Archives Departmentales de Loire-Atlantique, 1718</u>), Nantes, France, Serie B 4578 and Folio 90v–Folio 91v.
43. Exquemelin, Alexander Oliver (also Exquemelin, Exquemeling), Basil Ringrose, Raveneau de Lussan, <u>Buccaneers of America</u>, first published by Oliver L. Perkins, London, 1684.
44. Esquemeling, John (also Oexmelin, Exquemeling, or Esquemeling), <u>The Filibustiers of the New World</u>, first published in Dutch as De Americaensche Zee- Roovers, in Amsterdam, Jan ten Hoorn, in 1678.

45. Fage, J. D. "Slavery and the Slave Trade in the Context of West African History", Journal of African History, v. 10 #3, pp. 393-404.

46. Ferdinand, King of Castile, Aragon, Leon, etc., Letter to the Taino/Arawak Indians, Original source document.

47. Floyd, Troy S., The Columbus Dynasty in the Caribbean, 1492-1526, University of New Mexico Press, Albuquerque, 1973.

48. de Francisci, Leonard J., Indian River Journal: The Journal of the Brevard County Historical Commission, Vol. X, No. 1, (Summer 2011) "1715 Plate Fleet", p. 10.

49. De Gomara, Francisco Lopez, Historia General de las Indias, 1552 (Biblioteca Virtual Universal, www.biblioteca.org.ar/libros/92761.pdf). Ch. XXIII De Ovando, XXIV don Fernando de Toledo, de Leon, Balboa, and Pizarro.

50. Grinnell-Milne, G., Life of Lieut. Admiral de Ruyter, London, 1896.

51. Hale, Edward Everett, The Life of Christopher Columbus: From His Own Letters and Journals and Other Documents of His Time, Forgotten Books, 2012 (reprint).

52. Haring, C. H., The Buccaneers in the West Indies in the 17th Century, Methiuen & Co., London, 1966.

53. Harris, Graham, Treasure and Intrigue, the Legacy of Captain Kidd, Dundern, 2002.

54. Highfield, Arnold A., Guide to British Documents for the Danish West Indies and the Virgin Islands During the Colonial Period 1652-1739, Antilles Press, 2010.

55. 53. Highfield, Arnold A., Sainte Croix 1650-1733: A Plantation Society in the French Antilles, Antilles Press, 2013.

56. Virtual Library, "Modern Jewish History: The Jewish Expulsion (1492)", A project of AICE;

57. Johnson, Capt. Charles, A General History of the Robberies and Murders of the Most Notorious Pyrates,-

attributed by some to Danial Dafoe, and by others to
Nathaniel Mist, London, pub. 1728.

58. King, Noel (ed.), Ibn Battuta in Black Africa, Princeton
University, 2005, p. 54.

59. La America Espanola, "La Flota de Indias",
https://laamericaespanyola.wordpress.com/2015/09/29/la-
flota-de-indias, Publicado el 29 Septiembre 2015.

60. Lapouge, Gilles, pub. Phebus, 2001.

61. Edward Leslie, Desperate Journeys, Abandoned Souls,
Houghton Mifflin, 1988.

62. Lidz, Franz, "Tracking Balboa", Smithsonian Magazine,
Washington DC: 44 (5): 32–36. (Leoncico)

63. Marley, David, Pirates of the Americas, Santa Barbara,
August 2010.

64. Morgan, Edmund S., "Columbus' Confusion about the
New World", Smithsonian Magazine, October 2009.

65. Morison, Samuel Eliot, Admiral of the Ocean Sea: A Life
of Christopher Columbus, Boston, 1942, p. 617.

66. Morrison, Samuel Eliot, The European Discovery of
America: The Southern Voyages A.D. 1492-1616, Oxford
University Press, 1974 pp 502, 515.

67. Munich Dept. of Economics, "On English Pygmies and
Giants: The Physical Stature of English Youth in the Late
18th and Early 19th Centuries", University of Munich, 2005.

68. Museum of St. Eustatius, Founders' Letter, Oranjestad,
1636.

69. Newton, Lowell W., "Juan Esteban de Ubilla and the Flota
of 1715", The Americas, vol. 33, no. 2, October 1976, p.
267-81, Cambridge University Press.

70. Ogg, David, England in the Rein of James II and William
III, Oxford University Press, 1969.

71. Online Royal Genealogical Reference Handbook,
"Almanach de Saxe Gotha",
http://www.almanachdegotha.org/index.html.

72. Paiwonsky, Michael, Conquest of Eden 1493-1515, MAPes MONDe Ltd, St. Thomas, 1991.
73. Paiwonsky, Isidor, *La Trompeuse*, The Burning of a Pirate Ship in the Harbor of St. Thomas, July 31, 1683, Fordham University Press, New York, 1992.
74. Pelleprat, P., Relato de las Misiones de los Padres de la Compania de Jesus en las Islas y en Terra Firme de America Meridional, Biblioteca de la Academia Nacional de la Historia, v. 77, Caracas, reprinted from Colonial letters 1966.

75. Pope Alexander VI, "Inter Catera", World History Archives, Hartford Webb Publishing, http://www.hartford-hwp.com/archives/40/061.html.

76. Prescott, William H., History of the Conquest of Peru, v. 1 and v. 2, Philadelphia, J. B. Lippincott & Co. 1847.
77. Father Raynal, Philosophical and Political History of Settlements and Trade of the Europeans in the West Indies, J. Mundell & Co., London, 1798; 2nd printing by Negro University Press, div. of Greenwood Publishing, NY, 1969.
78. Rediker, Marcus, Between the Devil and the Deep Blue Sea: Merchant Seamen, Pirates, and the Anglo-American Maritime World, Cambridge University Press, 1989.

79. Rigarkivet, official online Danish colonial records of the Virgin Islands, https://www.virgin-islands-history.org/.

80. Ringrose, Basil (1685). Bucaniers of America the second volume: containing the dangerous voyage and bold attempts of Captain Bartholomew Sharp, and others, performed upon the coasts of the South Sea, for the space of two years, &c.: from the original journal of the said voyage / written by Basil Ringrose, Gent., who was all along present at those transactions. William Crooke, London, 1685; Retrieved 12 January 2018.

81. Ringrose, Basil, <u>A Buccaneer's Atlas: Basil Ringrose's South Sea Waggoner: A Sea Atlas and Sailing Directions of the Pacific Coast of the Americas, 1682</u>, University of California Press, Berkeley, 1991.
82. <u>St. Croix Avis</u>, "Ship Hard Aground off Judith's Fancy", Tuesday, October 18, 1977, #237, front page.
83. Sanders, Richard, <u>If a Pirate I Must Be</u>..., Aurum Press Ltd, 2007.
84. Sauer, Carl Orwin, <u>The Early Spanish Main</u>, University of California Press, Berkeley, 1969.
85. Society of Public Welfare, trans. Kappelhoff, <u>Biography of Celebrated Men and Women of Our Country, A School Book</u>, A. Loosjes, Haarlem, 1808.
86. Steward, Julian H., <u>Handbook of South American Indians, vol. 4: The Circum-Caribbean Tribes</u>, Smithsonian, USGP, Washington, D.C., 1948.
87. Taylor, Charles Edwain, <u>Leaflets From the Danish West Indies</u>, Wm. Dawson and Sons, 1888.
88. <u>(1523-1825)</u>, Island Resources Foundation, University of Texas, 1976.
89. Trinity Church (New York) website, https://www.trinitywallstreet.org/about.
90. Tyson, George, "John Gottliff: The Man Behind Buddhoe," *St. John Historical Society*, June 7, 2006.
91. Wafer, Lionel, <u>A New Voyage and Description of the Isthmus of America</u>, Edited by L.E. Elliott Joyce, Oxford, Hakluyt Society, 1933.

Photographs:

[1] Taino Deity figure, "Zemi", Archived December 5, 2009, at the Wayback Machine. In Heilbrunn Timeline of Art History. New York: The Metropolitan Museum of Art, 2000 October 2006; retrieved 22 September 2009, public domain.

[2] Reproduction of a Carib piragua canoe, Gli-Gli, 35' long. https://media.langleyphoto.com, with permission from Alison Langley.

[3] San Pelayo, reproduction of the flagship of Don Pedro Menendez de Aviles, http://www.wikinow.co/topic/san-pelayo, public domain photograph.

[4] "Gallos", sculptor Rubin Eynon, photo by MonikaP, Pixabay, CCO Creative Commons, free for commercial use.

[5] 1650 Salt River water windmill, de Poincy estate, author's photograph.

[6] Map by Spanish a spy circa 1655, courtesy of the Virgin Islands DPNR.

[7] *San Salvador*, a replica of Juan Rodriguez Cabrillo's ship that arrived at the port we now call San Diego on September 28, 1542. Maritime Museum of San Diego, https://sdmaritime.org/visit/the-ships/san-salvador/. Public domain photograph.

[8] "Sloop Providence Sails Again", New England Boating, April 21, 2011. Wikipedia stock photo, by permission of the magazine.

[9] Replica of a 17th century Dutch merchant ship exemplifying the "bluff-bowed" style of shipbuilding necessary because of shallow harbors, Pixabay, CCO Creative Commons, free for commercial use.

[10] Kalmar Nyckel, reproduction of a 17th century merchant ship. Wikipedia stock photo by Enricokamasa Public Domain, https://commons.wikimedia.org/w/index.php?curid=8637071

[11] Arial map of Salt River Bay, St. Croix, USVI, courtesy of the VI Department of Tourism.

[12] Diagram by the author showing the movements of the *Scarborough* and the *John and Martha*, the night of the 20th.

[13] Photographs of what I believe to be the John and Martha wreck site. Photographs by Lee Morris, with permission.

[14] Bronze spikes photograph by Barry Shipman, used with permission. Swivel cannon photographs by the author.

[15] "A sketch of the Capture of the El **Mosquito**" Early 20th-century illustration of the capture of Cofresí's flagship, the sloop *Anne(right)*, Historia de Puerto Rico, Paul Gerard Miller, 1928. http://archive.org> Ebook and Texts Archive > The Library of Congress.html, public domain.

[16] Statue of Don Roberto Confresi, Cabo Rojo, Puerto Rico, by Jerjes Medina Albino - Cropped version of this public domain image available under the CCO Creative Commons, 1.0 Universal Public Domain Dedication, free for commercial use.

[17] Photograph of schooner Vigilant, built in @1798, wrecked in 1928. Photograph circa 1898, "Centenary of the Schooner Vigilant", http://www.bisected-dwi.dk/412987410, Del siden. Common domain image.

[18] Bronze bust, a Crucian sounds a conch shell, the signal for freedom or death in 1848. Located in front of the old Danish scale house on Strand Street, Frederiksted.

[19] San Pelayo reproduction at sunset, Pexels.com, CCO License free for commercial use.

Appendix

Flags

Left to right: Though in the eighth century horsetail banners may
have been all the Umayyad warriors carried, this is the traditional
flag of the Berbers. Coat of arms awarded to Columbus by
Ferdinand and Isabella; Columbus' flagship wore this- the F stood
for (King) Ferdinand, the Y for (Queen) Isabela. The Flag of Aragon
and Castile, Columbus' other flag. The Cross of Burgundy, the
Conquistadores' flag and that of many Spanish pirates. The Cross of
St. George, often used by English buccaneers. The Flag of the

United Provinces of the Netherlands, used by Dutch buccaneers like de Ruyter. The Union Jack of Great Britain, flown after the act of union in 1707. The flag for French ships that were not part of the Bourbon navy. The flag of the Knights of St. John; an alternative used a black field, with a white cross. The French 'pavillion blanc' was the Bourbon flag, and thus the flag of the French colonies during the buccaneer period and during the 'Golden Age of Pirates', flown by LaBouse when privateering. 'Pavillion rouge', the solid red flag of no quarter used at times by English and French buccaneers and pirates. The flag of the 'Estates General', flown by many Dutch buccaneers. The Dannebrog, claimed by Denmark to be the oldest continuously used national flag. The English ensign probably flown by Henry Morgan. The seal of Puerto Rico, for Ponce de Leon. The seal of Peru, for Pizarro. The seal of Panama, for Balboa. The Stars and Stripes of the United States, and the flag of the territory of the United States Virgin Islands.

Pirate flags are paired with their captains in their biographical sketches above, as accurately as could be found at the time of publication. Blackbeard's flag was reported to be a simple death's head on a black field by witnesses; the one shown is popularly associated with him; perhaps this is handed down from the many crew who settled in North Carolina. LaBouse is said to have flown the same flag that Bellamy did until they split up, and then flew a "huge white flag with a dead man spread on it". The solid yellow flag is still the international flag for "Quarantine", denoting a place of isolation for contagious diseases, like malaria.

Notes, Letters, and Documents

A Hypocrisy: Using Jewish Money and Persecuting the Faith of their Fathers

The Fuggar family probably converted from Judaism to Catholicism in 1438, when Augsburg was purged of Jews. Jakob Fugger was related to the Goldsmiths, and some sources say the Rothschilds also. (26). King Ferdinand's great-grandfather was Jewish, as well.

B Re: Dr. Chanca's Letter

In the parallel passage to the two cited in Chapter 6 and 7, Dr. Chanca asserts that the fierce Caribs lived on and operated against the more timid Arawak from only three islands: St. Croix, Dominica, and Guadalupe, and that some of the other islands in the Eastern Caribbean were abandoned because the more peaceful Indians had moved on after Carib raids. He names 24 villages on St. Croix, with an estimated population he put at 4,000.

C The Papal Bull "Inter Caetera," (30)

Issued by Pope Alexander VI on May 4, 1493, played a central role in the Spanish conquest of the New World. The document supported Spain's strategy to ensure its exclusive right to the lands discovered by Columbus the previous year. It established a demarcation line one hundred leagues west of the Azores and Cape Verde Islands and assigned Spain the exclusive right to acquire territorial possessions and to trade in all lands west of that line. All others were forbidden to approach the lands west of the line without special license from the rulers of Spain. The Inter Caetera effectively gave Spain a monopoly on the lands in the New World (only Brazil was to the east, and thus granted to Portugal).

The Bull stated that any land not inhabited by Christians was available to be "discovered," claimed, and exploited by Christian rulers and declared that "the Catholic faith and the Christian religion be exalted and be everywhere increased and spread, that the health of souls be cared for and that barbarous nations be overthrown and brought to the faith itself." This "Doctrine of Discovery" became the basis of all European claims in the Americas as well as the foundation for the United States' western expansion. In the US Supreme Court in the 1823 case *Johnson v. McIntosh*, Chief Justice John Marshall's opinion in the unanimous decision held "that the principle of discovery gave European nations an absolute right to New World lands." In essence, American Indians had only a right of occupancy, which could be abolished.

The Bull Inter Caetera made headlines again throughout the 1990s and in 2000, when many Catholics petitioned Pope John Paul II to formally revoke it and recognize the human rights of indigenous "non-Christian peoples."

EXCERPT FROM THE INTER CATERA:

"Wherefore, as becomes Catholic kings and princes, after earnest
consideration of all matters, especially of the rise and spread of the
Catholic faith, as was the fashion of your ancestors, kings of renowned
memory, you have purposed with the favour of divine clemency to
bring under your sway the said mainlands and islands with their
residents and inhabitants and to bring them to the Catholic faith.
Hence, heartily commending in the Lord this your holy and
praiseworthy purpose, and desirous that it be duly accomplished, and
that the name of our Saviour be carried into those regions, we exhort
you very earnestly in the Lord and by your reception of holy baptism,
whereby you are bound to our apostolic commands, and by the
bowels of the mercy of our Lord Jesus Christ, enjoy strictly, that
inasmuch as with eager zeal for the true faith you design to equip and
dispatch this expedition, you purpose also, as is your duty, to lead the
peoples dwelling in those islands and countries to embrace the
Christian religion; nor at any time let dangers or hardships deter you
therefrom, with the stout hope and trust in your hearts that Almighty
God will further your undertakings. And, in order that you may enter
upon so great an undertaking with greater readiness and heartiness
endowed with benefit of our apostolic favor, we, of our own accord,
not at your instance nor the request of anyone else in your regard, but
out of our own sole largess and certain knowledge and out of the
fullness of our apostolic power, by the authority of Almighty God
conferred upon us in blessed Peter and of the vicarship of Jesus
Christ, which we hold on earth, do by tenor of these presents, should
any of said islands have been found by your envoys and captains, give,
grant, and assign to you and your heirs and successors, kings of Castile
and Leon, forever, together with all their dominions, cities, camps,
places, and villages, and all rights, jurisdictions, and appurtenances, all
islands and mainlands found and to be found, discovered and to be
discovered towards the west and south, by drawing and establishing a

line from the Arctic pole, namely the north, to the Antarctic pole, namely the south, no matter whether the said mainlands and islands are found and to be found in the direction of India or towards any other quarter, the said line to be distant one hundred leagues towards the west and south from any of the islands commonly known as the Azores and Cape Verde. With this proviso however that none of the islands and mainlands, found and to be found, discovered and to be discovered, beyond that said line towards the west and south, be in the actual possession of any Christian king or prince up to the birthday of our Lord Jesus Christ just past from which the present year one thousand four hundred ninety-three begins. And we make, appoint, and depute you and your said heirs and successors lords of them with full and free power, authority, and jurisdiction of every kind; with this proviso however, that by this our gift, grant, and assignment no right acquired by any Christian prince, who may be in actual possession of said islands and mainlands prior to the said birthday of our Lord Jesus Christ, is hereby to be understood to be withdrawn or taking away. Moreover we command you in virtue of holy obedience that, employing all due diligence in the premises, as you also promise—nor do we doubt your compliance therein in accordance with your loyalty and royal greatness of spirit—you should appoint to the aforesaid mainlands and islands worthy, God-fearing, learned, skilled, and experienced men, in order to instruct the aforesaid inhabitants and residents in the Catholic faith and train them in good morals. Furthermore, under penalty of excommunication "late sententie" to be incurred "ipso facto," should anyone thus contravene, we strictly forbid all persons of whatsoever rank, even imperial and royal, or of whatsoever estate, degree, order, or condition, to dare without your special permit or that of your aforesaid heirs and successors, to go for the purpose of trade or any other reason to the islands or mainlands, found and to be found, discovered and to be discovered, towards the west and south, by drawing and establishing a line from the Arctic pole to the Antarctic pole, no matter whether the mainlands and islands, found and to be found, lie in the direction of India or toward any other quarter whatsoever, the said line to be distant one hundred leagues towards the west and south, as is aforesaid, from any of the islands commonly known as the Azores and Cape Verde; apostolic constitutions and ordinances and other decrees whatsoever to the contrary notwithstanding. We trust in Him from whom empires and governments and all good things proceed, that, should you, with the Lord's guidance, pursue this holy and praiseworthy undertaking, in a short while your hardships and endeavours will attain the most felicitous result, to the happiness and glory of all Christendom." (30).

D King Ferdinand's letter to the Taino-Arawak Indians (1495):

"In the name of King Ferdinand and Juana, his daughter, Queen of Castile and Leon, etc., conquerors of barbarian nations, we notify you as best we can that our Lord God Eternal created Heaven and earth and a man and woman from whom we all descend for all times and all over the world. In the 5,000 years since creation the multitude of these generations caused men to divide and establish kingdoms in various parts of the world, among whom God chose St. Peter as leader of mankind, regardless of their law, sect or belief. He seated St. Peter in Rome as the best place from which to rule the world but he allowed him to establish his seat in all parts of the world and rule all people, whether Christians, Moors, Jews, Gentiles or any other sect. He was named Pope, which means admirable and greatest father, governor of all men. Those who lived at that time obeyed St. Peter as Lord and superior King of the universe, and so did their descendants obey his successors and so on to the end of time.

The late Pope gave these islands and mainland of the ocean and the contents hereof to the above-mentioned King and Queen, as is certified in writing, and you may see the documents if you should so desire. Therefore, Their Highnesses are lords and masters of this land; they were acknowledged as such when this notice was posted, and were and are being served willingly and without resistance; then, their religious envoys were acknowledged and obeyed without delay, and all subjects unconditionally and of their own free will became Christians and thus they remain. Their Highnesses received their allegiance with joy and benignity and decreed that they be treated in this spirit like good and loyal vassals and you are under the obligation to do the same.

Therefore, we request that you understand this text (in Spanish), deliberate on its contents within a reasonable time, and recognize the Church and its highest priest, the Pope, as rulers of the universe, and in their name the King and Queen of Spain as rulers of this land, allowing the religious fathers to preach our holy Faith to you. You own compliance as a duty to the King, and we in his name will receive you with love and charity, respecting your freedom and that of your wives and sons and your rights of possession and we shall not compel you to baptism unless you, informed of the Truth, wish to convert to our holy Catholic Faith as almost all your neighbours have done in other islands, in exchange for which Their Highnesses bestow many privileges and exemptions upon you. *Should you fail to comply, or delay maliciously in so doing, we assure you that with the help of God we shall use force against you, declaring war upon you from all sides and with all possible means, and we shall bind you to the yoke of the Church and of Their Highnesses; we shall enslave your persons, wives and sons, sell you or dispose of you as the King sees fit; we shall seize your possessions and harm you as much as we can as disobedient and resisting vassals. **And** we declare you guilty of resulting deaths and injuries, exempting Their Highnesses of such guilt as well as ourselves and the gentlemen who accompany us.* We hereby request that legal signatures be affixed to this text and pray those present to bear witness for us, etc. (25)."

"King Julian" gave a close version of this speech in the movie Madagascar, but I don't think anyone found it humorous in 1493.

[E]**Excerpt from Dr. Diego Alvarez Chanca's letter on the Second Voyage of Columbus:**

"The next day, at the hour of eating, we arrived at an island that appeared very good, because it seemed to be well populated according to the great quantity of tilled land there was upon it."

We went there and entered a harbor on the coast. Then the Admiral sent a boat to land well filled with people to see if they could talk with the natives in order to learn what people they were and also because it was necessary for us to obtain information about our course.

For this purpose, certain of the men who went in the boat landed and arrived at a village from which the people had already gone into hiding. They took there five or six women and certain boys, most of whom were (Taino) captives, for this island belonged to the Caribs.

Just as this boat was about to return to the ships with the captives which had been taken below this place, a canoe came along the coast containing four men, two women, and a boy, and as soon as they saw the wonderful fleet, they were so struck with amazement that for a good hour they did not move from one place at a distance of about two lombard shots from the vessels. In this position they were seen by those who were in the boat and even by all the fleet.

The men in our boat went toward them, keeping so near the land that in the amazed condition in which they were, they did not see the boat until it was very near them and so could not flee, although they made a great effort to do so. Our people went so fast that they could not get away.

The Caribs, as soon as they saw that their flight did not serve them, very boldly took up their bows, the women as well as the men. And I say very boldly, because there were not more than four men and two women and we numbered more than twenty-five, of whom they wounded two. One they hit twice with an arrow in the breast and the other they hit once in the side. And had it not been that our men carried shields of leather or wood and that they sheltered themselves with the boat and overturned their canoe, they would have wounded most of our men with their arms.

After their canoe was overturned they remained in the water, swimming and at times wading, as there were some shallow places there, and our men had to make great efforts to capture them, because they still fired upon them when they could. There was one whom they could not take until he was so badly wounded with a lance that he died, and in this condition they brought him to the ships...When on that day we started from that island, having remained there not more than about six or seven hours, we went toward another land which was visible to the eye and which lay on the route we had to take (to get to La Navidad) (29)."

[F]The Calendar of State Papers is filled with letters from Governors in the West Indies who said that the impressment of merchant sailors into the navy due to heavy losses in the area from malaria was leading to an increase in pirate volunteers. At the height of piracy in the West Indies, they petitioned the crown to put a moratorium on impressment for their area. The King agreed. Once in place, of course, Governors in other areas of the empire wanted the same moratorium, but did not get it (22).

[G] 'Renting a pew' meant that you tithed to the church, and you were given a pew reserved for your family and guests. This is how the church supported itself (Alexander Hamilton would be a future 'pew renter', also serving on the vestry and as comptroller, though never accepting communion.) (45)

[H] By the King,
A PROCLAMATION for Suppressing of PYRATES

GEORGE R.

Whereas we have received Information, that several Persons, Subjects of Great Britain, have, since the 24th Day of June, in the Year of our Lord, 1715, committed divers Pyracies and Robberies upon the High-Seas, in the West-Indies, or adjoining to our Plantations, which hath and may Occasion great Damage to the Merchants of Great Britain, and others trading into those Parts; and tho' we have appointed such a Force as we judge sufficient for suppressing the said Pyracies, yet the more effectually to put an End to the same, we have thought fit, by and with the Advice of our Privy Council, to Issue this our Royal Proclamation;

And we do hereby promise, and declare, that in Case any of the said Pyrates, shall on, or before, the 5th of September, in the Year of our Lord 1718, surrender him or themselves, to one of our Principal Secretaries of State in Great Britain or Ireland, or to any Governor or Deputy Governor of any of our Plantations beyond the Seas; every such Pyrate and Pyrates so surrendering him, or themselves, as aforesaid, shall have our gracious Pardon, of, and for such, his or their Pyracy, or Pyracies, by him or them committed, before the fifth of January next ensuing.

And we do hereby strictly charge and command all our Admirals, Captains, and other Officers at Sea, and all our Governors and Commanders of any Forts, Castles, or other Places in our Plantations, and all other our Officers Civil and Military, to seize and take such of the Pyrates, who shall refuse or neglect to surrender themselves accordingly.

And we do hereby further declare, that in Case any Person or Persons, on, or after, the 6th Day of September, 1718, shall discover or seize, or cause or procure to be discovered or seized, any one or more of the said Pyrates, so refusing or neglecting to surrender themselves as aforesaid, so as they may be brought to Justice, and convicted of the said Offence, such Person or Persons, so making such Discovery or Seizure, or causing or procuring such Discovery or Seizure to be made, shall have and receive as a Reward for the same, viz. for every Commander of any private Ship or Vessel, the Sum of 100 l. for every Lieutenant, Master, Boatswain, Carpenter, and Gunner, the Sum of 40 l. for every inferior Officer, the Sum of 30 l. and for every private Man, the Sum of 20 l.

And if any Person or Persons, belonging to, and being Part of the Crew, of any such Pyrate Ship and Vessel, shall, on or after the said sixth Day of September, 1718, seize and deliver, or cause to be seized or delivered, any Commander or Commanders, of such Pyrate Ship or Vessel, so as that he or they be brought to Justice, and convicted of the said Offence, such Person or Persons, as a Reward for the same, shall receive for every such Commander, the Sum of 200 l. which said Sums, the Lord Treasurer, or the Commissioners of our Treasury for the Time being, are hereby required, and desired to pay accordingly.

Given at our Court, at Hampton-Court, the fifth Day of September, 1717, in the fourth Year of our Reign.

George Rex

God save the KING.

Archaeology

"Gone with the wind."

Today, most of the site of the Taino/Carib village on the West side of Salt River Bay is part of the National Park Service. There are relics, mostly pottery, both in the museum on site and in Denmark, which the local government is negotiating to have returned. One such relic is an entire Taino ball court, currently in a museum in Denmark. The pirate village stood where the Indian one had been; the area is now a popular campsite for holiday weekends. You can still walk on the sand walls of Fort Flammand (Fort Salee, Fort de Sales) built originally by the Dutch in 1642 and improved by Henry Morgan 1646. It is slowly, inexorably sinking back into the earth and covered with bush; one day, if our government decides that accepting money from tourists is at least as easy as wheedling it from the federal government, maybe it will be restored. On the inside corner of the bay beside the old fort is good land where buildings --houses and businesses- once stood also, somewhat sheltered from wind and flood by the hill. Buildings would have been wood, with just stone pilings to support the runners. These foundation stones and garbage piles full of old bottles may be buried in there still. This area is now wild bush, but because of holiday campers over the years, littered with hundreds of modern beer bottles and cans. A metal detector will go crazy with the cans, driving the would-be archaeologist mad long before he could find a relic.

A map of Salt River Bay drawn by a Spanish spy in 1650 shows
clearly where the buildings stood, including the Dutch Reformed
Church. That site, which probably included a cemetery, is now the
site of a private home; bulldozers clearing the hilltop may have
destroyed historical evidence, or not. There were houses and
businesses all along the road inland from the fort on the west side.
There are still stone remnants of structures, pottery shards, and
probably more detritus in the bush.

On the eastern side of the bay the National Park Service
preserves a Taino burial site, and also owns the beach off of which
the remains of the *John and Martha* lie. This side of the bay was
bulldozed and completely reshaped during an abortive attempt to
build a hotel on the site in the 1970's. In 1716, it would have been
just a low, marshy swampland, with a sand island at its tip. The
southern peninsula in the middle of the bay would have been a
prime spot for pirate recreational facilities. It is a private residence
and has not been professionally examined for relics. Again, only
foundation stones and garbage piles would remain, and those may
have been moved for landscaping purposes.

As for Basin, the original wood buildings were torn down long
ago, and the charming Danish colonial town of Christiansted sits on
top of where it once stood. A recent archaeological dig on the
grounds of the fort uncovered foundations and a well dating back to
the French period; the structures were demolished long ago for a
clear field of fire from the Danish fort.

Many old plantation buildings lie in ruin all over the island.
Some have been renovated as wings of modern homes; others are
lawn ornaments. Still more lie undisturbed in the undergrowth.
Many French structures were incorporated into the buildings of the
Danish period, so ruins on the island are often a mix from different
periods.

The stone retaining wall for Fort Augusta (Fort St. Jean) on the
eastern side of Christiansted harbor is still there, as well as masonry

for a battery on Protestant Cay. The remnants of one of Governor DuBois's little batteries is on the south shore, covering long point bay, at a private residence that until recently belonged to the pastor of the St. Croix Reformed Church. The National Park Service has just cleared the land for a path to the first French water tower, built in 1651. It was still in use into the 1970s. Other water towers from the same period are still visible around the island as well. The ruins of the house De Poincy built in estate Judith's Fancy are still there.

SANG des FRANCAISE

Comparing the French census records of 1684-85 with the Beck map of 1754 (names that appear on both are in bold).

There were doubtless many families who did not appear on either of these records. Whether tradesman, indenture, slave, sailor or logger, many 'habitants' and transients in the French period were not important enough to list, nor were they shown on the Beck map, which only showed names of estate owners. Regardless, there are enough names that appear in both documents that are the same, and on the same land, to prove that some of the population from the French period remained on Saint Croix after the Danes took over.

FRENCH CENSUS RECORDS, 1680-1695:

M'estre de Camp:

Monsr. Camuset, Louis Girard, Charles Routier, Monsr. Lantier, Nicollas Claude, Claude Taisson, Le Gran Jacques, Pierre Blondaux, Charles Brisson, George LeMestre, Jacques Bachelet, Mang. Grouleaux, Rene Aligon, Pierre LeFebure, Louis Vibert(?), Robert Caillet, Denis Rondeaux, Pierre Munie, Anthoin Morin, Bois Galerant, Francois Goron, Andre (Jvage?), Vincent Perru(?), Nicollas Le Clerg, Gilles Chonneux, Jean Loinard, Connerot, Thomas Airain, *Charles Martel— (sons Charles, Jean Roux, and Francois Goron),* Andre Frage, Vincent Perru, Nocollas LeClerg, Gilles Phonneaur, Jean Boinard, Thomas Airain, Charles Martel, sons Charles and Jean,

Quarter du Nord:

Monsr de la Saulaye, Gouveneur, Charles de Cler, St. Jean, Duhamel, Gme. Barons, Lesr. Ste Joye, Monsr St. Lenoux, Lesr

Breuegat, Michel Vincent, Pierr Bereege, Jacques Lefebure, Jean
Metteraux, Francis Regnauld, Gme. Lannie, Jean Lenglois,
Francoisse Belleache,

Du Fond de Monery:

Mons. Lefebure, Capt.; Lesr Bernier, Francois Auge, Nicollass
Haran, Pierre Boitaux, Delgorgue, Gme. Estienne, Denis Soude,
Lesr Carbestain, Lauerdure, Jean Boste, Jean Martin, Pierre Aier,
Charles Lion, Bernier, Denis Soud, Carbestain, Jean Boste, Jean
Martin, Isaac Gilbert, Guilliaum Estienne, Carbestain, Lauerdure,
Charles Lion, Jean Courbet, Yves Bertaux, Thomas Torbuay, Louis
Chesnaux, Nichollas Bouffard, Henry Moisson, Jean Moisson, La
Jeunesse, Glme Etienne, Lasr Luchupec, Pierre Guistelec, Pierre
Boisilet, Charles Deselet, Llican, La vie Scerpestain, E. L. Salomon,
Francois Beard, Charles LeFebre, Martin Martin, Bme. Barbier, M.
Bled, Claude Langlois, Robert Bethelmy, Lesr Laroche, Pierre
Thiery, Pierre La Junette, Pierre Musinger, Isaac Gimbcus, Icar
Moztion

Pte. de Sable:

Lesr Derochette, Madlle Dubuisson, Monsr Guerin, Pierre
Soupel, Lade Jeruant, Mathurin Jiray, Jacques Daniel, Jean Feux,
Nicollas Bouche, Pierre Tiery, Pierre Jaueraux, Jacques Reuet, (?
Pitenne) Jaunache, Lesr Bernard, Laurant Lamielle, Jacques Gante,
Julien L'aigle, Jean LeLouf, Jean es Gante, Le Gascon LeGrand,
Lesr Le la Taille, Captain, Lesr Camuset, Lesr Girard, Lesr
Routtier, Andre Frage, Mr. Lantiery Juge, Francois Goron, Francis
Lance, bois Ealleran, Thomas Herpin, Lesr Bonnerot, Charles
Brisson, Nicollas Rocheton, Claude Tesson, Pierre Blondeaux,
Jacques Nafrichou, George Le Meshoe, Louis Gilbert, Jacques
Bachelet, Rene Aligon, Lesr Baron, Goroulaux, Pierre Le febure,

Denis Rondaure, Nicollas Le Clerq, Charles Martil, Jean Boinard, Charles Masse

Du Sud:

Lesr Du Blos Capitaine; Lasr Bernier, Major; Rene Robinaux, Gabriel Gournee, Jacques Gautier, Jean Lesr Es Toes, Noel Boureier, Francis D'Orleans, Nicollas Hubertan, Nicolas Tiollan, Le Gros Gierre, Martin Martin, Jean Coitttou, Denis DuCestre, Maturin Esty, Hustache LeRoy, Jean D'ollet, Pierre Perche, Thomas Gabe, Limond Lesne, Lesr Poduin, Claude Du Clos, Jacques Blec, Claude L'englois, Pierre Petit, Michel Houllet, Pierre Couturie, Jean Dupuis, Pierre Richard, Pierre Tuite

De La Majore:

Capt. Lesr Sotlzires, Lesr Dis Clufis, Denise Fonde, Hueviz De Gumul, Guilliaume Lumaue, Nicolaus Claude, Lesr Guiaus, Pierre Bivigure, Guittens, Pierre Guonol, Francois Rognuile (?), Guille Fouilnier, Gilles L'Gonneru, Givez Arguiz, Lesr Falinieue, Sa. Adget, Lesr Cinoua, Pierre Hueguin, Lesr. Arvinger, Lesr aliride, Guille. Buvay, Msr Lerutier, Alaus Cernnser, Pocuvern der Roy

Salee:

Lesr Ste. Joye Cappne, Lt. LaMiruille, Lesr Dumouchel-Ensigne, Phillipe Buices, Lesr Le Roziere, Louis Rigaude, Coessteau, Louis Menecee, Pierre Craminil, Barthelmy Cousture, Hiefure Guillaudes, Lesr Inbauls, Pierre Gaignes, Nocolaus Garbeaul, Estienne Cliz, Lesr Pierre Jaccobins

Beck map of 1754 (printed 1766)

(Notice how many of the names are the same as those found on the French census, above. On the map, the names are often in the same geographic location.)

Northside Quarter A:

Hams Bay: Roger; 35, Joseph Roger; 26, Manning/Roger, 16 Martin Roger; 24 P. Bleu, 13 Richards/Buntin, 12 William Roger; 15 AND 16, Daniel Barens and Martin Roger; 16 Henry Barens, 4 Roger Ferral, 7 Nicolay Tuite; 8 and 9 Robert Arvinger, 18 Piter Markoe/ Arvinger; 11; 10 Laurent Bodkin; 17 on borber with B, Andre Irvin; 18 Piter Markoe, Arvinger; 15 Daniel Barens, 16 Henry Barens; 24 Tham. Dunbavin and Piter Bleu; 13 Richard Buntin; 12 William Roger

Northside Quarter B:

16 Abraham Markoe; 15 Cathune; 14 Theob. Pourke; 13 Cornelis Stallard; 12 Boffron; 7 B. de Bretton; 6 Johnn Balta, sar Llytendaal, Baron de Breton; 23 Warner, Abraham, Rogers; 21 Daniel Poppin; 26 and 28, Cornelius; Romische Kirke 10

West Ende:

34, 35, 36 Markoe; 33, Fribiger; 32 Jordan; 18 Tuite; 2 Rodger; 3 Ferral; Hemer, 6-7 Cothune, 8-9 Pit. Heiliger and Felnior; 15; Bouver-Martin; 11 Arvinger; 18 Lourberg; Sand Pynt, Arvinger; 15 Roger/Feral; 56 Roger; 43, Phillippe Francis; 14 Georg; 2 Joh. Henry Barens; 2 Vaughan

Printsens Qvarteer:

51 Danbary, 45 Arvinger, 46 Thomas Laicefer(?); 36 Raivensher; 32 Theobald; 16 Newr; 15 Gouver; 17 Bagge; 18, 19 de Lucas; 22 Robbert Tounsen; 23 Purcel; 7 Ferrat/Kreky; Arvinger

Kongens Qvarteer, Dronningens Qvar:

1 and 5, Baron de Bretton; 6 and 7, Cothure; 16 Soren; 15 Abraham Dunker; 18 and 19, de Lucas, 23 Rapzard; 31 Meyer; 33 Nicholas Tuite; 35 Nully; 12 de Nielly(?); 44, 45 Saloman (near Wachthius Pynt); 46 Supte; 9 Nic. Tuitte; 33 and 11, Lillie; 46 Supt; 15-16 Gouverneur; Mathew Ferral; 17 Bagge; 15 Gouverneur; 6 Cothure

Dronningen's Qvarteer:

20 George; 27, 26 Tuite; 35 Nully; 30 Martin; 29 Markoe; 3 Callanon; 10 Francis; 11 Lillie; 12 de Nielly (Nully?); 1 Satornor(?); 2, 25, Salomon; 22 Lewry; 52 Fanson, 32 Meyer

Compagniets Qvarteer:

33, 11 Lillie, 3 Collanon, 2 and 1 N Tuite, 10 Francis; 6 Kortreigh; 25 and 7, Eilschow; 22 Joseph Richardson; 30 Sour Lain Tox (Jox?); Sour Lains 23 Egans 30 Francis Sourlain and Joxter (?); 18 Harris; 12 de Nielly; 46 Supte; 48 Liger 39 Bla=Jewel; 40 *Bastian* and Franck; 33 *Turnbull*; *Heyliger's* everywhere. 28 et. Selby; also 28 Fr. Sourlain; 41 Beral; 39 Hikey et Anderson;

Oost Ende:

Gallows Bay, 1, Satorner(?), 1 and 25, Salomon; 44 Shay; 8 Daniel Thomas; 10, 11, and 50 Cravin; 15 Richardson; 11 Daniel Williams; 12 Litton Adjett; 27 Bulls (?); 15 Quittel; 24 Samuel Adjett; 3 Daniel Mallet; 28 and 30 Thomas Hughs; 21 Henry Romney; 37 Mortimer Guittens; 18 Elms; 9 Coopman; 45 Darlons; 6 Shimoo; 10 Samuel Gibbs; 26 Richard Smith; 24 Samuel Adjett; 14 14 Darby Carty; 35 Francis Adjett; 36 Samuel Adjett; 13 Martin Borg; 35 George Beggs; 41 Beral; 26 Francois Sourlain; 29 Beral; 30 Stridiron; 31 Hasfel; 32 Arvinger; 53 Rowland; 23 Hansen; 26 Francois Sourlain; 52 Baron; 15 Richardson; 50 Cravin; 37 Moir; 18 Elms/Romney; 30 Hughes; 15 Quittel; 6 Abraham Markoe; 7 Mad.

Gumbs; 35 Lucas; 31 Hasfel; 23 Isaac Boffron; 24 Le Kipras; 36 Wm. Roger; Stridiron

'Queen Agnes,' Axeline Salomon, would help lead the Fireburn in 1878. In the 1685 census of Sainte Croix for Quarter fond du Monery, **E. L. Salomon** appears. While there are many other names that are both on the French census and the Beck map of 1754, this is the first one I have been able to make a connection for. The Jewish-French family of Salomon may or may not have converted to Catholicism by the time they arrived on Sainte Croix, but, either way, the white family members were relocated to San Domingue in 1695, where they mixed again. From 1879 to 1888 Louis Etienne Félicité Lysius Salomon was President of Haiti. I recently got in touch with a descendant of his, Yves Salomon, whose family moved from Haiti to New York when she was a little girl. She is now the President of Greenfield College in Massachusetts. I have not been able to prove that Louis came from this family of Salomon, but it is likely.

Agnes Salomon came from that family, as well. She is known as "Queen Agnes," as one of the three ladies who led the Fireburn rebellion in 1878. To 'restore order,' labor laws were rewritten to be more favorable, but the Danish government severely punished the leaders. One hundred men and women were shot to death by Danish soldiers during the riots and 12 were executed afterward. Thirty-nine were given a death sentence by the court and sent to Denmark for execution --among them the *Queens*-- but 34 of those, including the *Queens,* had their sentences commuted to life at hard labor. Freedom is never free.

The Beck map of 1754 shows two Salomon families on the same estate that the Salomon family had in 1685, in what was Quarter fond du Monery, near "Wachthius Pynt," now known as "Watch-ho Bay." Moth seems to have allowed some of those mulatto families who were on their ancestral land to keep farming it. I believe that Moth wanted to get St. Croix up and running as soon as possible and bringing in taxes. The quickest way to do that was to let the people already there buy their property on time and begin paying taxes. I am firmly convinced it is also why so many plantations on St. Croix still have French names.

Under the Sea

Captain Jean Roux Martel's eight-gun sloop *Renown* was anchored just inside the channel entrance to Salt River to cover the cut through the reef with her cannon (Johnson). European river rock ballast stones lay in a pile surrrounded by sand and chunks of coral in the spot exactly where *Renown* was supposed to have been anchored. So close to the beach, her eight cannons have long been salvaged to grace the yards of houses on St. Croix. The two Dutch ships sunk in 1650 could have washed in to the beach at "Columbus Landing", and the unusual sandbars just off the beach still hold the shape of what could very well be those ships.

Prizes left after being stripped of anything reusable were allowed to sink at their moorings. Other prizes were burned, as was the case with Blackbeard. A Dutch account speaks of Buccaneer vessels wrecked on the rocks of the western point of Salt River Bay under Fort Flammand. The National Park Service drug a magnetometer around the inside perimeter of Salt River Bay a few years ago, and detected nothing at all. The bottom of Salt River Bay probably has many such wrecks, but as they were wood, and stripped of most metal, there will be little evidence of them. Anything that did survive would be rotted wood, bronze or copper spikes, some iron hardware like pintles and gudgeons, and ballast stones under six feet of accumulated silt. Topsoil began washing into the bay when the land around was cleared for sugar cultivation and it is still washing in every time it rains. Other wrecks are lost beneath the tangled roots of encroaching red mangroves.

The remains of what is almost certainly the *John and Martha* lie near Salt River Bay (see photos above). It is a difficult place to snorkel or dive, however, and *John and Martha* had little treasure. One thousand pounds of silver came into Salt River Bay on board, but that was distributed among 120 crew, with some spent at local bars; anything on board would have been in 120 small bags.

Though readily identifiable, the cannons are now part of the reef, perforated with holes bored by black urchins and embeded in coral. The other north shore wreck at Cane Bay may be from the pirate era, or not, but this list represents all the physical evidence I know of on St. Croix from two and a half centuries of piracy.

Well over a hundred other ships were lost on reefs around St. Croix. Over a dozen wreck sites lie on the Buck Island reef. Others lie on Scotch Bank, Long Reef off of Christiansted, the Salt River Reef, White Horse Reef, and Sandy Point. Wherever pirate ships, their prizes, or smuggler ships died, no insurance could be collected; there are no records at Lloyd's of London for their wrecks, so many will rest unknown forever. The Smithsonian Institution sent a ship that ran a magnetometer all around St. Croix. They identified 114 shipwrecks that do not appear in insurance records on the reefs of St. Croix, not counting those in Christiansted or Salt River harbors. Most of those would have been loading molasses without paying taxes when the weather turned bad.

Famous treasure hunter Bert Kilbride lived by Salt River in the 1960s and early 1970s with his wife, whose family then owned Estate Judith's Fancy. According to mutual friend Lee Morris (photographer of the John and Martha cannons, above), Kilbride sold artifacts dived up from Salt River for many years, even advertising them in Florida newspapers. He and his wife purchased Mosquito Island off of Virgin Gorda. When they divorced, he bought Saba Rock and built a bar, and is famous for diving up artifacts from the Anegada Reef which he quietly sold. Queen Elizabeth II gave him the title, "Keeper of the Anegada Reef."

Richard Robbins, a man of literature and an alcoholic who never worked, made money for his habits by occasionally diving up swivel cannons from the bottom of Salt River. He once showed me a bronze one that was being picked up by a private buyer the next day. I saw another on a table the day before he died; it was taken by whoever discovered his body first the next day. Richard never disclosed the location of the wreck and took his secret to the grave.

Spanish convoys sometimes met with disaster; convoys leaving Spain in March left Havana for home in September, the height of hurricane season. Convoys sailing west in October could also run into late season storms. While not usually accompanied by dangerous winds, ferocious tropical downpours in November are common. For nearly 250 years (1543-1790) the New Spain Fleet sailed on schedule except during wartime, so it would be surprising if some of the New Spain Fleet did not leave their bones on Santa Cruz's west end beaches. The Sandy Point sandbar reaches almost two miles unseen under the waters of the southwest corner of Santa Cruz. Anchors are still in the sand, from where big ships that ran aground over the centuries tried to kedge off. Cannons thrown overboard to lighten these ships after running aground lie there, as well.

There are no reefs to protect the western anchorage of St. Croix from occasional huge swells. Twice between 2005 and 2015, swells from the west lifted all anchors out of the bottom of what is now known as Frederiksted Harbor and sent every vessel spinning into shore. The Fort Frederik museum has a line of cannons sitting in the grass pulled from the waters of the west end when holes for pilings were created for the new cruise ship dock (a small fraction of the harbor bottom). The cannons span four centuries, from 16th century Spanish (11 feet long) to a small mid-nineteenth century cannon probably from a ship caught in the tsunami of 1867 (the tsunami that washed the warship *USS Monongahela* two blocks from the waterfront in Frederiksted town).

Charlotte Amalie harbor contains the remains of *La Trompeuse* and the other privateer that blew up next to her, the remains of Prince Rupert's ships sunk in the hurricane of 1652, and hundreds of merchant wrecks from hurricanes through the centuries. For excellent wreck diving, Packet Rock -at the eastern approach to

Charlotte Amalie Harbor- claimed dozens of wrecks, and the Anagada reef has *hundreds* more.

Come to St. Croix and snorkel or dive the reefs with your metal detector; there is no telling what you may find, but if you believe it to be historic, share it with DPNR so that it can become a part of our island's story. As a further incentive, know that there are stiff fines and jail time if you do not! DPNR's office is in Fort Frederick (Frederiksted, West, where the cruise ships dock), one of two forts built by the Danes in the middle of the 18th century to protect the island, the other being Fort Christian. Each one has different artifacts, and both are worth a visit.

The Author

I have practiced storytelling for 37 years in front of the toughest audiences on the planet. My career has been teaching high school history, music, and sailing, thirty of those years in the Caribbean. I have sailed the waters, dived on and probably identified two pirate shipwrecks, and sailed through hurricanes. My voice is different from that of sedentary researchers or inexperienced fantasy writers. My voice is real.

Stanford Joines

Acknowledgments:

What is it about the sea? The stars begin to disappear and the wind freshens. You are desperately trying to get the clevis pin back in before the mast falls down. Pliers are between your teeth, the hammer is under your leg, and every wave breaks over your head. You're shivering so hard you can barely hold the tools. Lightning strikes the water around you, the headlamp goes out, and in a last-ditch effort, the pin goes home. The strange thing is, eager though we are to get to dry land, as soon as we are, we just want to be back out again.

Early critics are a writer's best friends. We are desperate for feedback to improve our work before it is out there and it is too late to fix anything and desperate for encouragement. My brother Ward savaged my paragraph structure; my sister Jill's response was always that it was brilliant and I must finish it; my son Jeremiah got his friends to read early parts, and their enthusiasm was inspirational. John Boyd said, "Stan, I have taken many blows, and they hurt. I urge you- *find original sources*." David Brewer, State Archaeologist for the Virgin Islands, was critical, yet always supportive and interested; he was invaluable. Dr. George Tyson was there to pull me back to historical accuracy. Warren Moseler supported the kids of team *Paladin* youth sailing program before hurricane Irma destroyed our J36. Lee Morris inspired me and supplied both the Avis cover from 1977 (MV Cumulus) and underwater photographs of what I am convinced is the wreck of the *John and Martha*. Brian Bishop found and showed me the wreck I knew must be there. Niarus Walker's cover is brilliant, and Bil Becker has put together a website which will introduce <u>The Eighth Flag</u> to potential readers all over the world. Thousands of historians have spent many thousands of hours putting archival material online; these are truly unsung heroes.

The sailors on these pages had a spirit of adventure and freedom which inspires me, and I am sure will inspire a passion for sailing in generations to come. Fair winds!

Made in the USA
Columbia, SC
11 June 2024